A CENTURY OF CAR
DESIGN

X942 HVC

A CENTURY OF CAR
DESIGN

PENNY SPARKE

BARRON'S

A CENTURY OF CAR DESIGN

PENNY SPARKE

First published in Great Britain in 2002 by Mitchell Beazley,
an imprint of Octopus Publishing Group Ltd,
2–4 Heron Quays, Docklands, London E14 4JP

First edition for the United States, its territories and dependencies,
and Canada published in 2002 by Barron's Educational Series, Inc.

Commissioning Editor Mark Fletcher
Managing Editor Hannah Barnes-Murphy
Art Director Viv Brar
Project Editor Emily Asquith
Designer Colin Goody
Picture Research Giles Chapman, Daffydd Bynon
Production Alex Wiltshire
Copy Editor Kirsty Seymour-Ure
Proof Reader Ian Pemberthy
Indexer Derek Copson

All inquiries should be addressed to:
Barron's Educational Series, Inc.
250 Wireless Boulevard
Hauppauge, NY 11788
http://www.barronseduc.com

Library of Congress Catalog Card No.: 2001097536

International Standard Book No.: 0-7641-5409-5

Set in Trade Gothic
Produced by Toppan Printing Co., (HK) Ltd.
Printed and bound in China
9 8 7 6 5 4 3 2 1

CONTENTS

FOREWORD

There are any number of books about cars but there are very few books about car design. Equally, while we probably all know the names Pininfarina and Alec Issigonis, who has heard of John Tjaarda or Ercole Spada? While real car enthusiasts may know the work of these inspired individuals the chances are that for most people they mean very little. The fact is that we know much more about the creators of the buildings, interiors, household goods, and decorative art objects around us than we do about the lumps of shiny metal that travel up and down our motorways and form a strong visual element of our urban and rural environments.

Why do we know so little about the designers who created the cars that surround us? It is partly, of course, because we all tend to think of cars first and foremost in terms of their performance and as pieces of moving technology rather than as pieces of sculpture enhancing our everyday lives. They are in reality both, a combination that is made possible by the designer working in tandem with the engineer. The numerous books about automobiles that line the shelves of the transportation sections of bookshops tend to focus on specific cars and treat them as classic cult objects. They frequently have a technical bias and they are usually aimed at the male enthusiast. Very few approach the car in its social or cultural context and even fewer name the people who created the cars in question.

However, we are becoming ever more familiar with the idea of car design and designers. Advertisements point them out to us and show us that cars are lifestyle objects *par excellence* as well as a means of travelling from A to B. Just as our hairstyles and our living rooms help to tell us who we are, so we define ourselves by our cars to a significant extent. They play an important role in the subliminal everyday landscape. Indeed it is harder and harder to escape from them. Venice is among the decreasing number of places where cars are absent. Whether or not we consciously acknowledge their presence they cannot fail to make an impact, one that involves an aesthetic experience of some kind.

The modern car is ubiquitous. However hard environmentalists call for its removal or its replacement by more efficient forms of public transport the car has found a fixed place in our communal and individual psyches. Drivers spend hours in cars complaining about the experience but many find it hard to give up that way of travelling. Some find much-needed solitude, others listen to radio programs they would otherwise not hear. Many people spend much of their time in cars looking at other cars.

This book is primarily about looking at cars. It serves to contradict that frequently voiced opinion that "all cars look the same" and demonstrates very clearly that they do not. As in any other sphere of visual culture, personal philosophies and taste preferences abound in car design. The more one examines the work of individual designers who have been influential the more one discovers a set of personal languages which reflect diverse emotional and aesthetic responses. Once one becomes sensitized to those individual languages it will never again be possible to confuse one designer's car with another's. Look at the lines of a Raymond Loewy Studebaker and compare them to Harley Earl's exuberance or Ercole Spada's subtlety. The differences are as interesting as those in paintings by different Renaissance masters or in buildings by Le Corbusier or Frank Lloyd Wright. We rarely hear the complaint that "all buildings look the same".

The other theme embraced by this text is the dramatic changes that took place in car design from the beginning of the 20th century to its end. Very little links the wooden "horseless carriage" of the early century to the sophisticated products of the late century. Developments in technology, materials, and production techniques made possible changes that radically transformed both the nature and the appearance of the modern automobile. It was designers that negotiated all those changes and translated them into forms with credibility and cultural validity. The middle years of the century mark the heroic period of automobile design, when all constraints were removed. Different nations and cultures interpreted that freedom in different ways: while the American designers, in collaboration with the American public, took that idea of liberty to visual extremes, the Italians retained a sense of tradition in the sense of the car's remaining an exclusive object of great beauty.

This book is, in essence, about the enormous diversity and richness of car design in the 20th century. From the millions of cars to choose from its author, Penny Sparke, has selected fewer than a thousand with which to show the wide range of variations that emerged, and from the hundreds of car designers who lived and worked through the 20th century she has selected around 50 in order to show a cross section of some of the personal visions that determined the path of modern car design. It is a book that will both inform and surprise its readers.

Patrick Le Quément

INTRODUCTION

RIGHT *The German engineer Gottfried Daimler's first four-wheel car with an internal combustion engine, dating from 1886. A real "horseless carriage", this basic automobile was to be transformed beyond all recognition over the following decade.*

*A*lthough it was an invention of the late 19th century, in the form in which we all recognize it the modern automobile belongs indubitably to the 20th century. Indeed the emergence of that familiar artifact and its penetration into everyday life were central to those years that were characterized by the impact of technological breakthroughs on the shape of human existence. The car became one of the most potent symbols of that phenomenon.

This book highlights the evolving face of the modern automobile, as determined by those creative individuals who visualized its forms and gave it its plethora of meanings. No apology is made for focusing on named designers, as many of them will be unfamiliar to many readers. While historians have brought to light most of the heroes (and heroines) of modern architectural and product design, the world of car design is still largely shrouded in anonymity. The names of the brands and the manufacturers of automobiles are well known to us, but very little is known of the men (and it was men in this industry for the most part) whose imaginations gave us so many familiar objects. Not only did they decide on the car's changing appearance, they also invented its symbolic language as it moved from plaything of the rich to marker of futurity. On it were projected the hopes and desires of large numbers of people. A means, at first, of objectifying their faith in modern technology, it quickly became an object through which that faith was put to the test.

Before the car's symbolic language could be formed, the object had to acquire its own visual identity. Like so many of the other goods that made up the visual landscape of the 20th century, in terms of its social and cultural functions it retained one foot in the past for some time. The carriage lent it its early format and it took a few decades for it to break loose from that powerful precursor and, aesthetically, to throw off its heritage. The early "horseless carriage" was exactly that and it borrowed its forms from existing carriage typologies: the phaeton, the berline, and the landaulet to name but a few. The first cars were basic structures with exposed seats and wooden bodies on a metal subframe, or chassis. The engine, beneath the seat, replaced the horse, whose absence gave this assembly of disparate components an unfinished, unbalanced appearance. For several years the focus on the technical challenges of the car pushed all thoughts about its appearance to the background, and form followed function as one technological solution followed another. A pragmatic approach meant that innovations such as steering wheels (replacing

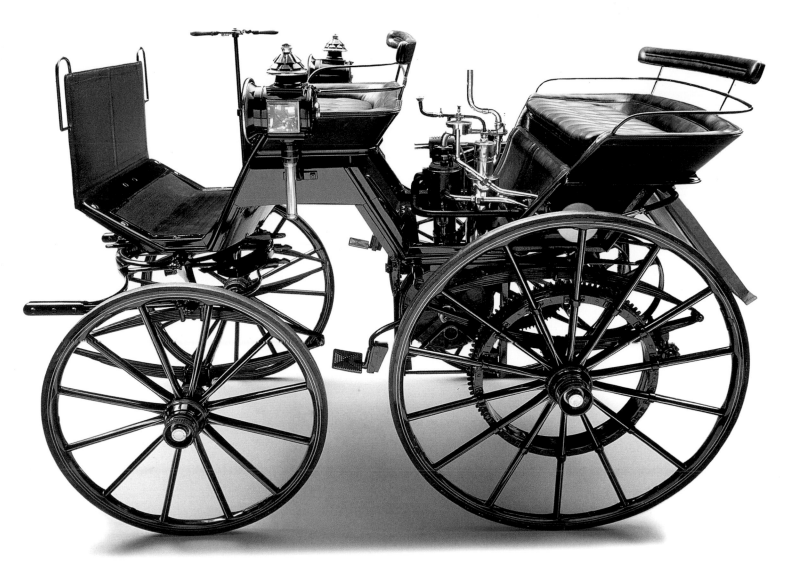

rudders) and the introduction of canopies were the sole agents of aesthetic change, while the continued use of carriage lamps and heavily upholstered seats were overt markers of the car's heritage.

The nature of the manufacturing process of early cars led to their conservative appearance. While the chassis were produced by the new automobile companies, keen to move forward, the bodies were the preserve of tradition-oriented carriage-builders. The work of the craftsmen employed by these firms was timber-based and they built car bodies, like carriages, on a wooden frame. Metalsmiths, painters, and trimmers completed the process. The level of visual elaboration and surface decoration was linked to the social status of the customer.

In applying their skills to the evolving car the carriage-builders were pragmatic, their aim being simply to create a box to fit on the chassis supplied, house the car's necessary components, and provide somewhere to sit. Gradually, changes to the car's structure, to the industry, and to manufacturing processes meant the carriage trade faded, and the reign of the automotive engineer began. Metal, often aluminium but more importantly steel, replaced wood. Soon the all-metal car was a reality. In 1914 the American car manufacturer Dodge created an all-metal car,

which was quickly emulated elsewhere. Across the Atlantic, the Italian maker Lancia created an all steel car body in 1918; the French firm Citroën launched its all-steel saloon in 1928. The use of steel for structural members and body panels facilitated the move towards prefabrication, standardization, and mass production, developed by the American automotive industry in the teens of the century, by Ford in particular. The carriage trade followed to some extent, developing standardized car bodies which were supplied to the large chassis producers.

In design terms, more significant was the shift from the chassis-based automobile to the unitary car – one that was made as a single unit. Developments in metal technology made this transition possible, allowing cars to be single structures rather than chassis/body combinations. The manufacturer Vincenzo Lancia launched his unitary Aurelia model in 1933, followed by the stylish Aprilia; the British firms Vauxhall and Morris and the German companies Opel and Adler produced their own unitary cars. Production methods were modified to accommodate this development. It was another blow for the carriage-builders.

The unitary car instigated a revolution in car design. For the first time a car could really be thought of, and conceived from the outset, as a single visual entity. Where design was concerned things had been moving in that direction for some time, beginning in Europe. In 1904 the Panhard Levassor company had crystallized the arrangement of the car's key components such that the architecture of the modern car had been put in place, and from that moment attempts were made to make the car look like a unified artifact. A sequence of developments – among them the raising of the bonnet and the lowering of the sitting position of the rear passengers – meant that the car acquired a strong horizontal emphasis and a "waistline" that held the components together visually. Developments in racing cars, responding to the emerging science of aerodynamics, especially the use of the "torpedo" body, also contributed to the process of visual unification.

By 1914 the visual language of the modern motor car had become distinct from that of the "horseless carriage". German designers played a key role in that shift in the years leading up to World War I. Working alongside architects and designers, such as Peter Behrens, who was employed by AEG, German car designers, such as Alex Kellner and Ernst Neumann, embraced the concept of visual simplicity and applied it to the car, removing extraneous mouldings and visible joints. The idea of the machine aesthetic that was being discussed in architectural and design circles penetrated the world of the automobile, ironically the ultimate consumer machine, and itself one of the key sources of inspiration for the avant-garde architectural modernists. Other objects of transport, notably aircraft and boats, which had evolved "modern" forms to facilitate their movement through air and water, were also important icons for the early protagonists of the architectural and design modern movement. By virtue of their status as real rather than metaphorical machines, cars never entered this exclusive arena, remaining on the periphery as raw objects of inspiration rather than self-consciously designed artifacts. This is not to say that cars did not have their own design trajectory, one within which the impact of aerodynamic theory was all-important. By 1914 Paul Jaray was working for the Zeppelin airship company and had begun to evolve his ideas about aerodynamic form which were to have a huge impact on car design two decades later.

The impetus behind the automobile's search for a modern visual identity of its own was not simply a rational one of visual simplification and scientific breakthroughs. Its role as a key marker of social status in the first half of the 20th century meant that there was an emotional side to its visual history as well.

LEFT *The R100 Airship at its mooring mast at Cardington, Bedford, UK, in 1929. Its highly evocative aerodynamic form significantly influenced car designers, who were looking for a shape that would both reduce air resistance and provide a fitting visual symbol of modernity.*

Particularly in France, the high-class carriage-builders pushed the form of the car to new levels of fantasy in the inter-war years, extending bonnets and developing long sweeping curves linking the fenders to the running-boards. Complex mouldings, multiple colours, and luxurious interior fittings reinforced the idea of the car as a fashion accessory. From then on, the push of scientific rationalism and the pull of fantasy and desire were to work alongside each other in modern car design, making the automobile at once an icon of modernity and a symbol of indulgence and consumer decadence. Such ambiguity helped to marginalize the car from most accounts of modern design.

At the other end of the spectrum, mass production brought the car within the reach of many people in the years following World War I. In that arena too, scientific rationalism vied with the "pleasure principle". With the demise of Henry Ford's Model T, which had brought the car to the mass market but was only available in black, General Motors took the lead in the late 1920s, showing that mass-produced cars could be objects of desire.

The late 1920s represented a turning point in modern car design, particularly where the professional side of the story is concerned. When General Motors hired the custom-car designer Harley Earl to head its new Art and Color Section, the prototype in-house styling studio, it initiated an approach to designing cars that was to be emulated worldwide and would dominate the profession for the rest of the century. Earl was an important catalyst, but his appointment coincided with several technological developments that also made a significant difference. Among them was the Dupont company's new cellulose paint, called Duco, which could be sprayed on to car bodies, eliminating lengthy drying and finishing processes. The late 1920s was also a time when manufacturers became aware of the role of women in car purchasing. This had a dramatic effect on the attitude towards designing cars. Women were believed to value the aesthetic and comfort properties of cars over their performance capacity. As a result visual design took on a new significance for the large manufacturers.

The late 1920s and early 1930s saw the emergence of many popular cars styled to suit the modern age, combining smooth curved surfaces derived from aerodynamic studies with the integration of components into the main body of the car. It was a symbolic moment in the creation of a car-styling paradigm which did not, in essence, change for the next 40 years. Although the silhouette and the visual characteristics of the car inevitably

RIGHT *Oldsmobile's Curved Dash model of 1895 was among the first automobiles to demonstrate that car bodies could be crafted in the fashionable styles of the day, in this case Art Nouveau.*

transmuted, the main approach towards creating single objects with a single identity and a modern look remained a constant.

Coachbuilders co-existed alongside the new profession of car stylists through the inter-war years, one community feeding fruitfully off the other and catering for different markets. A range of visual influences, from aircraft to boats to track-racing cars, fed the imaginations of both groups. By the early post-World War II years, however, the coachbuilders had all but disppeared, except in Italy. For the in-house and freelance car stylists the process of creating cars varied significantly from that of the traditional coach-builder. Once again it was Earl and his team at General Motors who established many of the working practices that were adopted by styling studios in general. The method of working from a sketch to a full-scale model, for instance, was to remain the norm for most of the century. Working with full-scale prototypes enabled designers to walk round their creations, work out the way in which their surfaces reflected light, and see how the proportions looked in three dimensions before production began. It has been suggested that the use of modelling clay in this context is one explanation for the curved surfaces of so many cars. Whether or not this is true, the methods used by car designers clearly affected

the appearance of the cars they created. In recent years the use of computers has become widespread and is dramatically modifying the methods evolved by Earl and his successors.

The term "styling", which has been used extensively to describe the car designer's "art", has been one of the causes of the marginalization of the work of the car designer from his peers. An assumption has been made that the stylist is more superficial and less responsible than his more serious furniture and product designer contemporaries. The strong commercial context of auto-motive manufacture has reinforced this view. Lately the term "car designer" has replaced "car stylist" and there is growing recognition that the process of designing cars is just as holistic and thorough as that of creating a chair or a household product. It is also as embedded in craft as furniture design and as complex as architectural design. There are exceptions to the car designer's historical marginalization, especially when the individuals concerned can be called engineers rather than stylists. Thus Pierre Boulanger's Citroën 2CV, Ferdinand Porsche's VW Beetle, and Alec Issigonis' BMC Mini have been taken out of the field of car styling and put into the arena of the "classic". These are iconic objects that have a recognized durability. Inevitably all car

designers aspire to this level of achievement in their work. Another escape is through the fine-art route; Sergio Pininfarina's creations for Ferrari are seen as exercises in sculpture. In recent years the work of the car designer has been equated more closely with that of the architect and the product designer, and the level of respect accorded has grown as a result.

Car designers have also been targeted by the anti-car lobby, which sees in the automobile the arch-enemy of the environment and of modern civilization. It is, of course, inappropriate to blame designers for the problematic relationship between the car and society. Indeed many designers are seeking to address the problems of pollution and diminishing resources. Along with other artists and designers of the 20th century, car designers played a key role in making technology culturally acceptable and in creating lasting symbols of the modern age. This book sets out to honour such achievements. It encourages its readers to encounter both the leading edge and the more mainstream faces of 20th-century car design acknowledging that both are equally important. It concentrates unashamedly on the aesthetic and symbolic aspects of the modern automobile. The emphasis is not on the automotive engineer, although many designers – including

Alec Issigonis and Dante Giacosa – have combined the skills of engineer and stylist. Others, such as Flaminio Bertoni, were artists applying their imagination to the problem of the automobile.

Cars are complex objects and their design is a complex operation involving large teams of people each bringing a different set of skills to the task. Increasingly designers have become vice-presidents of large companies heading teams of hundreds. The Fordist concept of the division of labour is alive and well in this context. Many men described in this book have headed large departments and may not have been responsible for anything more than the abstract concept underpinning a new design. Others have taken concepts from sketch to final production model. Many of the cars shown here were never produced; this is not to say they did not influence the way things moved forward. In the end, car design cannot be seen as the product of individuals alone: as with all mass-produced goods the design of cars is subject to technological, social, cultural, economic, ergonomic, and political forces and transformations. It needs individuals to harness those forces, however, and make them meaningful. This book tells the story of modern car design and highlights the work of a number of the key car designers who made it happen.

STYLING THE AUTOMOBILE

STYLING THE AUTOMOBILE

*B*y the second decade of the 20th century the mass-produced motor car had become a reality and the dramatic effects that it would have on the formation of modern life were beginning to be felt. Over the next three decades the car would be transformed from a means of road transport no longer dependent on the horse, to an icon of modernity complete with a new visual identity.

Only half a century earlier such a transformation could not have been anticipated. The process was made possible by a number of creative and far-sighted individuals whose visions were shaped by the huge changes – mass production, mass communications, the growth of the mass consumer society, and the technological revolution – that made the 20th century distinct from those that had preceded it. Most importantly, the modern automobile was not merely a symptom of those changes but a potent symbol of them all.

Artists and poets responding to the impact of modernization were enthralled by the car. The Italian futurists saw its speed and power as symptomatic of all that was changing in the urban environment. Giacomo Balla, in particular, used images of the moving automobile in many of his dynamic depictions of modern life in the early part of the century. Evocative turning wheels spiralled across his canvases in which he set out to create a painterly representation of modern existence. Filippo Marinetti, the leader of the futurist movement, famously claimed that "a roaring automobile, which seems to run on grapeshot, is more beautiful than the *Victory of Samothrace*" (a piece of classical sculpture in the Louvre), emphasizing his belief in the ability of the motor car to stand for modern life as a whole.

The imperative to create a new identity for the car that denied its roots in the "horseless carriage" grew from the same urge that

LEFT *A Ford Model T from the 1920s, viewed here outside an early petrol station. Although a modern machine by virtue of its existence, its appearance was not yet determined by studied consumer preferences.*

inspired the artists and architects of the turn-of-the-century Art Nouveau movement to search for a new style that had no history but looked for its visual stimulus to the world of nature. It is no coincidence that the French Art Nouveau designer René Lalique was asked to create a radiator mascot for the prestigious British car manufacturer Rolls-Royce, each belonging as they did to the same culture of change.

Apart from being an inspiration to artists, the car also belonged to the world of engineering and advanced technology. Indeed, the first designers were engineering experts who saw their role as one of improving the car's performance. The first important transformation of the horseless carriage – the democratization of the automobile – was made possible by technology. Henry Ford's great breakthroughs were the moving assembly line and the standardized automobile. His initiatives made possible the cheap

car, with the aim less of creating an object of beauty and more of bringing unprecedented mobility to all. In the United States Ford succeeded in providing affordable road transport for a huge rural population to whom it had never before been available. People's lives were transformed: they could shop in town in the afternoon and be home in time for tea.

As modernity extended man's control over nature the democratization of utility was soon joined by the democratization of desire. As Americans moved into cities and became mobile as never before, a useful car was no longer enough. They wanted to be able to outdo their neighbours and use their cars as a means of expressing their fashionable lifestyles. The mass-produced utility vehicle therefore had to learn to emulate the custom-made, coachbuilt cars of the wealthy and, like them, become a status symbol first and foremost. To meet these new needs men such as

Harley Earl, employed by General Motors in the late 1920s, were brought in from the parallel world of luxury custom cars to inject a new level of visual meaning into the production automobile.

The modern mass-produced motor car emerged in the 1930s as a mixture of scientific rationalism, expressed through the visual language of aerodynamics; Hollywood glamour (Harley Earl had worked for the Hollywood stars before arriving in Detroit); and the luxury and status symbolism associated with European and American hand-built cars for the wealthy. This heady cocktail was skilfully mixed by the "car stylists" emerging at that time who had the visualization abilities to make it possible. Refusing to look backward, they took their inspiration from the parallel technologies and objects of transport they saw around them, including airplanes and boats whose designers had to meet the challenges of air and water in their efforts to make their creations resist the

forces of nature. Many of the car stylists had acquired their own skills from working with planes and boats; Buckminster Fuller, John Tjaarda, and Eugene Gregorie all had backgrounds in these fields. In addition many of the new professionals, including Tjaarda, Gregorie, and Gordon Buehrig, worked with Harley Earl, who was the first to establish the currency of the new profession of "car styling": Earl's skilful transposition of custom-car aesthetics into the production automobile was emulated by many of his followers. Above all they came with hands-on experience rather than academic training. As a result they transformed the modern automobile beyond recognition and established a new profession which had its ear very close to the voice of the customer.

The aesthetic the car stylists admired, and which by the 1930s had come to characterize the modern car, was one that stressed the unity of the automobile as a simple entity, rather than

a complex one. It was a look that suggested man's control over nature and that, above all, emphasized the car's capacity for power and speed. Although frequently justified in rational language, and stressing features such as fuel economy and safety, these designs were primarily celebrations of the car's power to enthrall. The theory of functionalism – a design philosophy based on the principle that form should follow function, prevalent in architectural and design circles at this time – was called on to justify the appearance of cars, but in the end the symbolic function of automobiles won the day.

The inter-war years witnessed more than the emergence of the modern car. They also saw the arrival of a fully-fledged car culture in North America and Europe. With the democratization of the automobile came the growth of highways, gas (petrol) stations, motels, drive-in movies, and much more besides. The car was not

simply a symptom and a symbol of modernization: it was also a force behind its very creation, in terms of the material culture that accompanied modernization. The form of towns and cities was directly influenced by the car and, during this heroic period of the automobile, even buildings and consumer objects such as refrigerators began to look like cars.

By the outbreak of World War II it was clear that the mass-produced automobile had become central to modern existence in the Western industrialized world. Its passage from a machine to an icon was complete and, especially in the United States, the motor car had become a symbol of democracy. The car stylists, from Harley Earl onward, who had built their careers on the back of this phenomenon, had become key players in the creation of modernity, using their visualizing skills to create the important icons of the 20th century.

HENRY FORD

PRINCIPAL DESIGNS

1896	*Quadricycle*
1903	*Model A*
1905	*Model F*
1906	*Model K*
1908	*Model S*
1908	*Model T*
1927	*Model A*

The first major step towards the emergence of the modern mass-produced automobile was taken at the end of the first decade of the 20th century. The decision by Henry Ford (1863–1947) to abandon workshop practice and adopt instead the moving assembly line was a simple conceptual breakthrough. It transformed the manufacturing process and brought into being what we have referred to ever since as "mass production" on a hitherto unimagined scale.

TOWARDS THE TRANSFORMATION

In 1913 Ford was, in effect, putting in place the final piece in a jigsaw puzzle that had been emerging since the last years of the previous century. Learning lessons from flour mills, arms manufacture, and the meat-packing industry, he combined the use of standardized, interchangeable components and unskilled labour with the goal of large-scale manufacture. It was an ambition that stood at the other end of the spectrum from that of the skilled engineers and craftsmen who toiled to produce highly finished, hand-made automobiles for wealthy customers. The machines that flowed off Ford's production line at his Highland Park factory in Dearborn outside Detroit were as alike as peas in a pod: cheap, functional vehicles destined for the

ABOVE *The Model T Ford came in a number of different versions but remained a standardized automobile made from interchangeable parts. Still a "horseless carriage" in essence, visually it was a sum of its parts rather than a unified concept. However, it brought motoring within the reach of the American mass market for the first time.*

LEFT *The very last stage of the Model T Ford's assembly at the Highland Park plant brought the body in contact with the chassis to create the finished automobile. The cars were driven away at this point, alike as peas in a pod, without requiring additional fitting.*

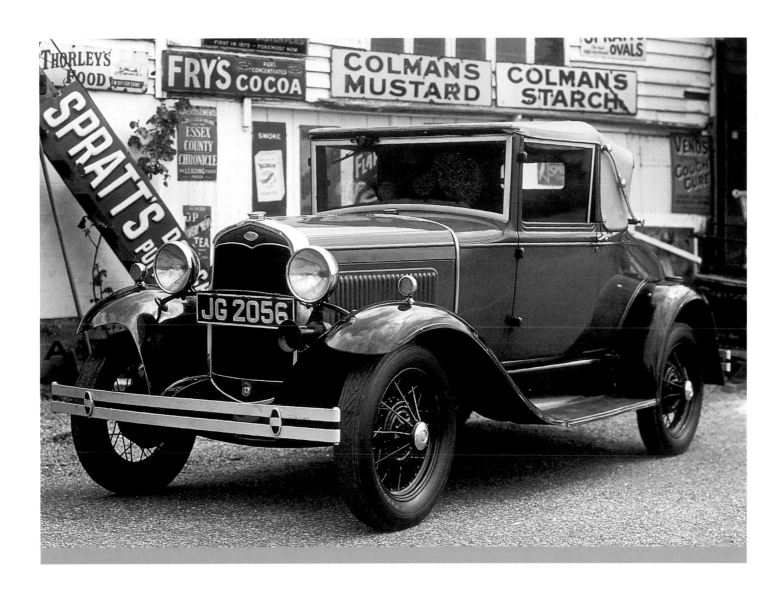

huge working population of the United States, especially those living in the rural areas whose lives would be transformed by ease of mobility.

Ford's revolution was not realized overnight. He developed his ideas for his first automobile in 1893; in 1896 he built his own car; in 1903 he formed the Ford Motor Company. His automobiles were named by the letters of the alphabet and 1908 saw the emergence of the model known by the letter T. This car appealed on the level of its functional simplicity, its hard-wearing qualities, and its ease of maintenance. It was not a beautiful car. Its appearance was dictated by the combination of its component parts rather than by a unified silhouette, but its utilitarian features gave it a high level of charm.

THE APPEAL OF UTILITY

Ford was less an aesthetic innovator than someone who understood that utility has its own inner beauty. The appeal of the "Tin Lizzie", as it came to be called, lay in its reliability. Ford's famous statement that his customers could have his car in any colour "so long as it's black" carried with it the promise that, although they would not get variety, the owners of his car would know that every Model T was as good as every other Model T.

ABOVE *The stylish Model A, launched in 1927, replaced its by then outmoded predecessor, the Model T. It was a response to the demands of the market, which looked increasingly for product differentiation in its automobiles.*

Ford came to the fore as a leading manufacturer in the teens of the 20th century. He paid his workers well and was able to lower the price of his cars, from $850 in 1908 to $260 by 1925. By that year two million Model Ts had rolled off his lines and he had built a new factory at River Rouge to cope with the enhanced scale of his manufacturing. By 1927 the production figures had risen to 15 million. But by the late 1920s, the unchanging nature of the Model T had become a problem. General Motors' new approach to styling, favouring diversity, began to make the Model T look old-fashioned and unappealing.

Ford was forced to close his River Rouge plant, and admit that he had to enter the style market. Although he re-opened the factory some months later and launched his much more style-conscious Model A automobile, his lead over his competitors was never again to be as great. From the late 1920s Ford cars were restyled on a regular basis like their General Motors and Chrysler counterparts. The era of the standardized mass-produced automobile was at an end.

HARLEY EARL

PRINCIPAL DESIGNS

In 1927, when Harley Earl (1893–1969) created the Art and Color Section of the General Motors Company, the concept of automobile styling, as we know it today, was born. The arrival of this tall Californian in the world of automotive manufacture had a transforming effect. Henry Ford (see pp.20–21) had had the vision to realize that the potential for car ownership was enormous, and in the early century ownership of a Model T Ford had been, in itself, enough to confer a high level of status on these new customers. Harley Earl went one stage further. He realized that once car ownership was more or less universal, Americans would want more from these feats of modern technology than mere reliability and low price. He went on to transform the automobile from an engineered object to a stylish consumer artifact – a subtle but dramatic conceptual shift that has never been overturned. His understanding, not so much of the rational needs of consumers, but rather of their deeper, emotionally rooted desires, turned the car from a utility object into a popular dream.

AFFORDABLE LUXURY FOR ALL

This transformation could not have happened without Alfred P. Sloan Jr, who became president of General Motors in 1923 and who oversaw a huge expansion of the company through that decade such that it overtook Ford as the leading automobile manufacturer in the United States. It achieved that unlikely feat by focusing on a new way of

ABOVE *Buick was revitalized in the 1930s by Harley Earl's Art and Color Section. This model, aimed at a market "on the threshold of the busy years of maturity", has a tapered rear and unified waistline.*

selling cars to the American market. Instead of providing one cheap, standardized model it brought in such concepts as product diversity, annual model changes, instalment purchasing, and trade-in deals. Most importantly, Sloan offered automobiles across the social spectrum, providing what he called "a car for every purse and every purpose". Crucial were the ideas of stylishness and comfort – qualities that had hitherto been available only in custom-made, luxury vehicles. Sloan aimed to offer every person a "luxury" car at a price he or she could afford, and to this end he offered a range, from the Buick as the cheapest brand to the Cadillac at the other end of the price band. He was tapping into the new urban American market in which social status was everything. No longer were car purchasers content with a democratic machine. The new sophisticated urban consumers sought, above all, to differentiate themselves from their neighbours. As with dress, so now with automobiles, the idea of fashion had penetrated right through American society and changed it irrevocably. With this marketing revolution came a change in manufacturing as well, from the heavily centralized world of Ford to the separate production plants of General Motors (GM).

Sloan's strategy was made possible by the introduction of Harley Earl into the GM picture by the general manager of Cadillac, Lawrence Fisher. Fisher had become aware of the progressive styling work done by Earl for his father's company, Earl Automotive Works, on luxury cars for the movie stars in Hollywood. Earl Sr had been a coachbuilder since 1889, making carriages for the wealthy of Los Angeles, but he had taken the initiative, after 20 years in the business, of forming a new company to make customized parts for luxury automobiles. After a spell at Stanford University his son, Harley, joined the business and quickly showed a talent for visualizing dramatically different-looking car bodies. The Hollywood stars for whom he created cars included "Fatty" Arbuckle and Tom Mix, a star of early Western films. For the latter he made a body that came complete with a saddle.

EARL'S FIRST DESIGNS FOR GENERAL MOTORS

Fisher's decision to bring Earl into GM stemmed from the company's need for a body design for a new model, the LaSalle, that was being planned to fill the gap in the market between Buick and Cadillac. Earl's proposal was heavily dependent on the custom-built cars

BELOW LEFT *The 1927 Cadillac LaSalle was the car that brought Harley Earl to General Motors. Alfred P. Sloan wanted a stylish model that was less expensive than the existing Cadillac, with which to target a new group of consumers. Its sleek lines and tapered rear were typical of Earl's designs.*

RIGHT *The 1934 LaSalle showed Earl's mastery of car styling at work. The teardrop mudguards and headlights, the "portholes", or "ventiports" as they came to be called, along the sides of the bonnet, and the single chrome strip along the car's waistline were all part of Earl's design strategy.*

produced by the Spanish manufacturer Hispano Suiza (see pp.68–9). By emulating these glamorous cars he brought the luxury look to a new audience of American car buyers for the first time. The LaSalle was a dramatically innovative design for a production car, which emphasized the long, low profile that was to become a hallmark of Earl's car designs over the next three decades. Its elegant shape suggested speed and modernity. Earl applied the lessons he had learned from Hollywood to this production car, showing that it was possible to combine luxury, comfort, and style in an automobile that was not out of the reach of most people. By 1929, in fact, 50,000 LaSalles had been sold. Although production was discontinued in the following year, the styling of the reworked 1934 LaSalle was even more streamlined than that of its predecessor.

The GM LaSalle was the first production car to be styled rather than merely engineered and it set an important precedent. Earl's next project for GM, a newly styled Buick, was less successful, however, as it ended up a compromise between the Art and Color Section and the engineering department, being dubbed the "pregnant" Buick as the result of a bulge just below its waistline.

THE HARLEY EARL HOTHOUSE

Through the 1930s Art and Color grew dramatically in size and made a significant impact. As a result GM became one of the most powerful manufacturers in the marketplace. Not only did Earl make its cars look good, he also helped define the modern automotive design process, pioneering the use of the two-dimensional rough sketch and the full-size clay model. His studio acted as a hothouse, training many stylists who would go on to become leading automotive designers in their own right. Among the "graduates" of Earl's section was the famous Cord designer, Gordon Buehrig (see pp.34–7).

In 1938, a year after the Art and Color Section became the fully-fledged Styling Division of General Motors – an initiative emulated by the other leading manufacturers – Earl pushed the world of car design yet another step forward with his design for the first "concept" car, the strikingly styled Buick Y Job. His intention was to design a car for the future, the stuff of dreams rather than reality. He created a stream-lined, stretched body with a continuously curved surface emblazoned with parallel, chromed metal strips emphasizing the form's essential horizontality. The clay modelling technique was an important factor in achieving the car's radical appearance. The car also exploited modern technology to the full, boasting an electrically controlled convertible top and windows. The Y Job was also the first car with concealed running boards, along with other innovative details, such as the flush door handles and the horizontal radiator grille. Earl's design was way ahead of its time and a model for others to follow.

ABOVE, LEFT AND RIGHT *Earl's experimental Y Job of 1938 represented a step forward in the professional practice of car styling. It was the first "concept car" created by a production car company to promote its forward-looking approach to automobile design and it displayed a number of innovative features.*

The marriage between Harley Earl and General Motors went on, in the postwar years, to produce even more innovative automobiles and set the pace for car styling internationally both as a profession and as a practice. Many young designers emerged from Earl's stable dependent on his design techniques and sharing his vision of the dream car of the 20th century. Bill Mitchell (see pp.146–9), who took over when Earl retired in 1959, had worked for him for several years, learning the trade at the master's elbow. Yet few others were to have the dramatic impact that Earl had over such a long period of time or to play such a seminal role in defining car styling as we know it today.

STREAMLINING

The move from the discovery of the scientific principles of aerodynamics (the study of the interaction between air and solid objects moving through it) to their application to automobiles and their influence on the shape of cars took between 20 and 30 years.

Aerodynamics had been preceded by hydrodynamics (the science of the movement of inert objects through fluid). The advent of air transportation in the early 20th century brought a corresponding need to think about speed and efficiency in movement through air. The elimination of air resistance or "turbulence", and the reduction of ground resistance or "drag", began to occupy automotive (as well as aircraft) engineers in Europe and the United States. Quite quickly the concept of the wind-tunnel test emerged as a scientific means of improving ground speed.

Hand in hand with these developments came the need on the part of car producers to improve the appearance of their goods; and the scientific, the commercial, and the aesthetic quickly became inextricably intertwined as the look of fast cars began to influence consumer choice. Precedents, such as the evocatively shaped dirigible airship, were pointed to, and proponents of the aerodynamic teardrop shape referred to the forms of porpoises and dolphins in their efforts to show how this shape was synonymous with speed.

STREAMFORM: SCIENCE AND ART

The new automobile body form came to be characterized by rounded edges, smooth surfaces, and low horizontal profiles. The emphasis was on the elimination of all protuberances – door handles, fenders, running-boards, and vertical grilles. The concept of "continuous flow" was all-important, as were a rounded front and a tapering rear in imitation of the teardrop.

"Streamform", as it came to be called, was as much a symbolic aesthetic denoting modernity and progress as it was a scientific principle facilitating greater speed and efficiency. Indeed, while

LEFT *Alfa Romeo's aerodynamic aluminium car was designed by Giuseppe Merosi for Count Ricotti in 1913. It was a highly innovative car and pioneered the teardrop shape and curved windscreen.*

justified by the scientific principles of aerodynamics, it was also derived from the forms that were being developed within avant-garde fine art in the first decades of the century. The work of the Italian futurists – Umberto Boccioni among them – and the early abstract sculptors – notably the Romanian Constantin Brancusi – used forms in their art that were not a million miles away from those being created in their cars by the "streamliners".

EUROPEAN STREAMLINING

Europe dominated the picture in these early years of automobile streamlining. Among the first car designs to show the way forward was a body designed for an Alfa Romeo chassis by Castagna for Count Ricotti in 1913. This lozenge-shaped design with a tapering rear, inspired by the contemporary Art Nouveau movement in the decorative arts, came complete with porthole windows, together with a wraparound windscreen decades before it was a common feature in

automobiles. Following on from this, a design in 1921 by the German engineer Count Rumpler, the Tropfenwagen, was formulated according to his ideas about aerodynamics and also marked an important breakthrough. But the most influential European in this context was undoubtedly the Hungarian Paul Jaray, who was head of design at the Zeppelin airship works in Germany between 1914 and 1923. Jaray used wind-tunnel testing to perfect the car that he designed in the early 1920s, a patent for which was eventually obtained in 1927 in the United States. The car featured a closed body with a rounded silhouette and a tapering back. To provide the driver with good visibility, however, the windshield was left in a vertical position, so the design fell short of being a perfect teardrop.

Jaray was among the first to reap the commercial benefits of streamlining. One of his companies, the Jaray Streamline Corporation, was formed in the United States, where his ideas were to have their greatest impact. His work was also evident in the design for a famous

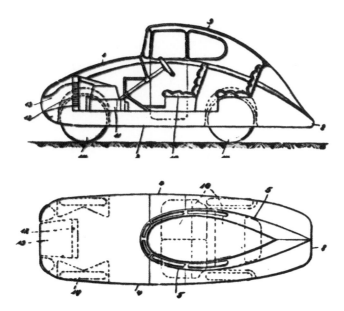

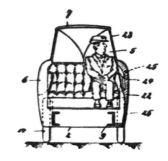

Czech automobile, the Tatra 77, which was produced from 1934 onward. Its radical appearance, made possible by the chassis created by the pioneering automotive engineer Hans Ledwinka, featured a rear fin that stabilized the car against the wind.

INDIVIDUAL DESIGNS

The early story of streamlining is of a sequence of "one-offs". Sir Charles Burney's Streamliner was one such example. Produced in about 1930 it featured a tapered back and a rear fin, although the grille at the front remained vertical and the headlights, while oval in form, were not integrated into the body. It was a hybrid showing the way forward but stopping short of embracing streamlining in all its glory. William Stout's Scarab of five years later was a similar lone experiment that has left its mark on the story of streamlining. Stout's background was in aircraft engineering and he was also involved with developments in railroad design. His strangely shaped Scarab car of 1935 was the result of his belief that a beetle or crab form was more effective aerodynamically than the teardrop shape, which he felt was faulty and adversely affected road-holding. He set out to design a car that would have better "roadability" and, in his view, an improved appearance. The interior of the Scarab was roomy and he made it flexible enough to include a folding table.

More scientific experiments took place in Europe with the discovery by Dr Wunibald Kamm of Stuttgart that the teardrop did not have to taper to a point to be effective. The vertical "Kamm tail" resulted from his work, eventually becoming, in the post-World War II years, a feature of a number of cars designed to manifest the latest in scientific thinking in this area.

STREAMLINING IN THE UNITED STATES

Perhaps the most significant impact of streamlining, however, was its incursion into the world of production cars, where its role was almost exclusively symbolic. In the United States streamlining fired the popular imagination more quickly than in Europe and the custom

coachmakers were quick to move into the production of lower, sleeker, longer cars that appealed to a wealthy clientele keen to participate in modern living. Leading designers, such as Raymond Dietrich, created a series of bodies for a range of producers, from Packard to Cadillac to Pierce Arrow, which were not streamlined in the radical teardrop sense but which owed their smooth body lines and integrated body features to that idiom.

STREAMLINING'S LASTING INFLUENCE

By the mid-1930s "streamlined" had become synonymous with "modern", denoting a look that was associated with glamour, speed, and sensuality. By the end of the decade the idea of the unified car-shell was a widespread reality and the "sit up and beg" automobile with its discrete elements was a thing of the past, an archaic throwback to a world in which the carriage had not fully evolved into the car. Such features as integrated headlights, running-boards, and enclosed wheels had become the norm and the car was perceived by most consumers as being less a piece of advanced engineering than an item of moving sculpture.

The story of streamlining, with its experimentation, its pioneers pushing forward the limits of the possible, and its manufacturers becoming confident enough to risk capital investment in its mass realization, was complete before World War II. After the war, only a handful of companies, among them Sweden's Saab (see pp.194–7) which continued the idea of air transportation influencing the shape of road-going vehicles, perpetuated the pre-war enthusiasm that had such a radical effect on car design in the 20th century. At the same time the unified body-shell, a *sine qua non* of streamlining, became the norm, and there can be no doubt that all car designers up to the present day owe an enormous debt to men such as Jaray, Bel Geddes (see pp.30–31), Buckminster Fuller (see pp.42–3), Breer, Stout, and Kamm – the intrepid pioneers of streamlining.

NORMAN BEL GEDDES

PRINCIPAL DESIGNS

1928 *Motor Car Number 1*
1931 *Motor Car Number 8*
1932 *Motor Coach Number 2*

Although Norman Bel Geddes (1893–1958) has been dubbed "the father of streamlining" he was not the first to apply the principles of aerodynamics to the motor car. But his ideas about the relationship between this new science and the appearance of automobiles played an important part in pushing forward the concept of the modern car in the years between the two world wars.

ALL-ROUND TALENT

Bel Geddes was an all-rounder. During his long career as a visual artist he contributed to the fields of painting, illustration, graphic design, set design, architecture, and interior and industrial design. His first foray into car design was the result of a 1928 commission from Ray Graham, of the Graham-Paige company, to design a car with a modern look for five years hence. Bel Geddes created five cars, one for each of the next five years, each increasingly futuristic in appearance. The model for the subsequent year already showed the influence of streamlining in its unified body-shell, rounded bonnet, and integrated fenders, but its use of a running-board linked it firmly with established conventions. Sadly the company did not use the proposals, fearing them to be too radical. Bel Geddes continued experimenting, in 1931 coming up

BELOW *Bel Geddes' little model for his open-topped Motor Car Number 1, created for the Graham-Paige company, although never manufactured, was the result of an exercise of imaginative projection into the future and bringing the results back to the present day.*

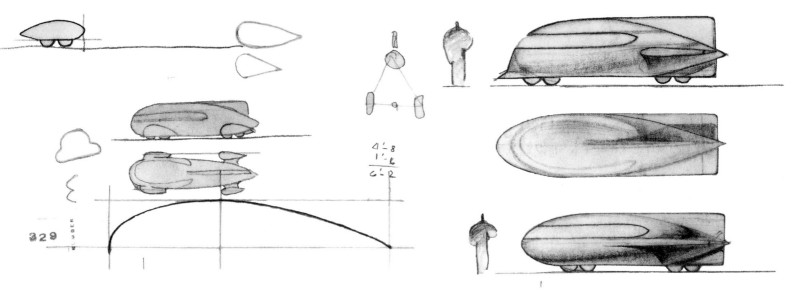

with a proposal for "Motor Car Number 8", which demonstrated the full extent of his visionary powers. Gone were the extended bonnet, fenders, and running-board, in their place a teardrop-shaped car body with two round rear windows and a fin emerging from the back.

VISIONS OF TOMORROW

In Motor Car Number 8 Bel Geddes had put into practice the principles of streamlining, including the elimination of all protuberances (such as headlights and fenders) and the creation of a clean continuous line from front to rear. Other factors included the space afforded to passengers, good visibility, and ease of driving and parking. He also maintained that the lack of air resistance would lead to a quieter ride. Other designs followed, including Motor Car Number 9 of 1932, a streamlined bus, a steam locomotive, and an ocean-going liner. So influential were his ideas that he was brought in as a consultant for Chrysler's Airflow car (see pp.32–3).

Bel Geddes predicted that the car would affect all areas of modern life, including the home, which, he ventured, would soon have an integrated garage facing the street. His contribution to General Motors' pavilion at the New York World's Fair of 1939, entitled "The World of Tomorrow", was an installation called "Futurama". This huge scale model of a city, made up of skyscrapers and a system of intersecting motorways, was dominated by the role of the automobile. In 1940 he published a book, *Magic Motorways*, in which he expressed his ideas about the key role of these constructions in the modern landscape.

In terms of mass production, Bel Geddes' work on gas stoves and beds was more influential, yet it was through his involvement with the world of automobiles that he was able fully to express his visionary ideals and play his key role as a prophet of modernity. Although none of his car designs reached the production stage his role as a stimulus to others, and his tireless commitment to the "world of the future", in which cars would show the way forward, cannot be underestimated.

ABOVE AND ABOVE LEFT *Preliminary sketches of streamlined Motor Car Number 9 of 1932 which was modelled on Number 8 of the previous year. By this time Bel Geddes had committed himself to developing the rear-engined, teardrop-shaped vehicle into a viable design. None of his creations was ever realized, however.*

RIGHT *A model of Motor Car Number 9 from 1932. This design had the same teardrop form and rear fin as the more futuristic Motor Car Number 8 of 1931 but, with its non-integrated mudguards, it was one stage nearer the state-of-the-art production car of that epoque.*

CHRYSLER AIRFLOW

Chrysler's Airflow model was launched at the Chicago *Century of Progress* exhibition in 1934, the work of a team of engineers who had dedicated the previous decade to making driving a car a more pleasant experience. Carl Breer, the head of research at Chrysler from 1925, was the man behind the Airflow. He had built his first steam-powered car in 1901, at the age of 17, and he studied engineering at Stanford University in California before working with a variety of automobile manufacturers. In 1921 he formed a firm of engineers along with two colleagues, Fred M. Zeder and Owen R. Skelton.

AERODYNAMIC STYLE

The demands of aerodynamics dictated a smoother, more rounded, more unified car body. In addition, with their sleeker body-shells and fewer protuberances, cars such as the Reo Royale of 1931 and the Graham Eight of 1932 were pointing the way forward, and Breer and his team were eager not to be left behind. Consultations with the aviation pioneer Orville Wright suggested that a new body be developed in which passengers were moved forward, and that wind-tunnel testing was needed if an aerodynamic result were to be

achieved. Chrysler funded the latter, and extensive experimentation took place. The resulting design played an important role in moving the car away from being a box towards it becoming an object of greater softness and fluidity. The Airflow was characterized by its continuous line from front to back, its sloping windshield, its integrated components – the headlights and front fenders were absorbed – and the incline of its rear.

Not only was the appearance of the Chrysler Airflow's body-shell visually innovative, it also abandoned the wooden frame mounted with separate steel panels, and adopted, instead, a single stressed-steel assembly, thereby pioneering a new concept for the structure of a car body. The interior was no less radical, boasting tubular steel-framed seats and marbled rubber floor-mats. The 1934 model was offered in five different body sizes, from the little De Soto model to a large limousine complete with a curved, one-piece windshield.

The least satisfactory feature of the 1934 Airflow from the outset was the appearance of its rounded nose with the chromed radiator grille giving it a very heavy appearance. Predictably the strongest public criticism was aimed at this feature, and the car was described

al different moments as "bug-eyed" and as resembling a rhinoceros. Its radical appearance, which made no concessions to the traditional appearance of motor cars, was just a little too much to take for most people and for many it became an object of ridicule.

TOO RADICAL

Although the car sold in reasonable numbers following the launch, it soon became apparent to Chrysler that public opposition outweighed support and that sales were dropping. Efforts to combat this trend concentrated on bringing in stylists who could give the front of the body a more traditional appearance. Ray Dietrich, a well-known coachbuilder of the period, provided some modifications, and the models produced in 1935, 1936, and 1937 all appeared with a different radiator grille in an attempt to make the car more conventional at the front. In addition the steel-framed seats and rubber flooring were replaced by more traditional components – upholstery and carpets – in the hope that these would be less offensive.

However, nothing succeeded in making the car more acceptable to the general public, and production was discontinued in 1937. On the surface it seemed as if the attempt to bring the automobile into the modern age had failed. Yet in spite of its poor sales, the Airflow cannot be thought of as a total failure. In terms of its influence it undoubtedly went a long way towards making the American market aware of the changing appearance of the modern car.

TOP *The sleek profile of Chrysler's Airflow CV Imperial Sedan was reinforced by horizontal chrome strips and "teardrop" mudguards, which provided a continuous line with the running-board.*

ABOVE *The interior of the Chrysler Airflow was as progressive as its exterior. It boasted seats with exposed tubular-steel frames and chrome highlights on details such as the steering wheel and foot-pedals.*

GORDON BUEHRIG

PRINCIPAL DESIGNS

1929	*Stutz Le Mans*
1929	*Duesenberg Tourster*
1931	*Duesenberg Torpedo Phaeton*
1933	*Duesenberg Sedan*
1934	*Auburn 851 Speedster*
1935	*Auburn 852 Speedster*
1935	*Cord 810*
1937	*Cord 812*
1952	*Ford Ranchwagon*

Gordon Buehrig (b.1904) is remembered for the stunningly original and elegant cars he created for America's best-known luxury car manufacturers, Duesenberg, Auburn, and Cord, in the late 1920s and early 1930s. These striking giants, with their huge fenders, dramatic grilles, tapering rears, and unified body-shells, looked ahead to the postwar years when American cars were to stun the rest of the world.

EARLY EXPERIENCE

Like many of his contemporaries, Buehrig was never formally trained as an automotive designer but entered the world of car styling as an enthusiastic amateur, and acquired his outstanding visualizing skills within the automotive industry. He learned all he knew from the car manufacturers who employed him and who gave his imagination the freedom it needed, so that his deep knowledge of cars and car culture was rooted in direct experience at several different levels.

Buehrig was attracted to cars from an early age and as a young man he worked for a sequence of car-body builders in Detroit, including C.R. Wilson and the Gotfredson Body Company. They taught

BELOW *The Hollywood film star James Cagney poses next to his open-topped Duesenberg in the late 1920s. Buehrig designed this dramatic Tourster model for that company and showed it at the New York Show of 1929. Gary Cooper also famously drove one of these luxurious cars.*

BELOW *The Auburn 851 supercharged Speedster model of 1934, the body of which was designed by Buehrig. Its elegant lines and teardrop-shaped mudguards made it a very desirable luxury car, while its chromed exhaust pipes added a touch of drama.*

him about the concept of car designing. His next job was to create luxury car bodies at the prestigious Packard Company, and he worked for a short while with Harley Earl (see pp.22–5) in the newly formed Art and Color Section of General Motors, where he was responsible for the instrument panel of the disastrous "pregnant" Buick of 1929.

Working with Earl introduced Buehrig to a new attitude towards car design that was predicated on the idea that cars were new and powerful symbols of the modern age. Undertaking his apprenticeship in the 1920s as he did, Buehrig witnessed at first hand the dramatic transformation of the American automobile from a high-performance piece of machinery to a new icon with a new meaning. He also saw that it was the stylist's job not only to make cars a part of the modern age but to make them look the part as well.

After his stint at General Motors, during which he became attuned to the potential of the automobile as a symbol, Buehrig moved to Stutz where he created the company's three boat-tailed Le Mans cars of 1929. There he began to find the confidence not only to apply the principles of aerodynamics to improve a car's performance but also to use them to create stunning sculptural forms. In the same year he was invited by Harold Ames, the sales manager of Duesenberg (which had

RIGHT *After the demise of Cord, Buehrig was employed for a while as a member of Raymond Loewy's design team, which was creating the revolutionary Tasco for Studebaker. His experiences to date made him a very useful team member.*

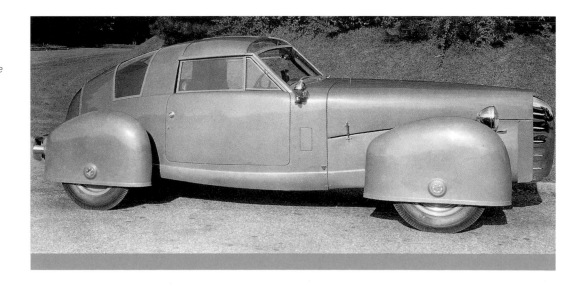

been bought by Cord in 1926 in the bankruptcy court), to revamp the appearance of its high-status automobiles. It was an important strategy employed by that exclusive car company to get through the difficult early years of the Depression.

THE YEARS WITH DUESENBERG

Duesenberg had previously bought in bodies from established coach-builders – LeBaron, Derham, and others – and had created some memorable luxury cars for wealthy clients. It was conscious that if it was to maintain its pre-eminence at the very high end of the market it had to provide something extra. The richness of Buehrig's combined experiences, his knowledge of car styling in the very different contexts of General Motors, Packard, and Stutz, and his growing confidence as a designer of cars with great individuality suggested to Duesenberg that he might be able to offer that something extra.

Buehrig was with Duesenberg for four years. It was an incredibly creative period for him, during which he created car designs that have remained iconic. Much of his work was experimental, and many projects only went as far as the drawing stage. During this period he visualized, among others, the famous Model J Duesenberg as well as the Judkins Victoria Coupé, the Beverley Berline, the Torpedo Phaeton, the Brunn Town Car, the Torpedo Victoria, the Whittel Speedster, La Grande Phaeton, and the Arlington. Buehrig's role was to stimulate the company to dare to move into the new automobile age and take on board all that modernity had to offer. Of the handful of his designs that went into production one stands out: the 1929 Tourster, built by Derham, a version of which was bought by Gary Cooper. Its long, low lines, unified form, and glamorous appearance soon gained

him a reputation as one of the most innovative car body designers of the day. Buehrig was also responsible for the Duesenberg radiator ornament, which quickly became a familiar icon.

After his enriching experience with Duesenberg, Buehrig returned to GM for a short period, during which he developed a radical design for a competition initiated by Earl. Although not appreciated by the GM head of styling, the design was noticed by Ames, by then president of Duesenberg. Ames asked him to return to the company. The design formed the basis of a new model which Buehrig was asked to create. The result was the cheaper, faster "baby" Duesenberg, which, when it was finally launched at the 1935 New York Automobile Show, had become transformed into the famous Cord 810. It confirmed Buehrig's reputation as one of the United States' most radical car designers.

The 810 looked like no other car: so dramatically different was it that Buehrig took out a patent for "a new, original and ornamental design for a car". It was known as the "coffin-nosed" Cord because of its rounded front; key features included its headlamps, adapted from aircraft landing lights, which could be made to lie flush with the front wings. Buehrig created two models for Cord, the 810 and the 812 of 1937, which were two of the most visually striking cars of the epoque.

Above all Buehrig is known for his designs for Auburn (the company that Errett Lobban Cord was invited to "put back on its feet"

in 1924), the 851 Speedster of 1934 being among the best-known models. The supercharged version of the 851 had four enormous exhaust pipes that swept from the side panel of the bonnet, giving the car a dramatic appearance and a strong sense of power.

YEARS OF CHANGE

Buehrig's two cars for Cord represented the last efforts by a failing company to withstand the effects of the Depression. By 1929 the holding company formed by E.L. Cord was owned by the Limousine Body Company and Century Airlines, as was Duesenberg which Cord had taken over in 1926/7. These were years of transition for the luxury coachbuilders who were having to adapt to a new culture which only a few of the individuals involved understood. In spite of Cord and Buehrig's efforts the company went into bankruptcy in 1937.

Following the demise of the Cord empire Buehrig was employed in a number of styling studios, including Studebaker's, where he worked on the Tasco. After World War II he worked for Ford, where he designed the 1952 Victoria Coupé, until his retirement in 1965. Among the many tributes bestowed on him was the inclusion of the Cord 812 in New York's Museum of Modern Art exhibition of 1951, *Eight Automobiles*, one of the first shows to recognize car design as an important facet of contemporary visual culture.

RIGHT *The famous Cord 810 was one of the 20th century's classic designs. With its "coffin-nosed" front, retracting headlights, and huge front mudguards, it represented all that was modern, forward-looking, and optimistic in the middle years of the US Depression.*

JOHN TJAARDA

PRINCIPAL DESIGNS

late 1920s *Sterkenberg series*
1932 *Briggs Dream Car*

In the story of the modernization of the American automobile the Dutch designer John Tjaarda (1897–1962) played a small but highly significant pioneering role – primarily through the design of a single automobile, the Briggs Dream Car of 1932.

Tjaarda brought a European background to bear on the challenge of the modern American automobile. He had trained as an aeronautical designer in England before serving in the Dutch airforce. In 1923 he arrived in Hollywood, where he helped to design custom-car bodies for Duesenberg and others. In the late 1920s Tjaarda designed a range of monocoque, streamlined car bodies known as the Sterkenberg series, inspired by the work of Paul Jaray, the father of aerodynamic car styling (see pp.26–9). He also created a series of bodies for Packard, Pierce Arrow, Stutz, and Duesenberg, characterized by their unified, elegant forms. His background in aeronautical design played its part in the sophisticated forms he created for these luxury cars.

BELOW *This sketch for a streamlined V8 automobile is part of a set of proposals made by Tjaarda known as his Sterkenberg series.*

BELOW *In 1932 the Briggs Manufacturing Co. was asked by Ford to work on a "Dream Car" for Lincoln. Tjaarda's proposal, shown here, was a dramatically styled streamlined model, which later was worked up to become the Lincoln Zephyr.*

Tjaarda moved on to work with Harley Earl (see pp.22–5) at General Motors and thence to run the newly formed design centre of the Briggs Manufacturing Company. Having just absorbed the influential custom body-maker LeBaron, Briggs was Detroit's most powerful company to have moved from the traditional arena of coach-building into the new world of car manufacture. It was also Ford's main body supplier, and among the many services it provided for Ford was assembling the Lincoln range. In 1932 it was clear to Ford that, with increasing competition from General Motors, it had to rethink its design for Lincoln. It was with Ford's approval, therefore, that Tjaarda was charged with developing a more progressive image for the marque.

THE BRIGGS DREAM CAR

Drawing on his earlier models Tjaarda created a prototype which came to be known as the Briggs Dream Car. With this car he established the practice, later to become widespread, of showing the public a car that was way ahead of its time but that helped it move towards acceptance of something inspired by the future. The Dream Car was a rear-engined design with an elongated, curved body. An indented ridge in the body-shell ran horizontally under the windows and down to the centre of the bonnet just above the bumper, giving a unified feel to the car's side profile. The door handles were recessed and the headlights were built into the front fenders, while the rear fenders hid the wheels from sight, helping to give the impression of an animal-like body with tensed rear haunches ready to take a leap forward. Every detail served

ABOVE *After World War II Tjaarda continued to make design proposals. Seen here are some sketches from 1951 featuring a long, low car with a single headlight at the front. These proposals owe much to contemporary aircraft styling.*

to reinforce its overriding image of speed, aggression, and modernity. The Dream Car was exhibited at Chicago's *Century of Progress* exhibition in 1933. It closely resembled Ferdinand Porsche's Type 32, or *Kleinauto*, designed for the German NSU company in 1932, though there can be no doubt that Tjaarda was already moving independently in this direction, as was clearly shown by his earlier models for the Sterkenberg series. It seems that Carl Breer at Chrysler, with the ill-fated Airflow (see pp.32–3), and Tjaarda for Ford were responding almost simultaneously to what was clearly a shared vision at that time.

Breer's attempt was unsuccessful, but Tjaarda's more imaginative solution proved to be a way forward for Ford inasmuch as the Dream Car was used as a prototype for the successful Lincoln Zephyr a few years later. Like Earl at General Motors and unlike Breer at Chrysler, Edsel Ford understood that the public's acceptance of the streamlined automobile would occur through the design that most successfully combined functional improvements – higher speed, lower fuel consumption, and so on – with a new look that spoke the language of the present and the near future but that did not alienate an essentially cautious buying public. This required the skills of an engineer and an artist as well as an understanding of the mass psychology of the day. It was a combination of skills that Tjaarda clearly possessed.

E.T. GREGORIE

PRINCIPAL DESIGNS

1933–4 *Fords*

1936 *Lincoln Zephyr (refinements)*

1935–7 *Fords*

1938 *Lincoln Zephyr*

1939 *Mercury*

1939 *Lincoln Continental*

1940s *Fords and Mercurys*

1949 *Lincoln*

The Lincoln Zephyr of 1935 has been described by New York's Museum of Modern Art as "the first successful streamlined car in the US". The tribute honours two people: Edsel Ford, president of Ford's new Lincoln Division since its takeover of Lincoln in 1922, and the head of Ford's in-house styling team, Eugene ("Bob") Gregorie. The two men worked closely together during the latter half of the 1930s and produced a number of highly innovative car designs, including the Lincoln Zephyr and the Lincoln Continental.

A BACKGROUND IN BOATS

Like many of his peers Gregorie brought to car styling a talent and a set of experiences that proved highly relevant. He came to cars from a boat-design background. Born in New York in 1908, he went to work at the age of 19 as a draftsman for the Elco Boat Works in New Jersey. A year later he moved on to yacht designers Cox and Stevens in New York. He enjoyed a spell under Harley Earl (see pp.22–5) at General Motors, a short working interlude at the coachbuilders Brewster, and ended up as a body draftsman at Lincoln in 1931. He witnessed the changes in appearance and meaning of the modern American car of the late 1920s and 1930s and he also saw the unfortunate story of the Chrysler Airflow (see pp.32–3) unfold before his eyes.

Unlike his father, Edsel Ford was committed to modern design. He employed the pioneer industrial designer W.D. Teague to create dramatic trade shows for Ford in the 1930s and to coordinate its visual

ABOVE *Edsel Ford, who collaborated closely with Eugene Gregorie.*

BELOW *The sleek lines of the car that Gregorie created for his boss, Edsel Ford, in 1939, which became the Lincoln Continental, owed much to his background in boat design. Its long low lines were stunningly different and the revealed spare wheel an exciting innovation.*

Lincoln Continentals are shown moving along the assembly line in 1947. Their stretched hoods and fenders, low lines, and integrated components owed much to the earlier Zephyr but took the streamlined look into a new era. This was Gregorie's most successful design.

image at events such as the 1933 Chicago *Century of Progress* exhibition. Ford worked closely with the internal styling division that he created in 1935 and promoted Gregorie to lead it.

SUCCESSFUL STREAMLINING

The Lincoln Zephyr was not Gregorie's work alone. It was based on the Briggs Dream Car designed by John Tjaarda (see pp.38–9), but Gregorie's reworking of certain elements undoubtedly led to its over-whelming success. Avoiding the ill-fated Chrysler Airflow's "bull-nose", Gregorie moved the engine to the front and created a form for the bonnet reminiscent of an inverted ship's prow, surely an inspiration from his boat-design days. The elegance of the form endeared it to the public and made the car acceptable despite the radical streamlining aesthetic that characterized the rest of the body. The car's name derived from America's first streamlined train, the *Burlington Zephyr*, and no attempt was made to conceal its futuristic associations. Nearly 15,000 Zephyrs were sold in its first year of production (1936). In 1938 Gregorie introduced the first horizontal radiator grille on an American production car. By the end of the decade the American public had accepted the streamlined automobile as its own.

The Lincoln Continental was launched a couple of years later, in 1939, after a request by Edsel Ford for a "special little sports car" for his personal use. Building on the Zephyr, Gregorie made a number of adaptations including lowering the chassis, stretching the fenders and hood, and reducing the length of the rear trunk. The great American architect Frank Lloyd Wright is claimed to have called the Continental "the most beautiful car in the world".

Gregorie worked on various successful Ford models through the 1930s and 1940s as well as several Mercurys. When Edsel Ford died in 1943 Gregorie left the company, to be brought back the following year by Henry Ford II. Two years later, the boat lover in him took over and he left to travel the seas in his trawler, the *Drifter*.

Gregorie's Lincoln Zephyr of 1936 was one of the first fully streamlined cars to leave the production line. It was based on the Briggs Dream Car designed by John Tjaarda. Gregorie developed it successfully into a production car and introduced a number of visual modifications.

R.BUCKMINSTER FULLER

Richard Buckminster Fuller (1895–1983) did not invent the streamlined car, but his interpretation of it was unique. Although he expressed his thoughts about automobile design in a mere handful of models, his "holistic" approach to the problem of the modern automobile makes him a pioneer of early car design. "Bucky" was not fomally trained in any discipline but, through his childhood experience in boat-making, his time in the navy in World War I, and his work with building materials with his architect father-in-law, he developed an interest in architecture, engineering, and mathematics. Moreover, the death of his first daughter lent him a determination to help humanity, a personal commitment that guided him through decades of activity which included designing, writing, lecturing, and experimenting.

Fuller's first experiment was his Dymaxion House of 1929, a lightweight hexagonal structure addressing the problem of housing shortages and the need for temporary buildings. Not a licensed

BELOW *The radical teardrop form of Fuller's prototype Dymaxion car no. 1 invited much public attention. It appeared at the Chicago Century of Progress exhibition, where it created a stir when its driver was killed outside the gates in a collision with another car.*

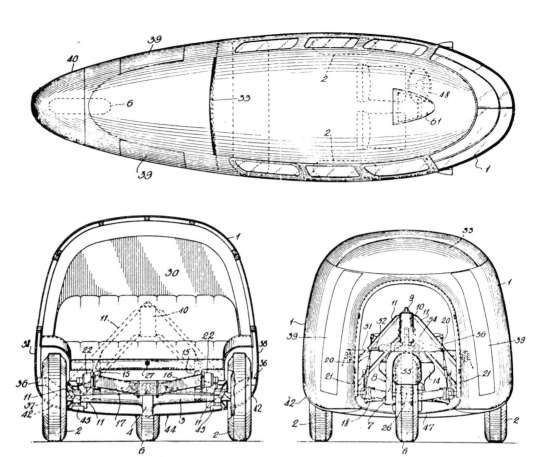

RIGHT *Aerial and front- and rear-section drawings of the Dymaxion car no. 1 showing its aerodynamic teardrop outline, its two front wheels, and its single rear wheel. Its narrow form allowed it to move through restricted spaces and turn very sharply.*

BELOW *The wooden and metal frame of the Dymaxion Car no. 1. Perforated steel was used for lightness, as was an aluminium body-shell and fabric roof. The prototype was constructed in Connecticut in the workshop of a former yacht designer, Starling Burgess.*

architect, he could not get far with the concept but it was exhibited in Chicago. Fuller defined the concept of "Dymaxion", a term he coined himself, as "yielding the greatest performance for the available technology", and he used it again for his next project, a streamlined car.

In 1928 Fuller had experimented with his "Zoomobile", a car that could metamorphose into an airplane. His Dymaxion car of 1933 was also designed on the principle that driving was the next best thing to flying. Fuller gave his car three wheels, one at the back and two at the front, and side rudders that would make it roll in the front and "fly" at the back. The engine was positioned at the back to maximize the interior space and give the driver maximum visibility.

Fuller built a full-size working model of the Dymaxion car with a naval architect, Starling Burgess, who played a key role in the design decisions. Built in Burgess's workshop in Bridgeport, Connecticut, it consisted of a wooden framework, an aluminium body, and a fabric roof. Burgess was expert in the design and construction of yachts and his skills contributed to the originality of the Dymaxion car.

THE REVOLUTIONARY NATURE OF THE DYMAXION

Visually the car was revolutionary and the public was stunned when it appeared in 1933. Its design aesthetic was only one of its virtues, however. Fuller was guided throughout his creative life by the principle of what he called "design science" and was a technocrat at heart. The Dymaxion's novelty lay in its ability to turn sharply in narrow streets, to steer through very narrow spaces, and to increase speed while decreasing fuel consumption. It was undoubtedly its science fiction-inspired appearance that enraptured the general public. Its teardrop body-shell, encasing the entire chassis and much of the wheels, helped to give the "horseless carriage" a whole new identity.

The car suffered a setback at its launch at the Chicago *Century of Progress* exhibition in 1933, where a collision ouside the gates killed the Dymaxion's driver. An investigation proved that Fuller's design was not at fault, but the incident cast a shadow over its future. Fuller created three versions of the Dymaxion car in 1933 and 1934, models 1, 2, and 3, each slightly different. In spite of its inventor's dreams, however, it never went beyond the model stage into production.

DESIGNING LUXURY

DESIGNING LUXURY

Most accounts of 20th-century car design stress the contribution that Harley Earl, pioneer of modern styling, made to the formation of the automobile design profession, and the impact of the aesthetic of streamlining on the appearance of the modern car. Equally, they take as their starting point the moment, in the late 1920s, when owners realized their cars did not simply take them from A to B but played a more complex role in social and cultural life. This realization forced the mass-production industry to begin to take style seriously and to move away from Henry Ford's vision of the standardized automobile available to all.

While this moment was certainly key to what came next, it is not true that the issue of style was absent from the minds of the creators of cars before the 1920s. In the custom-built luxury car, appearance had played a role from an early date, in the tradition of conspicuous display that had for centuries characterized the carriages of the upper classes. Unlike the transforming influence of aerodynamics, however, which made a break with the past, the class-laden aesthetic of the luxury carriage trade represented continuity and visual conservatism.

The luxury automobile of the inter-war years was a hybrid. Eager to become an icon of modernity, it was yet reluctant to lose its power as a status symbol. In that tussle it is important to recognize the pull of the coachbuilding tradition, which curbed the enthusiasm to move forward and introduced a note of caution into manufacturers' ideas about progressive styling in all levels of the market. Nowhere was this more evident than in the failure of the Chrysler Airflow to capture the imagination of the public.

The influence of the carriage trade was seminal in the evolution of modern car styling. From the late 19th century until after World War II, the appearance of luxury cars depended on the

coachbuilder. He it was who injected quality, craftsmanship, and refinement, long demanded of carriages by wealthy customers, into the car. Until the 1950s royalty, the aristocracy, and the wealthy required the maintenance of traditional values in their cars as a means of demonstrating their high social status.

The hybrid that was the modern luxury car of the inter-war years respected tradition in terms of materials, level of finish, and size and stature, but, with its flowing lines, integrated features, and long, low profile, it was unashamedly "of the moment". It reached its peak in the mid-1930s, with the classic cars of that era that are still highly regarded today.

From early in the 20th century, luxury car manufacturers existed in most European countries as well as in the United States. Britain could claim the greatest number of high-status, conservative car producers. While Rolls-Royce, Bentley, and Daimler

(the car associated with the British royal family) were luxury cars from the outset, the products of another group of British manufacturers that had links with racing – Jaguar, Lagonda, and Aston Martin among them – acquired a high level of prestige a little later; France had Bugatti, Delage, and Delahaye; Germany had Horch, Maybach, and Mercedes; Italy had Isotta Fraschini; Spain had Hispano Suiza; the United States had, among others, Cadillac, Packard, Duesenberg, Pierce Arrow, and Lincoln. While some concentrated on "grand tourers" and other road-going models, others gradually transferred their attention from the racetrack to the road. All understood the power of design to create a modern image of luxury and refinement that was forward-looking but dependent on carriage-making traditions.

As standardized production cars were turned off the factory assembly lines in increasing numbers so the need, at the top end

LEFT *The interiors of the inter-war luxury cars took their lead from train interiors, such as this observation coach of the LNER's* Coronation, *in which comfort had already been combined with a modern look, capturing the spirit of both the new technological age and the middle-class parlour of yesteryear.*

RIGHT *For the middle and upper classes of the inter-war years driving continued to be a leisure activity, in which women participated as well as men. Racing was particularly popular. Pictured here is the movie actress Greta Garbo driving her c. 1925 Lancia Lambda.*

of the market, for individuality and distinction became paramount. The manufacturers relied on the coachbuilders' skills in order to produce individualized cars for their wealthy customers. The coachbuilder aimed to provide every little luxury, and his working method involved creating models for the customer to approve before the body was produced and fitted to the chosen chassis.

By the 1920s the coachbuilders dictated high style in automobile design and others followed. The fact that Harley Earl's design for the LaSalle in 1927 was influenced by the up-market Hispano Suiza shows the importance of the look of luxury cars for production cars and also how coachbuilders influenced mass taste. All the car-manufacturing countries had their own coach-builders: Britain had, among others, H.J. Mulliner, Park Ward, Barker, and Vanden Plas; Germany had de Dietrich, Deutz, and Mathiz; France had Saoutchik, Figoni & Falaschi, and Chapron;

Italy had Alessio, Castagna, Zagato, and Farina; and the United States had Murphy, Le Baron, and Darrin and Hibbard. A few were cautious about moving forward too rapidly, while others experimented wildly with the possibilities open to them.

Obviously both the manufacturers and the coachbuilders depended on a market for their products. In the inter-war years the royalty and aristocracy who had made up most of their clients were replaced by a nouveau riche market of industrialists, movie stars, and gangsters who, with nothing to lose, were even more willing to embrace the future. Although the Depression made the going tougher, the luxury car lasted through to World War II.

As in fashion design, the French led the way where style was concerned in the inter-war years. Their experimentation and commitment to excess influenced the rest of the world. Indeed by this time luxury cars and their design were an international

business and French designers worked with American and European car manufacturers alike. The luxury car trade moved about as freely as the customers who patronized it.

The best examples of inter-war coachbuilt luxury cars were indisputably modern in appearance, with unified and sculptural body forms, exploiting the use of chrome as surface decoration and open to the stylistic influence of streamlining. Many of them maintained a sense of dignity that came from the past and was often manifested in conventional features such as a straight bonnet and a subtly sloping radiator grille and windshield. The coachbuilders were sensitive to the need to balance these conflicting idioms and they created models that had lasting appeal.

The inter-war coachbuilders rapidly refined their skills and reacted to new customer demands in a way that radicalized their practice. Their closeness to the customer gave them a privileged

position where changing tastes were concerned and they were able to respond swiftly to pendulum swings. But they could not respond as easily to the technology-led transformations that took place in car manufacturing. As the large car manufacturers found cheaper ways of making cars and styling them the application of heavy bodies to pre-existing chassis – the working practice of the coachbuilders – quickly became outdated. The advent of the one-piece body and chassis meant an end to the work of the traditional coachbuilder. Only a handful survived the transformations of the post-World War II years which allowed cheap, mass-produced cars to incorporate, at least on the surface, the same features as luxury cars. Only the Italian coachbuilders learned the lessons of the changing times and managed to survive in the new climate, finding new ways of providing a form of "added value" and injecting a level of modern luxury into the automobile.

ETTORE BUGATTI

In the rarefied world of custom-built cars the name of Bugatti stood out like a beacon in the first half of the 20th century. While in terms of the numbers of cars actually made, the contribution of Ettore Bugatti (1881–1947) and his son Jean (1909–39) to car design was, by mass-production standards, small (only 7,800 models were built), it was unequalled in terms of the technical and aesthetic standards they set for others to follow. As well as supplying its own bodywork Bugatti collaborated with a number of coachbuilders. It also worked across the boundaries between racing cars and road-going limousines, trans-ferring features from one to the other in the tradition of other early European car manufacturers such as Renault, Peugeot, and Fiat.

A CREATIVE FAMILY

Ettore and Jean came from a family of artists and craftsmen. Ettore's father, Carlo, had been a well-known Milanese furniture and interior designer, noted in the 1890s for his innovative designs linked with the flourishing Art Nouveau movement. Using exotic woods, parchment, and a range of other unusual materials he created interior schemes and furniture objects inspired by North African examples. His "Snail" room exhibited at the Turin exhibition of 1902, for example, brought

ABOVE *The front end of a Bugatti Type 41 Royale of 1931 showing the dramatic curve of the mudguard, the bank of headlights, and the famous elephant mascot. Together these elements work to create a sense of luxury and refinement.*

LEFT *Jean Bugatti in 1927 is photographed in a torpedo-shaped Type 43 Grand Sport, accompanied by his younger brother in a miniature version of a Bugatti sports car. Jean went on to create some stunning car bodies for the company in the 1930s.*

his work to international attention. In 1904 he closed his studio in Milan and moved with his family to Paris.

One of Carlo's sons, Rembrandt, followed his father into the world of art, specializing in animal sculptures. Sadly, afflicted with depression, he took his own life in 1916. His brother and nephew later paid tribute to him by using an elephant sculpture of his as the model for a silver radiator mascot on one of their most outstanding cars, the Type 41 Royale.

ETTORE BUGATTI'S BEGINNINGS

Although he attended the Art Academy at Brera, Carlo's other son, Ettore, moved in another direction, becoming interested in automobiles. His first job was with the Milanese bicycle manufacturer Prinetti and Stucchi and, at the age of 17, he bought a gas-powered tricycle which he spent time taking apart and putting together again. His first noted car design was a 64 km/h (40 mph) four-wheeler, for which he won a prize at the Milan exhibition of 1901.

Ettore Bugatti worked with three German coachbuilding firms before opening his own automobile factory in a former dyeworks in Molsheim in Alsace in 1909. In the same year his little Type 10

emerged from the drawing-board; four years later his first commercial success appeared and became known as his "little miracle". These years also saw his design for Peugeot's little Bébé automobile.

By the 1920s Ettore Bugatti was firmly established as a car manufacturer of high quality. His forte was engineering: his designs for engines were at the cutting edge and his chassis were always interesting. Visually the cars reflected their performance capacity. In 1923 he produced an aerodynamic car for the 1923 Grand Prix at Tours, named the Tank. Covered with a crudely riveted, half-teardrop body, with its large wheels visible under large arches, it was not a sophisticated design, but it showed that Bugatti was thinking along the same lines as other aerodynamically led designers of the period.

A NEW DESIGN AESTHETIC

After the design of the Tank Bugatti seems to have adopted a new approach towards the aesthetic of his cars. His models from the 1920s – from the Type 35 onward – demonstrated an enhanced alignment of function and beauty. To achieve this he had to design the chassis with the bodywork in mind from the start so that the two would work harmoniously together. Ettore's increased attention to the

aesthetic of his cars was undoubtedly a response to his competitors. When his son Jean took over the creation of many of the bodies for Bugatti's cars from around 1930, a new era in the company's history began – an era that was cut short by Jean's untimely death while test-driving one of his designs, the Type 57, in 1939.

Jean Bugatti had joined his father in the 1920s. He shared Ettore's love of racing, although he was not allowed to participate. His first contribution involved changes to the layout of the engine of the Type 50. When the factory opened a body shop in the late 1920s, it

was as a coachbuilder that his most significant contribution was made. Jean's influence began to be felt after 1930, with three cars standing out as tributes to him as a designer of enormous talent.

THE GREAT DESIGNS OF JEAN BUGATTI

The Type 41 Royale Roadster, of which only six models were made, was a disaster inasmuch as it never reached any of the royal clientele for whom it was clearly intended, but as a design it remains one of Bugatti's greatest successes. The best-known example of this design

LEFT *A ceramic model of one of Jean Bugatti's most stunning body designs, the Type 57SC Atalante. The teardrop side window and headlights, curved mudguards, sloping boot, and raked windscreen were all his hallmarks.*

is a model created in 1932 for a clothing manufacturer, Armand Esders, who never drove at night and therefore had no need of headlights. The Type 55 sports car also came from Jean's drawing-board and has been described as the sports car with the most beautiful body ever. A wheel fixed to the back emphasized the raciness of the model. The streamlined profile recalled the Profilée body that Jean created for a number of Bugatti models; it was a controlled streamlining, however, tempered by more traditional features, such as the vertical radiator grille that visually balanced the rest of the body outline.

Jean's *tour de force* was the bodies he created for the Type 57, namely the Ventoux, the Stelvio, and the Atalante. The last, in particular, was a radical design, with a very low stretched hood, a rounded rear, large front fenders, a set-back angled radiator grille, and teardrop headlights. Above all it was the unity of line and the visual balance of its features that made this car one of the most sculpturally pleasing objects of its time.

THE END OF THE GOLDEN ERA

Bugatti's limousines and sports cars made no concessions to the principle of democratization. They were unashamedly expensive and élitist and appealed to an aristocratic, style-conscious audience. The combination of advanced engineering and sophisticated styling earned them a reputation for quality and innovation. With Jean's death in 1939, however, the formula was lost.

Ettore Bugatti continued to design road cars, racing cars, and boats but none of them could compete with the achievements of the 1930s. The factory was used for producing bombs and torpedoes during World War II but the firm never really recovered and Ettore died in 1947. In spite of efforts made to keep the factory open it closed in 1963.

BUGATTI BECOMES A LEGEND

The Bugattis' achievement quickly became mythologized and the remaining cars became collectors' items, reaching high prices in auction houses. In an effort to sustain the myth the Italian Romano Artioli opened a new Bugatti factory in Campogalliano, Modena, in 1987, and in 1990 a new model was launched, the EB 110. But the revival proved unsuccessful, and the Bugatti company is now owned by Volkswagen. In the story of modern car design the decades of the 1920s and the 1930s stand out as years of near perfection, when the combined skills of automotive engineering design and car styling were indivisible, the one informing the other to produce a series of outstanding automobiles.

LEFT *A Bugatti racing car, the Type 59 of 1933, which was based on the Type 57 touring car. It owed much to the ideas of Jean Bugatti, who began to develop an interest in body forms in the early 1930s.*

ROLLS-ROYCE

The subtle imagery created for Rolls-Royce cars over the last hundred years, evoking a world of tradition, quality, and craftsmanship, is testimony to the role of the coachbuilder in the creation of luxury automobiles. Formed in 1906 by the engineer Frederick Henry Royce (1863–1933) and his partner Charles Rolls (1877–1910), the Rolls-Royce company set out to create the "best car in the world" in terms of reliability and performance. With their Silver Ghost model of 1907 there was a general consensus that they achieved just that.

LUXURY AND TRADITION

Britain was slow to develop a mass-production car industry along American and continental European lines, instead producing very high-quality cars for a very wealthy clientele. The manufacturing companies provided the chassis and engine, while the customer commissioned a body from one of the many coachbuilders available. The early part of the century saw Rolls-Royce establish a link with the coachbuilding firm H.J. Mulliner (which became increasingly dependent on the manufacturer and, from 1959, owned by it). Park Ward was the second coachbuilding firm to develop a close relationship with Rolls-Royce; by the 1930s it was providing a number of standard bodies that could be bought directly from the car manufacturer. It too was absorbed by Rolls-Royce, just before World War II. Like Mulliner's, its body designs were conservative – long upright forms with running-boards; picnic baskets attached to the rear – created to sustain the traditional image.

Rolls-Royce did not place much importance on the issue of style until the late 1920s, when the Depression years caused even this company to seek to expand its market; the appeal of stylishness could

ABOVE *The neoclassical lines of Rolls-Royce's geometric radiator grille serve to enhance the authoritative visual presence of these cars. Topped by the ever-present mascot, the Rolls has come to symbolize the idea of high-class luxury.*

LEFT *The materials used in the interior of Rolls-Royce's cars reinforce the image of luxury. Here walnut veneer and leather upholstery combine to evoke tradition and craftsmanship, qualities that define, in part, the company's contribution to 20th-century car design.*

no longer be ignored. This was apparent in the Phantom II of 1929, for which a number of designers created a range of strikingly modern-looking bodies in an attempt to bring Rolls-Royce up to date.

SUBTLE INNOVATIONS

John Blatchley, a former employee of the coachbuilders Gurney Nutting, became Rolls-Royce's chief stylist soon after the war. He initiated a program of designs that moved Rolls-Royce subtly forward without sacrificing its traditional image of quality and reliability. Impressed by Cadillac's designs of the postwar years, he made efforts to bring Rolls-Royce nearer to that American definition of luxury. The Silver Dawn model of the late 1940s was the first to demonstrate these new tendencies, followed by the Silver Cloud and the revolutionary Silver Shadow. Blatchley claims that his vision of the Rolls-Royce was of a "flying drawing room", and that he saw his task as to create a high level of comfort. He took the Rolls-Royce from an automobile with a separate chassis and body to an integrated car that could be driven by an "owner-driver". Yet his continued sensitivity to the importance of tradition prompted him to introduce "retro" features into the Corniche model of 1971. Throughout his years with the company Blatchley trod a delicate path between past and future, managing not to alienate the old customers while attracting the new.

Blatchley left Rolls-Royce in the early 1970s. With the market for this status car to end all status cars expanding, so its association with a "nouveau riche" image became more and more deeply entrenched. However, as a company using design to hold on to tradition while simultaneously responding to the needs of the future, the example of Rolls-Royce cannot be surpassed.

ABOVE *The Silver Ghost model of 1907 established Rolls-Royce as a manufacturer of luxurious and reliable cars. The commitment to craftsmanship that underpinned its production and the impact of its size and elegance combined to create a memorable automobile.*

RIGHT *Rolls-Royce's Corniche two-door saloon with Mulliner/Park Ward coachwork. The design of this classic car's elegant form was carried out under the watchful eye of John Blatchley, who was the company's head of styling for a number of years.*

BENTLEY

The name of Bentley is inextricably linked with the British upper classes: throughout its 80-year history, the firm has maintained its reputation for quality and for giving customers the trappings of high social status. Its cars have reflected that reputation, favouring tradition over novelty and formal aesthetics over experimentation.

EARLY SUCCESSES

The company's founder, W.O. Bentley (1888–1971), had a background in the railways and in car sales but he desperately wanted to produce his own car. His first attempt, in the early 1920s, doubled as a tourer and a racer. The appearance of the company's first cars depended on the input of coachbuilders, among them the well-known firm of Vanden Plas, which developed a strong alliance with Bentley through the inter-war years. From early on the pointed radiator became an almost universal feature of Bentley cars.

The fast tourers were soon joined by cars with more heavy, closed bodywork; many coachbuilders, including H.J. Mulliner, Freestone and Webb, Barker, Hooper, and Gurney Nutting, worked with Bentley in creating the large saloons, characterized by their length, solidity, and attention to detail. In 1931 financial difficulties led to a buy-out by Rolls-Royce (see pp.54–5) and an end to independence. Until the early 1980s Bentley's designs were influenced by Rolls-Royce and, for a time after World War II, the models were almost indistinguishable, only their radiator grilles and mascots serving to separate them.

RIGHT *The Bentley company first earned a reputation through its high-performance racing cars. This 1931 4.5 Litre supercharged model epitomizes the look of the powerful and elegant cars it produced in the inter-war years.*

BOTH CLASSIC AND STYLISH

The 1930s saw a continuation of Bentley's successes on the racetrack. As well as maintaining the "classic" Bentley image the coachbuilders also reflected the changes in styling fashions on its road cars. Even streamlining entered the picture in certain models. A two-door "airline" saloon by Barker of 1935, created for the Marquesa de Portago, was one such example, while a Park Ward two-seater coupé of 1938 displayed similarly sophisticated lines. A 1939 model, designed by the French bodymaker Georges Paulin, went the whole way, boasting a completely streamlined body-shell.

The postwar years at Bentley inevitably echoed those at Rolls-Royce. The 1950s marked the beginning of the end for the British coachbuilders but Bentley and Rolls-Royce worked with them for a while longer. Alongside the standard bodies, a number of styling masterpieces were created. Even the Italian coachbuilder Pininfarina

(see pp.162–5) created a coupé design for a Bentley Continental. For a short period the British coachbuilders showed that they could create innovative designs in line with the Americans and the Italians.

John Blatchley, head of Rolls-Royce styling, had a significant input into Bentley styling after the war, creating, among other cars, the standard Bentley Mark VI body at the same time as the Rolls-Royce Silver Dawn. The latter firm dominated the former where sales were concerned. However, in the early 1980s Bentley began to reassert itself both as an individual brand and as a design-led company, showing with the Mulsanne and Continental models that it was possible to produce progressively styled, high-status cars. Other striking designs from these years included a car shown at Geneva in 1985, named Project 90 and styled by John Heffernan and Ken Greenley, which showed just how far Bentley had come in creating a new identity for itself through design.

ABOVE *This stylish 1950s R-type Bentley Continental, with its unified, aerodynamically inspired body-shell, represents a high point of achievement in the luxurious cars the company created in collaboration with high-quality coachbuilders.*

LEFT *Brand identity, tradition, and a forward-looking approach to styling were combined into a single visual formula with the classic, elegant Bentley Continental R model (1991). Its low sleek lines suggest power and speed, while the pointed radiator grille provides a link with the past.*

JAGUAR

The British car company Jaguar has created a legend, closely tied up with the post-World War II concept of "British style", that is known the world over. Its cars have come to denote a sense of quality and timeless elegance and can be listed alongside Burberry raincoats and Church's shoes as great British success stories. Jaguar cars depend on a seamless alliance of appearance and performance, creating a total Jaguar "experience" that is hard to put into words

JAGUAR'S ROOTS

The unique aesthetic of Jaguar cars is a result of the discerning taste of the man who created the company, William Lyons. With a handful of engineers and stylists, he created the Jaguar image and oversaw every detail of every car. An expert marketing man, he understood not only how to create a unique product but also how to sell it.

Jaguar's roots lay in the production of sidecars for motorcycles. An enthusiastic motorcyclist himself, Lyons began producing sidecars on an amateur basis but soon teamed up with a partner, William Walmsley, to create the Swallow Sidecar Company in Blackpool in 1922. The Stockport Zeppelin sidecar became the company's first product. Its torpedo form showed the pair's interest in the aesthetic of streamlining, a visual language that was to become an important part of Jaguar's progressive image. Their use of aluminium was a manifestation of their forward-looking approach to modern manufacturing methods and materials.

The late 1920s saw Lyons and Walmesley producing elegant car bodies for a range of manufacturers, among them Austin, Fiat, and Wolseley. They made their mark with a stylish body, created for an Austin Seven chassis, that boasted a dramatic, chrome-surrounded

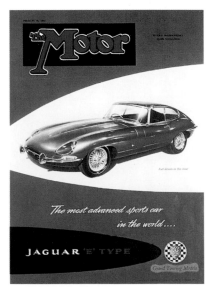

RIGHT *The hard-top version of Jaguar's stylish E Type sports car is depicted on the cover of an issue of* The Motor *magazine from the mid-1960s. Most people considered this version to be the most aesthetically pleasing of all.*

ABOVE *The Jaguar company began life as the Swallow Sidecar Company, a manufacturer of motorcycle sidecars. The torpedo form of the example illustrated here demonstrates the influence of aerodynamics. William Lyons went on to create cars with equally stylish lines.*

LEFT *Jaguar's 3.8 litre E Type of 1964, the body of which was designed by the company's in-house stylist, Malcolm Sayer. This model opened up Jaguar's appeal to a new, youthful market which sought racy sports cars. Its long low lines were inspired by the racetrack.*

radiator and a rounded trunk. As a result of its success the company expanded and moved to Coventry, the home of the British car manufacturing industry.

ELEGANCE AND MODERNITY

From its modest beginnings the Swallow Sidecar Company had built up a flourishing coachbuilding side. It soon earned a reputation for providing elegant bodies with a modern look. The coachbuilder Cyril Holland played an important role in these early days, his acute eye introducing a level of stylishness into the firm's bodies. Nineteen thirty-one marked the launch at the London Motor Show of the company's first car, the SS1, an elongated model with an integrated form. This was followed by the SS2 which, with its flowing front fenders, pushed the company's aesthetic a stage further.

In the early 1930s Lyons created an engineering department headed by William Haynes, who stayed with Lyons until 1969. The name "Jaguar" was used for the first time in 1935, and in 1937 the famous leaping cat mascot was designed for the company by F. Gordon Crosby. By the late 1930s Jaguar cars were beginning to acquire a reputation for high stylishness. A dramatic-looking two-seater version of the SS100 with rounded wings, enclosed wheels and flowing tail, known as the Airline, was shown in 1938, proving that Britain could produce streamlined cars that were as elegant as anything produced elsewhere. Lyons was equally innovative in his approach to modern manufacturing techniques, moving from the wooden-framed to the all-steel car body in the late 1930s. Features such as leather seats and the use of wood on the dashboard were retained as a sign of quality; leather seats were a standard component

LEFT *While the exteriors of Jaguar's cars pushed forward the limits of styling, their interiors retained links with tradition through the use of luxury materials, such as leather, which were worked by craftsmen. The combination served to earn Jaguar a reputation for both quality and progressiveness.*

of all the Jaguar saloons up until the early 1960s when they became optional. This element of conservatism enabled Lyons to shape a car company known as much for its links with British traditions as for its commitment to the future.

JAGUAR IS LAUNCHED

It was in the years after 1945, when the Jaguar Company was finally created, that Lyons' greatest successes came. He saw the importance of producing racing cars alongside road vehicles, aware that the technical reputation of the racers influenced customers' perceptions of the roadsters. One fed off the other in commercial terms.

From the 1940s Jaguar became known both for its stylish sports cars and for its saloons. Among the former was the elegant XK120, first seen at the Earls Court Motor Show of 1948, which overshadowed the Mark V saloon launched in the same year. The first model boasted an aluminium body (which would later be replaced by steel). The XK120 was launched to gain publicity for Jaguar's new XK six-cylinder engine but it gained its immediate impact as a result of its stunning curvaceous form, evocative of an animal with tensed haunches about to leap into action.

The early 1950s were the beginning of an era of design at Jaguar with which the name of Malcolm Sayer is inextricably associated. Sayer came to Jaguar with a background in aerodynamics, and for a decade used his extensive knowledge of that science to influence both the performance and the appearance of Jaguar's racing cars. Working closely with Lyons and Haynes, Sayer took Jaguar cars into a new era. His first efforts resulted in the C Type Jaguar, a racing car launched in 1951. Its simple, aerodynamic curves were repeated in the D Type of a few years later.

The shift from the track to the road came full circle with the emergence of the E Type Jaguar of 1961, probably the most "classic" of all the company's products. The stylish saloons of the 1950s and early 1960s, culminating in the broad Mark X, had become hallmarks of luxury, albeit more attainable and more modern than that offered by Rolls-Royces and Bentleys. The E Type, by contrast, had a much more racy, youthful image. Once again the body was styled by Sayer, closely overseen by Lyons. Its low, long lines, its dramatically extended bonnet with built-in headlights and miniature radiator grille, came directly from the racetrack. The experience of driving the car was part and parcel of its aesthetic appeal. As a piece of pure sculpture its sleek profile – particularly the coupé version – was strikingly harmonious. Its quality was later confirmed by the Museum of Modern Art in New York which, in 1996, selected it as only the third car to be added to its permanent design collection.

The early 1960s saw a peak in Jaguar's reputation. In 1968 the XJ6 was launched which, once again, won acclaim for the elegance of its design. It was an unostentatious car confirming the company's reputation for attention to visual detail and commitment to quiet, tasteful luxury. In the mid-1960s the company moved through a series of changes of ownership – from a merger with BMC in 1966 to becoming part of British Leyland in 1968. Lyons retired in 1972; the company was privatized again in 1984 and was bought by Ford in 1989. In design terms, very little happened until the launch of the new XJ6 in 1986.

THE JAGUAR IS REBORN

Geoff Lawson, a graduate of London's Royal College of Art, was employed as Jaguar's head of styling in 1984 and was personally responsible for the renaissance in the company's reputation for innovative and high-quality design. He achieved this by building on the company's reputation for elegance, sophistication, attention to detail, luxury, and comfort combined wth "Jaguar appeal". Lawson managed to bring the company back to the fore as one that valued the concept of design. Above all he understood the important role that William Lyons, who died in 1985, had played in carefully controlling Jaguar's image and in balancing tradition with innovation. In turn he understood that the modern tradition that Jaguar had created over half a century deserved respect and a level of humility. Following his premature death in 1999, Lawson was succeeded as Jaguar's head of styling by Ian Callum, who has sustained his predecessor's philosophy ensuring that tradition works hand in hand with innovation.

ASTON MARTIN

The products of the British manufacturer of exclusive sports cars and saloons, Aston Martin, belong unambiguously to the 20th century. At the same time they owe everything to the traditional skills of the coachbuilder. Lionel Martin and Robert Bamford set out, in 1913, to create quality cars for discerning customers. In the 1990s consumers buying a DB7 could still choose their own preferred colour, and their own Connolly leather fittings and Wilton carpet. Back in the 1920s and 1930s firms such as H.J. Mulliner of Birmingham had supplied elegant bodies for the technologically innovative chassis and engines that Aston Martin developed. Later Italian coachbuilders, such as Touring and Zagato, created special bodies for the company.

THE MAKING OF THE NAME

The firm's name came into being after World War I, formed from a combination of its founder's surname with a competition event called the Aston Clinton Hill Climb. Aston Martin focused on the creation of racing cars that would beat all others – they saw Bugatti (see pp.50–53) as a key competitor – and from this base they branched

out into high-quality sports cars in the years leading up to World War II. Financial problems led the company through a sequence of owners, however, until, in 1947, it was bought by David Brown.

THE DB SERIES

Brown initiated the design and production of the DB (the initials of his name) series of Aston Martins which have become classics. His DB1 emerged in 1948, followed by the DB2 and DB3 of 1950 and 1951. In 1955 Brown moved Aston Martin to a new factory in Newport Pagnell, on the site of Salmon and Sons, a coachbuilder to nobility established in 1820. Tickford Motor Bodies, as that old coachbuilding firm was now known, became a main supplier of bodies to Aston Martin.

The DB4 of 1958 was classic Aston Martin: Carrozzeria Touring styled the saloon model. Its wraparound windshield and bumpers, gently sloping extended bonnet, and sloping roof typified the Italian company's sculptural approach to car design. Aston Martin called on Italian car-styling skills again in 1960 to create bodies for 19 examples of its DB4GT model. This time it was Zagato, a company with which

Aston Martin was to work fairly frequently, that, through the eyes and hands of Ercole Spada (see pp.172–3), created a strikingly sculptural lightweight body with bubble headlights and a gently sloping roof. In the mid-1960s the cult status of Aston Martin cars was enhanced when DB5s were featured in two James Bond films, *Goldfinger* and *Thunderball*. Complete with futuristic add-ons, the car had a sophisticated image that was ideal for the slick, handsome hero who always won the day and the girl.

CONTINUING STYLE

David Brown withdrew his involvement from the company in 1963, and Aston Martin's next design success was the 1967 DBS. This model was styled at Newport Pagnell by William Towns, who had come

from Rover and is also well known for the huge Aston Martin Lagonda that he created. He continued to produce models for Aston Martin, notably the Bulldog of 1980 with its striking gull-wing doors. Zagato also collaborated with the company again, creating a version of the 1986 Vantage of which only 50 were built.

Increasingly in the 1990s British designers showed their worth by styling innovative Aston Martins. John Heffernan was responsible for the 1988 Virage while Ian Callum styled the 1993 DB7. Ford took control of the company in 1987 and there were fears for its future. The unique image of Aston Martin was not under threat, however, and its bespoke elegance and design were maintained in the hands of a new generation of designers who understood where the company had come from and, equally importantly, where it was going.

ABOVE *A luxurious Lagonda M45 from the late 1930s demonstrates an effective use of two-tone paintwork. Attention to detail and the superb craftsmanship of the coachbuilt body marked out Lagonda's cars of this era as among the most sumptuous in Britain.*

RIGHT *The interior of this Aston Martin DB6 from the 1970s shows how the luxurious nature of the exterior body was continued inside, where high-quality leatherwork gave a high level of comfort. The dial design reflected the distinctive radiator grille and contributed to the stylishness of this desirable car.*

FRENCH CARROSSIERS

Between the two world wars, where women's clothing and interior decoration were concerned, Paris was the centre of the world: all judgments about fashion and taste emanated from this powerful city. And this extended to cars as well. Stylish Parisians considered the automobile to be an essential accessory of their modern lifestyles, especially for their journeys down to the Côte d'Azur which had just become fashionable.

COUTURE AND CARS

A decade earlier the designer Sonia Delaunay had designed a car body to match a coat she had created, thereby showing just how closely the two worlds of fashion and cars were intertwined. The bespoke nature of Parisian couture extended into car production such that wealthy, fashion-conscious customers could create their own personalized automobiles to match their clothing and their lifestyles. In this process the skills of the coachbuilders were all-important.

FRENCH DOMINANCE

French coachbuilders, or *carrossiers*, dominated the appearance of the high-end, high-fashion, luxury vehicles used by the wealthy internationally. What they decreed was followed by coachbuilders in Britain, the United States, and elsewhere. The extravagant forms of their creations were, however, symbols of an era that was fated to fade away after the end of World War II. It was an era that clung to the aristocratic values of the past but that, at the same time, embraced the possibilities of modernity. In car design terms this meant combining the paraphernalia of luxury, such as exotic woods and the use of leather in luggage and interiors, with aerodynamic and futuristic shapes.

The French car industry had been a pioneering one in the early century, with manufacturing firms such as Panhard, Talbot, Delage, and Delahaye playing a key role in the development of the modern automobile. While they supplied the chassis, the coachbuilding

companies created the bodies selected by the wealthy clients who could create their individualized objects of transport. The tradition of individualism underpinning the work of the coachbuilders continued well into the century, until the coachbuilders finally had to admit defeat after World War II, when the conditions of car production and consumption changed beyond all recognition.

France boasted a large number of coachbuilding firms. Prominent among them were the names of Saoutchik, Figoni & Falaschi, Chapron, Faget Varnet, Facel, Franay, and Pourtout. All of them worked with a range of automobile manufacturers. Their system of creating models in wood, and frequently full-size mockups, was a common one and played a crucial role in the manufacture of unique, one-off automobiles.

SAOUTCHIK

Saoutchik was one of the first coachbuilding firms to be founded in the 20th century and, by the mid-century, was known internationally as a supplier of luxurious, highly fashionable bodies for prestigious manufacturers, from Hispano Suiza (see pp.68–9) and Mercedes-Benz to Voisin, Cadillac (see pp.76–7), Daimler, and Rolls-Royce (see pp.54–5). Russian in origin, Iacov (or Jacques as he became known)

ABOVE *A view of a range of cars displayed within the Grand Palais building in Paris in 1948. In the years just following World War II the French luxury car, with its coachbuilt body created by Saoutchik, Figoni & Falaschi, and others, was still in existence.*

BELOW *The elegant, elongated body of this Delage D8 model, with its two-tone paintwork, created in the 1930s, epitomizes the French luxury car of that period. While the body form betrays a level of conservatism the flowing line of the mudguard/running-board is overtly modern.*

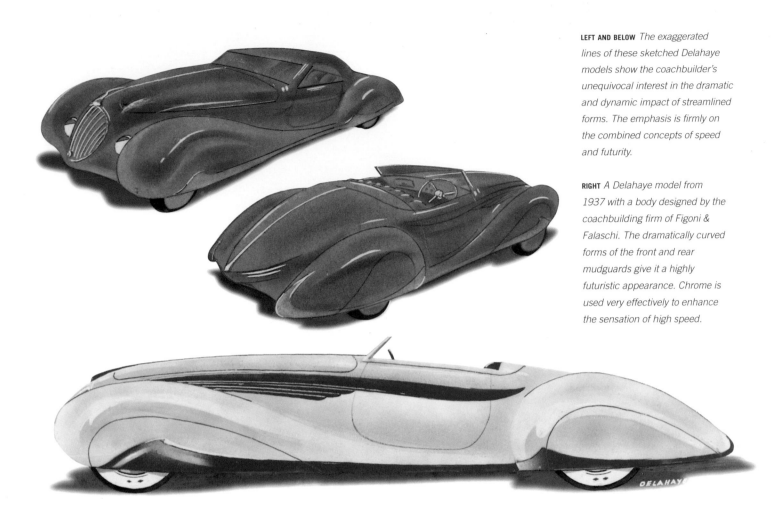

known) Saoutchik began his working life as an artist but then moved into designing car bodies, to which he applied his artistic skills to good effect. From 1906 onward he created an enormous number of stunning cars, which have all become classics.

The 1930s were particularly productive years for Saoutchik, and models of note include a Bucciali TA V30 of 1932 and a 1939 T57C Bugatti (see pp.50–53). In 1939 Saoutchik's workshop created a cabriolet which was to become, after the war, the Delage D8-120 that was used by De Gaulle at the time of the Liberation. Like all coachbuilt cars, it was a heavy vehicle – more than 2 tons in weight – but its elegant, streamlined forms effectively succeeded in creating an illusion of lightness.

A few years later, in 1949, Saoutchik created a body for the Delahaye 135M. The result was an extravagant white automobile with rounded and teardrop-shaped forms and a dramatically slanted windshield. The extensive use of chrome around the radiator grille and the headlights was reminiscent of contemporary American cars, with the difference that in the Saoutchik body the material was an intrinsic element of the design rather than an add-on for dramatic effect. The interiors of Saoutchik's cars were always sumptuous, featuring leather and other luxury materials.

FIGONI & FALASCHI

The firm of Figoni & Falaschi was equally visible through its designs for wealthy clients. Like Saoutchik, its clientele encompassed royalty, including the Shah of Iran, for whom they created a body for the Bugatti T57C in 1937. Among the numerous bodies that Giuseppe Figoni and Ovidio Falaschi created were those for a famous 8C 2300 Alfa Romeo of 1932, a Delage D8, a Delahaye 135 of 1937, and a Talbot Lago T120 of the following year. The last had an extra-long chassis which allowed the coachbuilders to create an extended body. In this model they indulged their long-standing interest in the front wings of cars by giving it huge, aerodynamic examples complete with chrome trim.

HENRI CHAPRON

Another highly successful French coachbuilder, Henri Chapron, set up his establishment in 1919. Once again he worked with Delage on the D6 and the D8. He made his fortune, however, through a contract with Delahaye that allowed him to create nearly all the bodies for the 135 model. Like the other coachbuilders, he worked primarily on sports cars and grand tourers (*grands routiers*). A Delage D8 tourer of 1930, for example, with its huge, stretched body and its boot packed behind the spare wheel at the back, demonstrated just how

"grand" these vehicles could be. No expense was spared on these luxurious, elegant monsters.

After World War II Chapron changed direction somewhat in an attempt to move with the times, and he worked for a period with Citroën. His Citroën designs included the Croisette cabriolet version of the DS. Key features of the design included the addition of a chrome strip to conceal the join between the wing and the rear door. The most successful result of Chapron's collaboration with Citroën was the design of the Usine cabriolet version of the DS, which was included in the official range.

THE END OF THE ROAD

Chapron's success with Citroën was a rare exception. In general the luxury car market disappeared in France after the war and with it the coachbuilders. This was partly a result of a tax on luxury cars that was brought in at that time, and partly, as far as the coachbuilders were concerned, a result of the lack of availability of wood (still the main material used to build models), together with the growing appeal of the mass-produced car aimed at the popular market. Although the international market for one-off custom cars remained fairly buoyant, from the 1950s onward it was no longer to France that the

manufacturers looked, but rather to Italy, where the coachbuilders had managed to transform themselves to suit the new climate.

With the demise of the French coachbuilders came the end of an era in which craftsmanship and status linked with traditional values and elegance came together in car design. In the story of 20th-century car styling this period was an important transitional moment which stood between coachbuilding practices and modern car design. It had sustained the idea of motoring for pleasure and the link between motoring and the social élite. Despite the fact that the customers now included a new wealthy market, which had made its money through the new "glamour industries", this age had encompassed a world in which car ownership had been the exception rather than the rule.

After 1945 mass car ownership became ever more real in the industrialized world, and car ownership was no longer a means of differentiating the "haves" from the "have-nots". In line with such socio-cultural changes car design also moved into a new era, becoming less preoccupied with luxury and more concerned to offer dreams to the mass of the consuming population. While the French coachbuilders faded from view the Italians rose to the fore, able to combine this old craft with a new approach to mass manufacturing and aware that desire was stimulated by a whole new set of automotive values.

HISPANO SUIZA

*F*ormed in 1902, the result of a collaboration between a renowned Swiss engineer named Marc Birkigt and a Spanish manufacturer of electric cars, La Cuidra, the Fabrica La Hispano Suiza de Automovils was evidence of burgeoning internationalism in the car industry. This was reinforced by the establishment of a French Hispano Suiza factory in 1911, which moved to its permanent location in Bois Colombes, outside Paris, three years later. As a result Hispano Suizas were believed by many to be French automobiles and they quickly became linked with the concept of luxurious high fashion.

In spite of this reputation the first Hispano Suiza of international renown derived its name from the Spanish king, Alfonso XIII, who commissioned a 15T grand tourer in 1912. Over the next few years

BELOW *The earliest Hispano Suizas were elegant touring cars. This was one of the first models, designed for the king of Spain in 1912. From the outset, the company created a luxurious, aristocratic image for its cars.*

Hispano Suiza led the field in grand tourers built for enjoyment and not just for utility. Birkigt's sophisticated engineering, combined with elegant coachwork provided by the leading coachbuilders of the day, produced cars that were the envy of many.

RACERS AND TOURERS

During World War I Birkigt designed a V8 aircraft engine; in 1919, he adapted his success to the needs of the automotive industry and Hispano Suiza in particular, with the creation of the H6 model. That year also saw the adoption by the Spanish company of the stork as its mascot – an icon that also had World War I associations, since it had been painted on the side of a victorious Spad fighter plane. The H6 was the star of the 1919 Paris motor show.

In 1928 the American coachbuilding firm of Hibbard and Darrin, active in Paris from the early 1920s, created a coupé de ville body for an H6B. Such was the appeal of these grand, hand-crafted Hispano

LEFT *The ultimate luxury car, the Hispano Suiza reached its apogee in models such as the two-tone 12-cylinder 9.4 litre car pictured here. The extravagant and dramatic sweeping boot of this inter-war car is accentuated by the chrome strip positioned along its waistline.*

BELOW *The front of this Sedanca Coupé V12 of 1936 shows the juxtaposition of the curve of the exaggerated fender and the vertical lines of the radiator grille. The stork mascot completes the composition, creating a strong brand identity for this powerful, luxurious touring car.*

Suizas that Harley Earl (see pp.22–5) looked closely at them when creating his first designs for General Motors in the late 1920s, aiming to translate the appeal of the ultimate luxury car into an affordable, mass-produced automobile. Binder was another coachbuilder to work on an H6B coupé de ville. Its design was a little more staid and upright in form but its use of two-tone purple-and-mauve paintwork reinforced the company's racy image. A large number of other cabriolets and coupés were available with bodies that ranged from the conventional to the streamlined depending on the requirements of the customer. Not only did they function as touring cars, as originally intended, but the power of their engines also meant that they could be used as sports cars; many H6s won eminent racing prizes through the 1920s.

TRADITION AND MODERNITY

The production span of the Hispano Suiza J12, which took over from the H6, stretched from 1931 to 1938. Once again, pre-eminent coachbuilders were charged with providing bodies. A Saoutchik of 1935, for example, demonstrated the way in which it was possible to combine the conservative image required of the high-status car with a racy profile conveying just the right level of modernity for Europe's wealthiest customers. The interior was crucially important in this context and the Saoutchik model came complete with a drinks cabinet equipped with a glass decanter and glasses, while the female passenger was supplied with a mirror and comb and her male companion with a box of cigars. Every detail enhanced the important leisure role that cars such as these played in the lives of the wealthy in the inter-war years.

The consumer lifestyle that was part and parcel of the Hispano Suiza mythology vanished after World War II but the car manufacturer had been forced to close its Spanish and French factories for financial reasons a year before hostilities broke out. The company survived but moved away from the production of luxury cars to the more pragmatic and realistic world of engineering.

ITALIAN CARROZZERIE

In the years after 1945 the world of car design was dominated by the work of the Italian coachbuilders (*carrozzerie*) – Pininfarina, Bertone, Zagato, Touring, Ghia, and others. Their roots were firmly embedded in the first half of the 20th century, however. Between 1900 and 1945 the coachbuilders helped the car industry understand that cars should not be thought of as a set of disjointed components but as unified objects with a powerful sculptural appeal.

THE EARLY COACHBUILDERS

The first coachbuilding workshops formed specifically to service the car industry were set up at the turn of the century. One of the earliest was Castagna, which moved from carriage-building into automotive bodies. It quickly became known as a leader in the field and produced bodies for royalty, as well as creating the extraordinary streamlined body for Count Ricotti's special Alfa Romeo of 1913. Ercole Castagna, the son of the founder, was one of the first coachbuilders to be specifically trained in car mechanics and design and, with his brother Emilio, who had been art school-trained, took over the workshop from his father during World War I. Castagna proved not to be the most radical of the Italian coachbuilding firms but it succeeded in creating a number of impressive designs with a strikingly modern feel to them, including examples for Alfa Romeo (such as the RL Supersport of 1925) and Isotta Fraschini (among them the Tipo 8A of 1933).

Stabilimenti Farina set up its business in Turin in 1906. Led by Giovanni Farina, who had worked previously in the established workshop of Marcello Alessio, it collaborated with a wide range of French and Italian manufacturers, among them De Dion, Itala, Peugeot, and Lancia. Farina was also involved in the creation of the body for Fiat's Zero, the Italian manufacturer's attempt to produce a car in response to Ford's Model T (see pp.20–1). The inter-war years saw the Farina workshop move into the modern era with some interesting designs for individual Lancia models, some of them embracing the new streamlining idiom. A 1934 Dilambda and the 1936 Asturia Cabriolet Aerodinamico were among Farina's most memorable achievements. However, as was also the case with

RIGHT *A chassis with a wooden body framework created by Bertone in the early 1920s. This provided the basis on which the coachbuilders constructed their elegant bodies. Their task was to create an image of luxury and comfort and to hide the mechanical innards of the automobile.*

Castagna, the company's early formation held it back, preventing it from moving into the postwar era, and it closed in 1952.

Bertone (see also pp.166–9) and Ghia also had their origins in the early century, the former in 1912 and the latter three years later. Bertone's achievements included a body for Fiat's 501 racing car of 1921, and a range of designs for Lancia, created in the inter-war years, which came about as a result of Giuseppe Bertone's friendship with Vincenzo Lancia. Giacinto Ghia's coachbuilding firm was successful in the inter-war years, producing bodies for Italian racing cars renowned for their speed and elegance. Once again the leading Italian manufacturers, Lancia, Fiat, and Alfa Romeo, were key clients, and notable cars included a Lancia Kappa and the Alfa Romeo 6C 1500, which won the Mille Miglia race of 1929.

Nineteen nineteen was the year of the foundation of Carrozzeria Zagato. Like so many other leading car designers of those years, Ugo Zagato had learned a great deal from his World War I experience in aircraft construction. At the Pomilio aircraft construction company he

ABOVE *A body created by the Carrozzeria Pininfarina of Turin. Pininfarina created elegant forms for this Lancia Dilambda model and others in the 1930s in his factory on Corso Trapani. The overt luxury and comfort of this stylish model, with its raked radiator grille and extended bonnet, are typical of his work.*

had acquired first-hand knowledge of new construction techniques leading to lighter and stronger metal products, and it was with the intention of applying that knowledge to cars that he founded his own bodymaking firm. In the shift from traditional carriage-making to modern car styling this transfer of knowledge was to prove key, and Zagato undoubtedly played an important role in the process. He applied his new skills to racing cars in the first instance and Alfa Romeo, Fiat, and Lancia were quick to realize the advantages he offered. In the 1930s the firm stayed with sports cars but also ventured into the world of saloons. Clients included Isotta Fraschini and Alfa Romeo, with the 6C 2300 Pescara of 1936 and the 8C 2900 B Spider Carenato starring among the designs. The 1938 Lancia

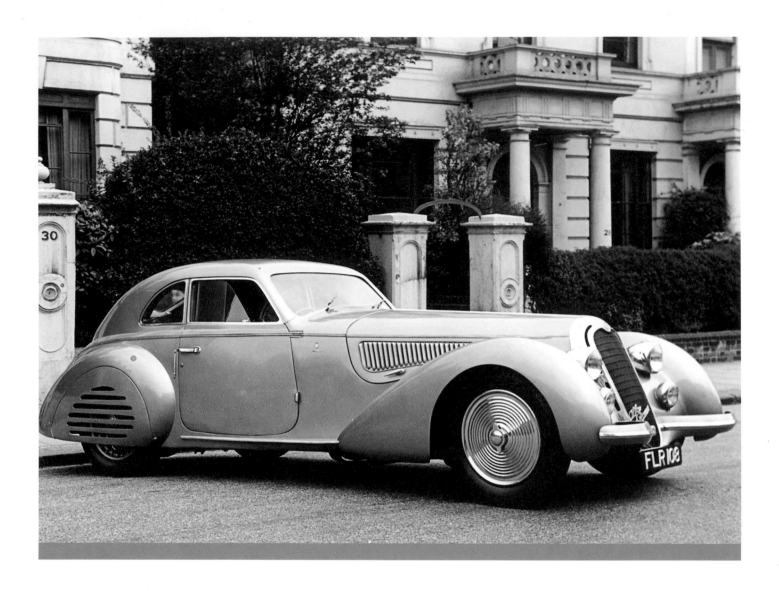

Aprilia Panciona introduced what came to be known as the "panoramic look". During World War II Zagato designed lorries for Isotta Fraschini, and in 1945 Ugo and his sons Elio and Gianni established La Zagato, opening a new factory in Milan in the following year.

The Touring workshop opened its doors in 1926 – the name indicates the high level of cultural capital that was attached to an English name at that time. From the outset the firm's main client was Alfa Romeo, with which Felice Anderloni, Touring's founder, had a formal relationship from 1927. The workshop also offered a number of stunning designs for saloon cars to Alfa.

PININFARINA

The Italian coachbuilder to make the greatest impact in the pre-World War II years was undoubtedly Battista "Pinin" Farina (see also pp.162–5), the brother of Giovanni. Pininfarina was introduced to car

design at an early age in the workshop of his older brother, and claims to have designed the radiator for the Fiat Zero while still a boy. As it did for Ugo Zagato, World War I provided a crucial training ground for him. He was involved in the construction of the Aviatic trainer planes and his education was rounded off by a trip to the United States and a meeting with Henry Ford. In the 1920s he set up a workshop, began designing car bodies, and developed his ideas about metal construction. Pininfarina has written about his interest in the influence of nature on forms, particularly the effect of wind on snow formations and on the shape of trees. When he finally came to designing real car bodies in the 1930s these influences were apparent in the simple streamlined profiles and flowing lines that he achieved.

Pininfarina founded a company in 1930 in Turin to work on the design and construction of special car bodies. Early examples included designs for Alfa Romeo and the Hispano Suiza Coupé but

LEFT *Carrozzeria Touring's 8C 2900 B Lungo model created for Alfa Romeo in 1935 is one of the most dramatic statements of style and power to appear in car design in this era.*

LEFT *The body for Alfa Romeo's 6C 1750 was created by Pininfarina in 1931 and represents his early foray into body design. The most innovative feature of this model is the way the wings are blended into the running-board. The headlights are still separate components.*

his most striking designs were those he created for Lancia: the DiLambda of 1930, the Astura of 1936, and the streamlined Aprilia coupé of 1937. They all exhibited a simple sculptural aesthetic which was artistically inspired and which became a hallmark of Italian postwar styling. The Aprilia, with its dramatically curved windscreen, was particularly advanced in its conception, and its subtly curved profile was echoed in a number of later Pininfarina designs.

THE SHIFT TO THE MODERN

By 1939 the stage had been set for what was to come next. Most importantly the shift from traditional to modern practice had taken place and many of the close collaborations between the manufacturers and the bodymakers had been established. While the older firms did not make the transition, for the most part the younger ones were more flexible and open to change, particularly when, as in

the cases of Pininfarina and Bertone, there was a younger generation able and ready to take on the baton in the tradition of Italian family firms. Most significantly, individuals such as Pininfarina and Zagato were not merely responding to the new techniques of car construction and manufacture that were widespread by 1945, but had played a part in making them happen.

The role played by the Italian coachbuilding firms in the years after 1945 has been widely documented. However, it was in the earlier part of the century that the roots of these firms were established and their approach to innovation developed. Their skill in adapting to changing circumstances in the automobile industry, together with their ability to come up with new solutions, was unequalled. After 1945 they went on to apply those skills to the creation of the luxury, fantasy vehicles that earned Italy a leading role in the world of automotive design.

MASCOTS

ABOVE *The Spanish car manufacturer Hispano Suiza used the stork mascot after World War I. This symbolic reference to the company's role in World War I served to link its cars with progress and modernity.*

RIGHT *Bugatti used this upright elephant as a mascot on its Type 41 Royale as a tribute to Rembrandt Bugatti, the sculptor son of Ettore Bugatti and brother of Jean. Its use served to demonstrate the closeness of the family.*

The heroic era of car mascots fixed to the top of gleaming radiator caps belongs to the inter-war years. The mascots were instant symbols of luxury, differentiating the individualized, custom-built automobile, replete with all the other signs of affluence and privilege such as exotic wood finishes and dashboards and leather upholstery, from the run-of-the-mill factory-made car. The mascot was, above all, a trademark that served to remove the car from the technological context that had spawned it and place it within the more mythic sphere of speed, glamour, and elegance. The chosen imagery – for the most part ethereal women and winged creatures – suggested a world of beauty, speed, and serenity that was far removed from the reality of the dirty machinery hidden beneath the bonnet.

The first mascots were decorative emblems fixed by owners of luxury cars to their own vehicles through which they personalized and tamed their often wayward machines. Soon such items could be purchased from shops and gradually car manufacturers themselves became sensitized to their appeal and sought to sell them with their vehicles as a kind of added value. As mass-produced cars began to flow off the factory lines and the difference between these cheap transport machines and the hand-built, custom-made equivalents became increasingly apparent, the addition of an "art" detail served to emphasize the difference even further.

SPIRIT OF STYLE

Rolls-Royce (see pp.54–5) was among the first of the car manufacturers to utilize this strategy effectively. Its famous "Spirit of Ecstasy" figurine, an elegant female figure with outstretched arms and billowing dress, was cast from a sculpture by Charles Robinson Sykes for the Silver Ghost in 1911. A little later the well-known Art Nouveau decorative artist René Lalique created a glass mascot for Rolls-Royce, thereby helping to bring what had hitherto been valued as an engineered object into the world of contemporary art, fashion,

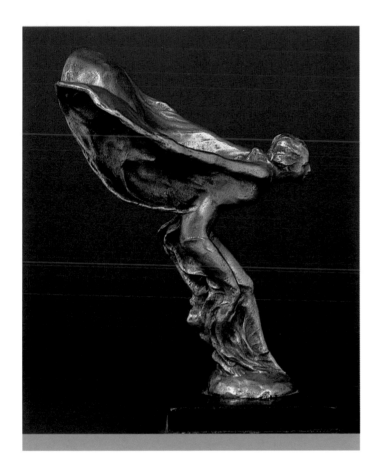

LEFT *Rolls-Royce led the way in mascot design with the "Spirit of Ecstasy" in 1911, modelled on a woman called Eleanor Velasco Thornton. Known affectionately as the "Flying Lady", it was used on all subsequent cars.*

ABOVE *This mascot, used on Jaguar cars from 1937, was designed by the sculptor F. Gordon Crosby. The "Leaping Cat" emulated the sinuous forms of the automobiles themselves and became synonymous with the Jaguar brand.*

and style. The prestige British company quickly established a trend, which was widely emulated and which, by the inter-war years, had engendered a whole menagerie of streamlined creatures.

EMBLEMS OF LUXURY

The stork of the Spanish company Hispano Suiza (see pp.68–9) is among the best known, and owes its origin to the motif on the side of a World War I fighter plane, a Spad, the engine of which was made by the Hispano Suiza company. The "Leaper" of the British car manufacturer Jaguar (see pp.58–61) was introduced in 1937, commissioned by the owner, William Lyons, from the sculptor F. Gordon Crosby; the sight of an inferior emblem that Lyons had seen attached to the radiator of one of his cars inspired him to create his own mascot. France's prestige car manufacturer *par excellence*, Bugatti (see pp.50–3), used a mascot on only one of its models, the luxurious Type 41. The object selected was an elephant cast in silver

from an original sculpture by Rembrandt Bugatti, the brother of the car designer, as a form of commemoration for the young sculptor who had killed himself. Other European car manufacturers followed the same path – the French company Voisin, for example, boasted a styled bird from the late 1920s, while Horch, a German manufacturer of luxury cars, attached a winged ball to the bonnets of its cars. Mercedes introduced its simple star.

MASCOTS IN AMERICA

The inter-war American luxury cars were quick to exploit the power of the mascot. Pierce Arrow's archer, Chevrolet's eagle, Packard's cormorant, Chrysler's gazelle, Lincoln's leaping greyhound, and Stutz's head of the sun god Ra, were yet more signs of American car design's debt to Europe. However, in the post-World War II years, as the concept of safety came increasingly to the fore, the mascot – a dangerous protuberance – faded from view in all but a very few cases.

CADILLAC

Through the middle years of the 20th century Cadillac was, for many people, the premier luxury American automobile. Its cars were immediately recognizable by the coat of arms of the Marquis de la Mothe de Cadillac, the founder of the Detroit company, which was positioned on the top of their chromed radiator grilles. The company acquired its prestige status gradually in the years after World War I, as the forms of its automobiles became increasingly elongated.

FROM THE TECHNICAL TO THE SYMBOLIC

Before this, its claim to fame had been technological rather than symbolic. The Cadillac Automobile Company had been founded in 1902 with H.M. Leland as co-founder. It first achieved renown through its standard use of electric headlights and then, in 1912, by being the first manufacturer to create a car with a self-starter motor. However technically advanced it was though, its cars were still "horseless carriages", and it was not until the late 1920s that Cadillac styling really began to capture the attention of the general public.

In 1908 General Motors had bought Cadillac so as to have a car at the top of the range but had kept it relatively independent. In 1925 Laurence Fisher, one of the Fisher coachbuilding brothers, became Cadillac's general manager. (He it was who brought Harley Earl into General Motors to revolutionize the appearance of the LaSalle, Cadillac's cheaper equivalent.) The Cadillac remained top of the range, styled from the late 1920s onward by the coachbuilders Fisher and Fleetwood. This was the era of the great Cadillacs. Although there were many different models they were all based on a handful of basic body-shells with the variations of bonnets, body sills, windshields, window frames, and roof pillars making it seem as if there were hundreds of different designs available. The Cadillac V16, the first production V16 ever, was launched in 1930 and the next couple of

LEFT *This early custom-built model from 1925, the Suburban 7, is traditionally styled, but its size indicates the social status that was already associated with ownership of a Cadillac. This luxury car was geared towards the top end of the American market.*

years saw the emergence of some of the classic Cadillac designs. The size, length, luxurious finish, subtle colours, and coachwork details of these impressive machines attracted hordes of owners eager to show off their wealth and status, from Al Capone to the Maharaja of Tikar.

STATUS, POWER, AND STYLE

In 1928 the Cadillac was among the first car manufacturers to use chrome plating over its nickel trim to prevent the metal from tarnishing. The use of chrome to create visual highlights was extended in the late 1930s and early 1940s by Cadillac's designers, who established a new vogue in car design. Harley Earl and Bill Mitchell's famous "egg-crate" grille of 1941 used this finish effectively to draw attention to the powerful front end of this huge car, which was now characterized by its large, separate, streamform wings, giving it an impressive presence on America's highways.

Cadillac also pioneered the use of tailfins in American car design. They first made an appearance as little growths on the back end of the 1948 model and grew to have rear lights embedded in them by the end of the 1950s. The most dramatic models of the 1950s were the Eldorado of 1954 and the Brougham of 1955, which, with their sloping roofs, finned rear ends, and four headlights, had an authoritative presence. In addition to their "dream car" exteriors their range of interior fittings bore testimony to Cadillac's continued status as *the* American luxury car. A limited-edition model from the mid-decade included, as well as a self-seeking radio and central locking, a tissue dispenser and a built-in powder compact for the female passenger.

Cadillac maintained its reputation as a status car through the 1960s but, with the demise of the American dream car, went into decline after that decade. The era of the car as a mobile symbol of a wealth and status that could be bought into was at an end.

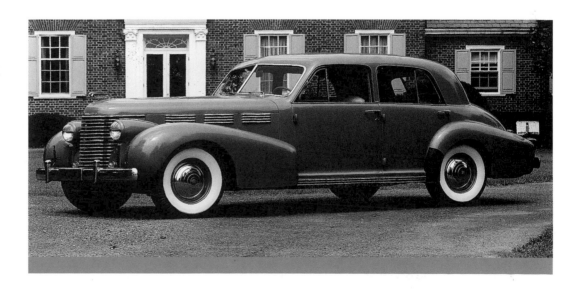

PACKARD

*A*long with those of Cadillac, Lincoln, Peerless, and Pierce Arrow, the name of Packard is inextricably linked with the notion of the mid-century American luxury car. Indeed Packard outsold the other marques at the height of the Depression and, for many people, was considered the pre-eminent status car. Certainly royalty and politicians – including Franklin D. Roosevelt, who drove a customized Packard Twelve – were of this opinion. Unlike Cadillac (see pp.76–7), however, Packard remained an independent company almost to the end and, perhaps because of that fact, did not manage to survive long into the post-World War II period.

A SOLID REPUTATION

Like Cadillac, Packard was established at the beginning of the 20th century and rapidly established a reputation for quality, reliability, and technological bravura. Packards were among the first American cars with steering wheels – replacements for the earlier rudder. Confident in its product, the company did not develop sophisticated marketing strategies but simply suggested that a prospective buyer "ask the man who owns one" if they wanted information. Nor, later, did Packard go along with the idea of the annual model change, preferring to let its "old money" customers buy Packard cars on the basis of their

reputation for quality. The first significant sign that the company valued the importance of modern design was its appointment of the distinguished architect of so many of America's early factories, Albert Kahn, to build its Detroit plant.

"AMERICA'S ROLLS-ROYCE"

Packard did not entirely ignore the attractions of modern styling and, like its competitors, worked from the late 1920s onward with some of the best coachbuilders of the day – Raymond Dietrich, LeBaron, Rollston, and Brunn among them – to create a range of memorable cars which were all visually distinctive. From the outset the Packard marque could be recognized by its yoke-shaped radiator and fluted bonnet, and its body designers were careful to integrate this strong visual signal into their creations. Nineteen-thirties models also boasted extravagant radiator mascots – flowing forms of animals and women. The bodies were long and low with impeccably finished coachwork, coloured paintwork, and trim. The russet-brown body of a 1934 LeBaron V12 Convertible, for example, boasted dramatically styled teardrop fenders and rear end, while the parallel lines of the bonnet retained the grace and elegance of an earlier era. In 1935, as the Depression bit deeper, the smaller V8 120 model was launched.

ABOVE *A traditionally styled Packard from the 1920s complete with its chauffeur and passenger. These large, comfortable cars maintained a conservative appearance which only added to their image of high-class luxury.*

LEFT *Employees of the Packard Motor Car Company gather in one of the courtyards between the two outer quadrangles of the company's plant at Detroit. The Packard firm was one of Detroit's largest in the early years of the century and it produced some of America's first luxury cars.*

Its teardrop styling, along with its relatively modest price, quickly made it a popular car. Late 1930s Packards embraced the aesthetic of streamlining enthusiastically, showing that modern styling and luxury appeal were not incompatible in cars where attention to detail remained the order of the day. The firm's reputation as the "Rolls-Royce of the USA" was well earned, but it was interested also in making the luxury car more widely available. With the appearance of the Packard V6 in 1937 this ambition was quickly realized.

PEAK OF SUCCESS

As well as its more economical models the Packard company continued to supply the wealthy market with remarkable cars that were noteworthy for their modern apearance. The Convertible Victoria 1940 and 1941, styled by Howard Darrin (see pp.128–9), competed with the Lincoln Continental as a design breakthrough. By the early 1940s the company had reached the peak of its success, but it was to be shortlived. Unlike Cadillac which had the power of General Motors behind it, Packard was vulnerable and ended up being merged with Studebaker in 1954. Chrysler bought the coachbuilders who had supplied Packard with its bodies.

Packard limped on until the late 1950s but had disappeared from the scene by the early 1960s. Its dependence on its reputation and its slowness to move forward with design and marketing in the postwar years brought about its demise.

ABOVE *A headlight of a 1934 Packard Super-light Coupé Sedan.*

AMERICAN COACHBUILDERS

Although the American automobile started life primarily as an object of utility for the rural community, by the turn of the century it had also become a mark of a high-class lifestyle in an urban setting. To cater for this market the long-established carriage-building trade began to transfer its attention to the provision of finely crafted automobile bodies for the social élite. As a result, by the time the first Ford Model T came off the production line in 1913 the American custom-built luxury car was a well-established reality.

ADAPTING TO THE NEW

As it was in Europe, coachbuilding in the United States was an old trade. Firms such as Brewster, Willoughby, Locke, Derham, Rollstone, Judkins, and Brunn had deep roots. In the early 20th century, in response to the arrival of the automobile, the trade moved into a new era. Brewster and Company, established in 1810, saw the emergence of two men from its ranks, Raymond Dietrich and Thomas Hibbard, who were to play an important role in this transformation. In 1913

William Brewster sent Dietrich to study body design and advanced drafting in New York. After graduating the young coachbuilder worked for a spell at Chevrolet, returning to Brewster in 1918. Two years later he set up his own company with Hibbard named LeBaron Carrossiers, the name giving their work a distinctly European flavour. With the assistance of Ralph W. Roberts and the illustrator Roland P. Stickney, Dietrich and Hibbard were to play a key role in American luxury car styling over the next two decades. Edsel Ford, for example, commissioned them to design car bodies for Lincoln chassis.

Dietrich broke away from Hibbard in 1925: Dietrich Inc. of Detroit worked with a range of luxury car manufacturers, including Cadillac, Packard, and Pierce Arrow. His stylish automobiles were characterized by their long, low profiles and streamlined fenders. In the late 1920s the Depression took its toll and the firm was absorbed by the Murray Body Company. In 1932 Dietrich moved to Chrysler, becoming its head of Art and Color until World War II, the equivalent of General Motors' Harley Earl (see pp.22–5) in the same period.

The American luxury car thrived at a time when a certain clientele, including industrialists and movie stars (both Gloria Swanson and Rudolph Valentino owned cars styled by Dietrich), openly aspired to have access to the status symbols of European royalty and aristocracy. Where automobiles were concerned it was a symbolism achieved by a mix of traditional values and a sense of futurity expressed in styling details. Above all, however, it was expressed through a commitment to craftsmanship and quality, features that all the coachbuilders were skilled at injecting into the luxury objects they created.

SURVIVAL BETWEEN THE WARS AND AFTER

By the interwar years the coachbuilding firms had fallen into two camps. On the one hand, a few of the older small firms managed to survive by adapting their skills to the needs of the luxury car makers to whom they supplied bodies on a relatively modest scale. On the other,

the new mass-production industries created a need for large-scale body suppliers that was met by a number of firms which secured their future through these new relationships. Fleetwood and Fisher, for example, provided bodies for General Motors. Le Baron continued to design custom cars, without Dietrich, in the 1920s under the leadership of Ralph W. Roberts until it was absorbed first by the Briggs Manufacturing Company and eventually by the Chrysler Corporation.

By the 1950s most of the familiar names in coachbuilding had faded from view. Mass production had taken over from custom building, and the new democratic attitude towards car ownership, pioneered by Henry Ford (see pp.20–21), had become a reality. With it came a new attitude towards luxury that was less about craftsmanship and more about showiness, less about refinement and more about exaggerated display. Now, it was the in-house stylist, albeit frequently with his roots in carriage-making, who had moved centre stage.

ABOVE *A 1933 Duesenberg passenger sedan with a body designed by Derham. In this model, two-tone paintwork and an integrated boot make this luxurious car both modern and attractive. There is still a conservative feel to this high-class automobile, however.*

RIGHT *A view of the interior of a 1934 Packard Super-light Coupé Sedan. Coachbuilders were responsible for the fact that interiors were given as luxurious a treatment as exteriors, as the leather upholstery and the chromed dashboard of this model bear witness.*

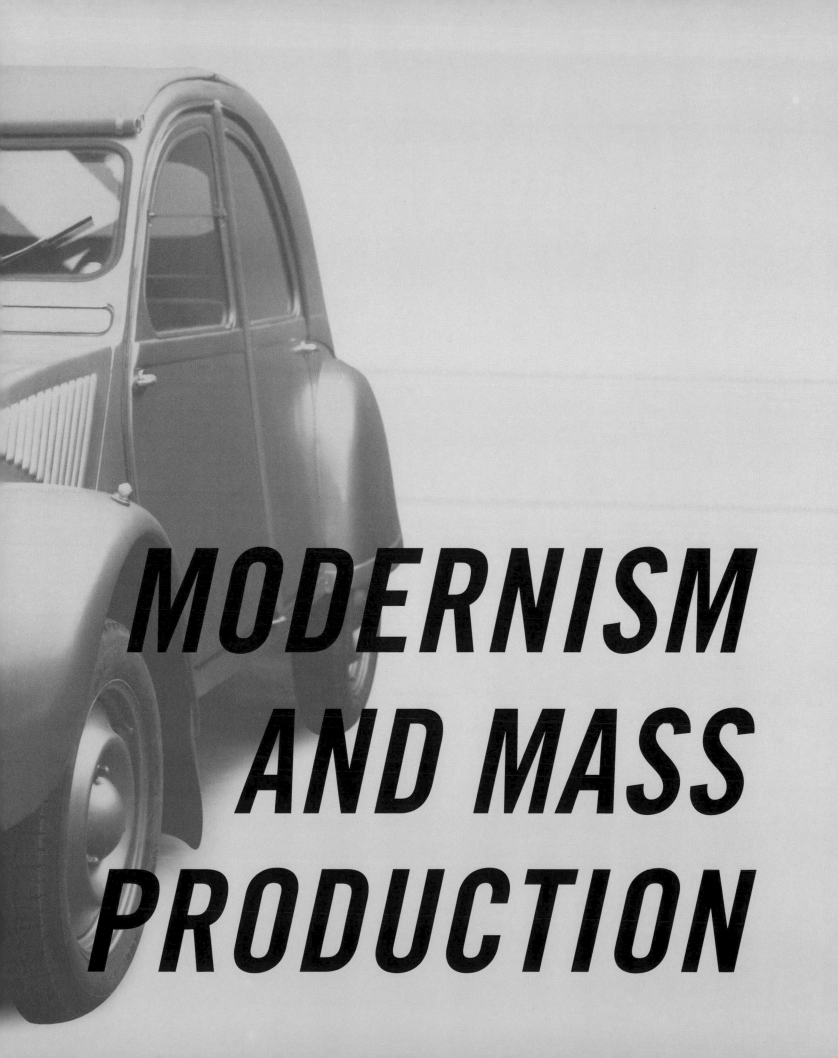

MODERNISM AND MASS PRODUCTION

MODERNISM AND MASS PRODUCTION

*D*uring the Depression (1929–34) the United States was obsessed with turning the science of aerodynamics into an acceptable vision of the future for the automobile consumers of the time; trying, that is, to make them forget the horrors of the period they were living through. Meanwhile Europe was busy catching up, attempting to turn its car-manufacturing base into a mass-production industry in the manner of Henry Ford more than a decade earlier. A number of companies – for example Fiat in Italy, Citroën and Renault in France, and Morris and Austin in England – made enormous efforts to introduce efficient production methods into their factories in order to make the European mass-production car a reality. By the 1920s they had gone a long way towards achieving this goal.

The quest for a standardized automobile that everyone could afford was not just an economic goal: in Europe it also had political overtones. The creation of a "car for the people", a symbol of the entry of the masses into modernity, was required by the fascist and the liberal regimes of Europe alike. They both needed to have the masses on their side and the best way to do this seemed to be to provide the kind of consumer goods the people wanted. A number of car manufacturers in Britain, France, Italy, and Germany focused on this ambition and the 1920s and 1930s saw a variety of "people's cars" – from the British Morris Eight to the Italian Fiat Topolino – coming on to the streets in Europe's urban centres. In this context Henry Ford's achievement took on a new meaning.

Whereas during these years in the United States the gap between cars aimed at the wealthy and those for the mass market began to close, with producers such as Ford and Chrysler emulating the luxury "carriages" of Cadillac and Packard, the

difference between the automobiles aimed at the rich and the poor in Europe remained more clearly demarcated. The luxurious, chauffeur-driven cars produced by Rolls-Royce and Hispano Suiza had nothing in common with the tiny cars that began to be produced for the other end of the market. In the latter context price was everything and the cars destined for the masses had to be as small as possible. By 1945 the VW Beetle, the Fiat 500, the Citroën 2CV, the Morris Minor, and the Renault 4CV had all emerged to meet the needs of poorly paid workers and their families. With the restricted supplies of fuel, low consumption was also a key requirement of these diminutive automobiles.

These were the years in which workers all over Europe exchanged their bicycles and motorcycles for cars. The spate of low-priced bubble cars that also appeared made it even easier to move into car ownership, even if these were less than totally

stable. Yet the postwar European people's car was more than a mere consumer object: more significantly it was also a mark of national identity in the new Europe. While the small cars of the 1950s had some features in common they were all visually distinctive and all created for the specific nature of the roads that had to carry them, whether the highly efficient autobahns of Germany or the less well developed rural roads of France. Very few cars moved across national borders in these years. Instead they served to help create a sense of nationhood for their owners.

There was also a very particular philosophy underpinning the design of mass-production cars in Europe at this time. Price and utility outweighed luxury and overt status symbolism, and the relationship between engineering and the outward appearance of the cars was more crucial than ever before. As sheet-steel bodies and monocoque construction became the norm, the tradition of

the coachbuilder's creating a body that could be fitted on to a separate chassis became increasingly redundant: a more holistic approach to design emerged in which the engineer and the stylist had to work closely together.

Ideas that were prevalent in avant-garde architecture and design also began to infiltrate car design in Europe. Indeed a number of leading modern architects believed that the car should serve as a key source of inspiration, bringing to architecture rational ideas emanating from factory practices – fundamental tenets of the design philosophy of functionalism. Several of them even had a go at designing a car, although the lesson quickly learned was that architect-designed cars usually ended up as little more than "houses on wheels" in which attention was paid to the interior but very little thought was given to the working parts or to the exterior. However car designers learned from contemporary

architecture that structural and spatial concerns were as important in cars as in buildings. The work of the designers Dante Giacosa at Fiat and Alec Issigonis at Morris and the British Motor Corporation reflected architectural thinking to the extent that their designs for the Fiat 600 and the BMC Mini respectively were, for the first time, conceived from the inside out.

What Giacosa and Issigonis had that the architects Le Corbusier and Walter Gropius did not was a thorough engineering knowledge that enabled them to design every individual component of the car as well as its final form. Interestingly the "machine aesthetic", so admired by Le Corbusier and his followers, which they applied metaphorically to their architectural designs, existed literally in the context of the automobile.

The holistic approach embraced by certain European engineer-designers – Ferdinand Porsche, Dante Giacosa, Alec

Issigonis and a handful of others – stood in direct oppostion to the approach of the American car stylists. It also effectively meant an end to the work of the European and American coachbuilders (with the notable exception of the Italians).

The way in which this new breed of automobile designer worked was nearer to product design than to car styling. They embraced the functionalist tradition of design, deriving from the ideas propagated by the Bauhaus school of design in Germany in the 1920s, which suggested that the form of an object should result from its internal structure and its functional necessities. Indeed the Citroën 2CV emerged directly from a list of tight specifications and is often described as resembling a Bauhaus design. The fact that a sculptor, Flaminio Bertoni, was involved in the team that created the pioneering car is an indication that its overall form needed to be evocative as well. As at the Bauhaus,

artists and designers worked closely together ensuring not only that their creations were functionally correct but also that they looked as if they were.

While tight specifications and utility underpinned all the designs described in this chapter, aesthetics played an important role as well. The case studies of the Jeep and the Land Rover serve to demonstrate how vehicles designed on a utilitarian basis can be as visually appealing as those in which designers have had an aesthetic free hand. The constraints of utility can, and often do, result in forms that appeal in very fundamental ways. Issigonis was always adamant that he worked outside the arena of fashion. Like him the designers described in the following pages worked with new automotive concepts that radically transformed the car as it had existed up to then. The results are some of the most timeless automobile designs of the 20th century.

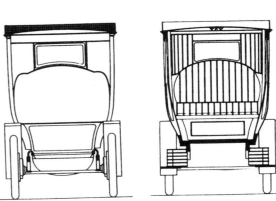

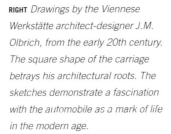

RIGHT *Drawings by the Viennese Werkstätte architect-designer J.M. Olbrich, from the early 20th century. The square shape of the carriage betrays his architectural roots. The sketches demonstrate a fascination with the automobile as a mark of life in the modern age.*

ARCHITECTS AND CARS

From the very early years of their existence cars have acted as sources of inspiration for artists and architects who were keen to demonstrate that they were indisputably a part of the 20th century. For these creative individuals the "horseless carriage's" unremitting commitment to progress and its dependence on advanced technology rendered it a perfect symbol of modernity, an icon of the machine age, which they frequently took as an aesthetic starting point. It mattered little who had created these visions: they existed, simply, as manifestations of an era, innocent carriers of aesthetic values that were part and parcel of modernity itself.

ART AND DEMOCRACY

For many early 20th-century painters, such as the Italian futurist Umberto Boccioni, the automobile inspired a move towards visual abstraction, its essential dynamism suggesting forms that aspired to represent movement itself. The relationship between cars and architects was a little different: on the one hand, the achievements of

Ford, Fiat, Citroën, and others showed how mass-produced, standardized components could be used to democratize objects, a lesson that many architects have been keen to apply to buildings; on the other, cars were seen as a form of "architecture on wheels", which some architects saw as a natural extension of their territory.

MORE THAN A HOUSE ON WHEELS?

From early in the century architects responded to the challenge of the automobile on both these levels, especially in Europe where the architectural modern movement held most sway. Their desire to reject 19th-century historical styles, and to embrace the cultural and technological imperatives of the modern age, focused their attention on what for them were raw manifestations of technology and function. In Vienna, for example, where architects attached to a group known as the Wiener Werkstätte were attempting to find a new way forward, Josef Maria Olbrich and Josef Hoffmann, leading Austrian architects, both tried their hands at visualizing cars, if only on the back of

envelopes. Olbrich's design was little more than a box on wheels; as was to prove characteristic of several architect-designed cars, the greatest attention was paid to the interior which, in keeping with many contemporary Viennese interiors, was decorated with horizontal stripes. A little later, in 1923, another Viennese architect, Adolf Loos, famous for his writings about the need for modern architecture to reject ornamentation, also created a thumbnail sketch for a motor car. His idea was more radical than those of his predecessors and proposed a car with three rows of seats and two front windows, one behind the other and at different levels.

THE CAR AS SPIRIT OF THE AGE

In the 1920s, the heroic decade of the architectural modern movement, the relationship between architects and cars reached a high point. This coincided with the years in which automobiles ceased to be mere products of their technology and aspired to acquire a visual identity all their own. In the search for such an identity engineers, sculptors, and architects all played seminal roles. The pioneer Swiss-born architect Le Corbusier was, like the futurists before him, deeply affected by the impact of the objects of transport – aircraft, cars, and steamships – that he saw around him. In his writings he referred frequently to the power of these machines, claiming that they encapsulated as nothing else did the spirit of the age, and that they were as much a valid expression of the contemporary era as temples had been for the ancient Greeks.

Le Corbusier's enthusiasm for the motor car extended to his ownership of a Voisin 10CV which he frequently used as visual foil for his architectural creations. The architect's first contact with the Voisin company, creator of luxury automobiles, had been when it sponsored his contribution to the French Exhibition of Decorative Arts in 1925, at which he showed his highly innovative Pavillon de l'Esprit Nouveau ("pavilion of the new spirit"). He maintained a strong relationship with the firm for several years. His own car was a luxurious, custom-made, highly finished vehicle, as far away from a

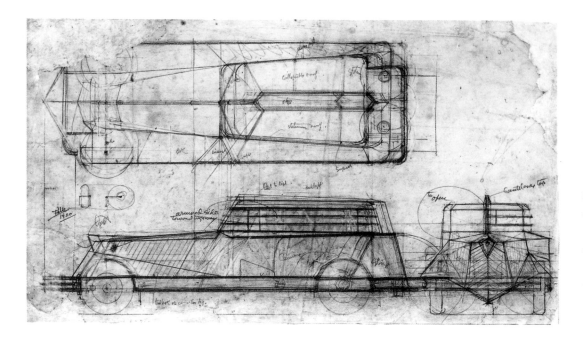

Model T Ford as could be imagined. Ironically, in spite of his commitment to what he perceived as a raw machine aesthetic, Le Corbusier's car was styled by an architect, André Noël-Telmont, who had been brought in to head Voisin's body design department after the end of World War I.

Although undoubtedly Le Corbusier's contribution to car design was, like that of Adolf Loos and Josef Hoffmann before him, primarily a visualizing exercise, between 1928 and 1936 he created, with his cousin Pierre Jeanneret, a number of studies of a "people's car", the Voiture Minimum. Once again, the interior received the greater part of the attention, featuring three seats at the front and room for luggage at the back. Although the rear end was curved this was in reality less the result of aerodynamic experimentation than a golden-section (that is, an aesthetically determined) composition. The working elements of the car were never visualized. The body, like the shell of one of Le Corbusier's buildings, was more a result of the inner requirements

than an exercise in styling. It served to show the extent to which architectural thinking could provide an alternative route into car design to that of the stylist.

INTERIOR DESIGN

In Germany the modern architect Walter Gropius was brought in by an automobile manufacturer, Adler, to assist it in creating visually acceptable bodies for its engineered products. Gropius created six different models, among them the Favorit cabriolet of 1930, the Standard 6 cabriolet of 1931, and a later Standard 6 limousine, all of which were put into production by the Frankfurt-based firm. As with the designs of his fellow architects, Gropius' shell showed no signs of the dramatic, elongated forms created by Harley Earl (see pp.22–5) and his followers across the Atlantic. This was an entirely different vision of the automobile, one that stressed the object at rest rather than in movement, that ignored social status and luxury and that

RIGHT *The Voiture Minimum (Minimum Car) designed by the French architects Le Corbusier and Pierre Jeanneret in response to a competition for a "people's car". Both these architects were fascinated by the idea of the automobile and worked on sketches and models through the late 1920s and up to the mid-1930s.*

emphasized instead the possibilities inherent in its internal space and its relationship with its external structure. Gropius' Adler Standard 6 cabriolet of 1931 was, in essence, a box, in which, ingeniously, the front seat could recline and turn into a bed.

The fascination of architects with cars remained a constant through the 20th century. In the United States, Frank Lloyd Wright, like his European counterparts, fantasized about a car built according to architectural principles; a drawing of 1920 showed a car with a structural cantilever, a device that was to come into its own in Wright's famous Falling Water house of a few years later.

Richard Neutra, Gio Ponti, and Jean Prouvé are other names belonging to the long list of architects who designed cars. Like Le Corbusier and Gropius they all viewed the automobile as an expression of a sense of modernity and as a communicator of the values that they wanted to incorporate in their buildings. More

recently, latter-day modernists such as Jan Kaplicky and Norman Foster have sustained this tradition. The relationship between cars and architects has not been just a one-way infatuation, however: car manufacturers have also looked to architects in their search for creative individuals who might be able to supply what engineers could not, an aesthetic for the machine.

A DEBT TO ARCHITECTS

Nevertheless, in the end, there have been few truly successful architect-designed cars. Ultimately the 20th-century car did not follow the path of "architecture on wheels" but rather that of "a dream that money can buy". What the architects did help to prioritize was the importance of a car's internal space in relation to its external structure. The lesson proved to be of enormous importance to the evolution of the postwar European "people's car".

BRITISH "PEOPLE'S CARS"

Although Britain was late to enter the world of automobile manufacture, both Herbert Austin and William Morris had, by the 1920s, set up companies that were eager to produce small, affordable cars for the mass market. This coincided with a thirst for cars by the sector of the population that hitherto had had to make do with a bicycle or, at best, a motorcycle and sidecar. As with the Model T Ford in the United States (see pp.20–1), the revolution that took place in car production and ownership at this time focused more on price than on styling or design. The automobiles that Austin and Morris created were, like their American equivalents, simple, conservative vehicles, the appeal of which lay principally in their price, their reliability, and their ease of maintenance.

WILLIAM MORRIS

William Morris emerged from the world of bicycles and motorcycles to produce his first car – the Bullnose Morris, thus named because of the curved shape of its radiator – in 1912. From the outset Morris was committed to the concept of high-volume, low-price production, and he assembled his simple, affordable cars in a small factory outside Oxford using components sourced from elsewhere. The formula was highly successful, and by the mid-1920s Morris cars constituted 41

per cent of Britain's total car output. The Oxford model of 1912 was joined by the Cowley in 1915; both cars were unexceptional to look at but they helped to bring motoring within the reach of vast numbers of British consumers for the first time.

HERBERT AUSTIN

Having designed a car for Wolseley back in 1895, Herbert Austin launched his own manufacturing concern in 1906. Like Morris, he oriented his manufacture towards the lower end of the market, but it was not until 1922 that he launched the mass-produced car that was to make Britain truly a road-going nation. "Chummy", as the little Austin Seven came to be called, was undoubtedly a response to the Model T, although its tiny size and low price gave it an edge in Britain. Austin travelled to the United States in the same year to observe American manufacturing techniques at first hand. His car targeted the mass of the British families for whom a motorcycle and sidecar had been the only option and it could be bought for the same price.

The Austin Seven had four seats, although the two at the back were only really big enough for children. The standard model was a tourer which came complete with a windshield and hood. The emphasis was on simplicity and, as an Austin advertisement for an

LEFT *The Bullnose Morris Tourer of 1913 was Great Britain's first answer to the Model T Ford, and it had the same effect of making a significant part of the population mobile for the first time. However, it took a little longer for mass-production techniques to penetrate fully into British manufacturing.*

LEFT *Austin's little A30 of the post-World War II years was a direct descendant of the original Austin Seven of 1922, Britain's first mass-market, mass-production "people's car". Like its predecessor, this model could seat four adults. A Countryman estate version was launched in 1955.*

earlier model had explained, "Austin design avoids the startling, content to concentrate upon the simply good". A new model with a little more space was launched in 1925, one version featuring blue-enamelled bodywork. Sporty models, including the Brooklands type, appeared soon afterwards. In 1928 an architect called Ronald Aver Duncan produced a body for a model called the Merlyn. The "baby" Seven remained in production until 1939, by which time it had acquired a special place in the context of British car manufacturing. The company tried to manufacture an American version in the early 1930s but it was too small for American tastes and proved attractive only to a few Hollywood stars, including Buster Keaton and Al Jolson, for whom it had a special appeal.

GREAT SMALL SUCCESSES

Morris launched the Minor in 1928, its first really small car, in competition with the Austin Seven. Once again price won over style, although by this date the body had a more unifed appearance and the front fenders boasted a tapering rear. The Morris 8 of 1934 had a more progressive look, albeit one borrowed from the Ford Model Y.

The success of Austin and Morris small cars in the Britain of the inter-war years marked the desire, in that country, to find a formula for the affordable car. When, in the postwar years, the skills of the engineer Alec Issigonis (see pp.106–9) were brought to bear on two cars that inherited many features of the Morris Minor and the Austin Seven, that formula would be complete.

LEFT *The Ford Popular, in production in Britain from 1953 to 1959, was launched as a cheap family car. Although not progressive stylistically it was a basic, colourful car that was ideal for family outings. Living up to its name, it was extremely popular throughout the 1950s.*

VW BEETLE

The VW Beetle, as the "people's car" developed by the German Volkswagen company in the years just before and after World War II came to be called, emerged in the 1930s as the result of a project spearheaded by the car designer Ferdinand Porsche and backed by the Nazi leader Adolf Hitler. The idea of making Germany mobile by improving the roads and making a low-price, high-quality car widely available was a part of the Chancellor's agenda and Porsche's design proved the ideal way of fulfilling it.

THE PORSCHE PEDIGREE

Porsche had impeccable credentials as an automotive engineer and car designer long before he came to Hitler's notice. In 1900 he had won a prize at the Paris Exhibition for an electric-motored car created for the Lohner company, based in Vienna, and he followed this by a long stint (1906–23) as chief engineering designer for the Austro-Daimler company. In 1910 he created a stunningly progressive streamlined car, and his work for this Austrian branch of the German manufacturer earned him a reputation as one of his country's leading automotive engineers. However, Porsche's strong character resulted in his dismissal from Austro-Daimler – they wanted to concentrate on luxury sedans while he was more interested in sports models – and again from Daimler, Stuttgart, three years later.

In 1931 Porsche established his own automotive design consultancy in Stuttgart. In addition to his sons he employed many of the men he had worked with for many years who had been able to turn his radical ideas into reality. He was keen at this time to develop a small, affordable car for the masses, a challenge that had not yet been confronted adequately by Germany's automobile manufacturers. His first opportunity to create such a car came through his collaboration with a firm called Zündapp which was working on

ABOVE *Ferdinand Porsche's aerodynamically styled Type 32 was created for the NSU company in 1932, and had been preceded by the Type 12 designed for Zündapp. Although both projects failed to reach fruition owing to lack of funds they put in place the innovative design ideas that would later be realized in the production Beetle.*

RIGHT *When Adolf Hitler came to power in 1933 one of his projects was the development of a German "people's car". He is seen here in April 1938 looking at the prototype that Porsche created for him.*

motorcycle manufacture. With its rounded, streamlined back, unified body lines, and rear engine the Kleinwagen ("small car") prototype, which he developed with them in 1930, was undoubtedly a forerunner of the Beetle, although the windshield was raked sharply and the front not yet rounded. The following eight years would see an unprecedented program of research and development.

THE BEGINNINGS OF THE BEETLE

A couple of years after the Kleinwagen, Porsche pursued his interest in the small car with a second prototype, produced by the NSU company. The Kleinauto Type 32, with its bodywork by Reutter coachworks, was rounded at the front and rear but the hood was high and sloped abruptly. The model had a distinctly front-heavy feel to it and the front door opened from a central hinge. The sophisticated and futuristic body styling of the Type 32 was undertaken by Erwin Komenda, one of Porsche's close collaborators, who styled several of his designs. Three prototypes of the NSU car were built but development went no further. Nonetheless the iconic form of the Beetle had been put in place and the many modifications that took place from that year onward served to improve the engineering and design details so that, once perfected, the car would remain relatively unchanged for several decades.

Nineteen thirty-three was the year of Hitler's accession to power, and by the following year he had not only had Porsche's experiments brought to his notice, but he had also commissioned the construction of two prototypes of what came to be called the Type 60. It seems that Hitler had a considerable interest in car design, although he did not possess a driver's licence, and he made suggestions to Porsche – which were dutifully followed – with respect to lowering the line of the hood to balance the look of the car and removing the headlights from the bonnet. Sketches made by Hitler showing his vision of a people's car are still in existence.

HITLER'S REQUIREMENTS

The most notable feature of the next version of the Beetle was the absence of a rear window; in other respects it had become recognizably the rounded form that was to become the Beetle from the 1940s onward. Most importantly, by this point Porsche and his team had perfected the engineering requirements that would allow Hitler's specifications for a people's car to be realized. Hitler had made it clear that his car should not cost more than 1,000 Reichsmarks, that it should be air-cooled, and that it should have a top speed of 100 km/h (62 mph) together with a fuel consumption of 7 litres (1½ gal) per 100 km (62 miles). Other requirements included the fact that, as this was intended to be a family car, it had to be big enough to hold two adults and three children.

The Type 60 was rigorously tested by the Nazis and subsequent prototypes of the 1936 model, the VW3, were made until further testing declared the model a success. To ensure that the car would perform well it was driven nearly 800 km (500 miles) daily. The next models, the Series 30 of 1936 (30 models built) were put together by Daimler-Benz but the styling was left once again to Erwin Komenda, whose task was to refine and simplify the car. The headlamps were mounted in the fenders and the line of the hood made to slope right down to the front. A 1937 model, the body for which was made by Reutter, introduced a split rear window – the "pretzel" as it came affectionately to be called – and a row of vertical louvres beneath it. The car was getting nearer and nearer to the final version that would eventually roll off the production lines in the postwar years. Nineteen thirty-seven was also the year in which Hitler

decided that the project should be state-funded, and the Society for the Development of the German Volkswagen (the name means "people's car") was formed.

THE FIRST BEETLES

The last stage of Hitler's program for his people's car lay in the creation of a factory to build it. A town was chosen and renamed KdF (*Kraft durch Freude*) Stadt ("work through joy town"). It was designated the home of the manufacture of Hitler's project, the KdF Wagen, and the factory was opened in 1939, just before the outbreak of the war. The town was more than a factory, also incorporating workers' housing and other facilities, and it became part of Hitler's achievements in the area of town planning.

Only slightly more than 200 KdF Wagens were produced before the factory went over to war production and was bombed by the Allies. Those early cars – all of which were manufactured in a bluish-

ABOVE *The interior of this postwar Beetle shows its small rear window and minimal detailing. A level of comfort is introduced with the inclusion of upholstered armrests on the rear seat. Although space was limited the Beetle could seat four adults with some ease.*

LEFT *Production of the postwar Beetle in the Wolfsburg factory. Sales of this little car, with its aerodynamic form, expanded dramatically through the 1950s, penetrating the American market in the mid-decade.*

grey colour – were allocated to Nazi chiefs and ironically, although perhaps not surprisingly, did not reach the people for whom they had been so painstakingly researched and constructed.

AFTER THE WAR: SURVIVAL AND SUCCESS

The survival of the Beetle into the postwar years was the result of initiatives made by the British. In 1946 Major Ivan Hurst initiated the production of about 1,000 cars a year for the British Army. Ownership of the factory was returned to Germany and Heinz Nordhoff, a German car industry chief, supervised the restructuring of the Volkswagen

plant in what by then had been renamed Wolfsburg. Porsche was imprisoned for almost 20 months for his collaboration and survived his freedom for only five years. By the time of his death Volkswagen had become one of Germany's leading car manufacturers, producing more than 40 per cent of the country's output of automobiles.

The consolidation of the postwar success of the Beetle came with its introduction in 1949 into the United States, which was facilitated by a Dutch distributor. Volkswagen of America was established six years later and by that date its acceptance as the European people's car *par excellence* was complete.

ABOVE *Postwar cars from the Wolfsburg factory are shown being taken on a train to Switzerland. Once production was re-established the number of Beetles coming off the assembly line increased significantly and they were exported widely.*

RIGHT *The KdF Wagen featured a split rear window known affectionately as the "pretzel". This model shows the louvres below the window that became one of the hallmarks of the rear-engined Beetle. Its integrated headlights and curved form were also familiar features.*

DANTE GIACOSA

PRINCIPAL DESIGNS

1936 *Fiat 500*
1946 *Cisitalia 202*
1950 *Fiat 1400*
1956 *Fiat 600*
1957 *Fiat Nuova 500*
1964 *Autobianchi Primula*
1969 *Fiat 128*

The car manufacturer Fiat (Fabbrica Italiana di Automobili Torino) and the engineer-designer Dante Giacosa (1905–96) enjoyed one of the longest and most fruitful relationships in the story of 20th-century car design. Between 1928 and 1975 they worked together to produce some of the century's most lasting automobile icons, especially in terms of small cars for the mass market.

FIAT

Fiat had a history before the arrival of Giacosa. Formed in 1899 by nine entrepreneurs, Giovanni Agnelli among them, it created a wide range of cars – from the impressive racers of the early century to the compact Zero of 1912 to the large touring cars of the 1920s. It was a progressive firm from the outset and in 1921 built a modern factory in Turin. The architect, Giacomo Matte-Trucco, was a member of a group of avant-garde Italian architects and, in the spirit of futurism, he built a racetrack on the roof of the factory to test-drive Fiat's models, which, more importantly, marked the company's forward-looking approach

BELOW *Fiat's small 500 model of 1936. This cute little car was nicknamed "Topolino" (Italian for Mickey Mouse) because of its visual resemblance to the cartoon character. Giacosa worked on the engine of this successful car.*

towards speed and modern life. Nineteen twenty-five saw the arrival of Fiat's little 509 model, while the 508 Balilla of seven years later showed the company's interest in creating cars that visually announced the speed of which they were capable.

THE FIRST ITALIAN "PEOPLE'S CAR"

Giacosa had trained as an engineer in Turin and joined Fiat soon after his graduation. Not long after his arrival the company began to think about a car for the Italian masses. Its little postwar 501 model had anticipated Britain's Austin Seven and Morris Minor (see pp.92–3). The arrival of the Morris Eight in Britain and the early stages of Porsche's work on the VW Beetle (see pp.94–7) were clear signs that a "people's car" need not only be cheap, small, and reliable: it could also be stylish.

The idea of creating an Italian people's car came from Giovanni Agnelli himself. The first proposal was made by one of his engineers, Oreste Lardone, but his air-cooled prototype caught fire and Agnelli turned instead to Giacosa's version, which was water-cooled with a front-mounted engine. Giacosa's proposal was a one-man design, from the engine through to the body-shell. His design method involved sketching on paper and working up to full-size maquettes in wood and clay. His work demonstrated a unity of engineering and styling such that the two aspects were indistinguishable one from the other.

The little Fiat 500, or Topolino (Mickey Mouse) as it became known, was the fruit of Giacosa's efforts. It was launched in 1936 at the Milan show and was an immediate success. Two people could travel comfortably in the Topolino and its pert, softly streamlined form and small wheels gave it a friendly appearance. Unlike the VW Beetle its headlights were not integrated into its fenders, nor were its rounded forms as dramatic as its German equivalent but, to the Italian people, it stood for democratized mobility like no car before it. Production resumed after the war; between 1936 and 1948, 122,000 Topolinos came off the assembly lines, making it Italy's most popular car.

Giacosa's work for Fiat was supplemented by designs he created for the Italian racing car manufacturer Cisitalia in the early postwar years. In total he created 30 cars for them. The 202 CMM coupé, designed with Giovanni Savonuzzi in 1946, stands out as one of the most elegant examples. From 1948 onward he resumed work on the Fiat 500, creating the 500B and the 500C versions of this little classic.

MAKING ITALY MOBILE

Things did not stop there. Unlike Britain and Germany, Italy was still a largely rural country in the early postwar years and the process of urbanization went on through the 1950s. Italy was still not fully mobilized, and many Italians made do with a bicycle or, from the late 1940s onward, the new, modern-looking little motor scooters, the

FIAT 500
la nuova

LEFT *An advertisement from 1957 showing the launch of the Fiat 500. Along with the 600, the 500 provided Italy with a car for the people. Giacosa managed to capture the popular imagination and appeal to the growing sense of modernity in that country.*

ABOVE *Small as it was (even smaller than the earlier 600) Fiat's "new" 500 model was conceived as a family car. By the late 1950s it had become virtually ubiquitous in the Italian everyday environment, its rounded form soon becoming familiar to everyone.*

Lambrettas and Vespas, that were easy to manoeuvre through the narrow medieval streets in the centre of so many of Italy's cities. The challenge to mobilize Italy fully was still there in 1950, therefore.

The scooters showed that the car to do this had to be very small, easy to park, and, to compete with the Vespa, full of character. Above all it had to symbolize modernity for a population that was just beginning to familiarize itself with the concept.

THE FIAT 600

In 1951 Giacosa began work on a design for a 600 model, once again using full-size clay and wooden models. Although it was a radical and costly change he opted for a rear engine. The car that emerged had an expanded interior and four seats, but a reduced bonnet and boot, so that the overall form was more integrated. Launched in 1955, the 600 was an overnight success. It was cheap and provided everything that was needed by Italy's new motorists.

THE NEW 500

The next development undertaken by Fiat and Giacosa, the Nuova 500 ("new 500") took the idea of size reduction even further and revived the popularity of the Topolino. The design drew on the work undertaken for the 600 as well as on research done on a prototype for a small, two-seater utility car called the 400. Launched in 1957, the Nuova 500, with its fold-back sunroof, was the ideal car with which to navigate Italy's narrow streets and could be parked in the smallest of spaces. Its sloping back gave it a more rakish appearance than the more bulky 600 and new engineering gave it improved acceleration. It was highly popular with Italy's youth. The following years saw a range of modifications: a late-1957 version had wind-up windows, and a sports model with a solid roof was available in 1958. In 1965 the doors acquired front hinges (a safer option) and a luxury version with carpeting appeared in 1969. The car remained in production until 1975, by which time it had become part and parcel of the Italian landscape.

ABOVE *Giacosa was responsible for the design of the British Hillman Imp de luxe. This compact little car from the mid-1960s set out to provide the British public with a "people's car", although Issigonis' Mini arrived first.*

Giacosa retired that same year, 1975. As Fiat's head of research and development he had been responsible for dozens of models, from the 128 to the 850. He had been a highly intuitive designer, crossing the divide that, for many others, separated technology and art. His holistic approach came from an understanding of the engineering principles of the car together with an ability to grasp the spatial and visual implications of engineering decisions applied to the car as both physical artifact and object of desire. He also understood the cultural and socio-economic imperatives that determined the evolution of the modern automobile. His was an approach shared by only a handful of other car designers in the 20th century and one that enabled not mere evolution but radical change to enter the world of automobile design.

CITROËN 2CV

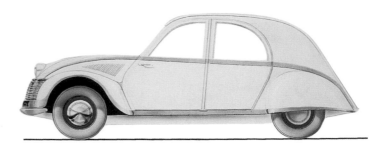

*I*n an account of the design of 20th-century "people's cars" Citroën's 2CV has a special place. On one level, its curved, streamlined body-shell can be seen as just one more example of the influence of aerodynamics on car design in the inter-war years. On another level, however, its striking visual idiosyncracies and peculiarities – the use of corrugated metal, the cloth-covered tubular-steel seats, the crude finish on its flat body panels, and the roll-back canvas roof – indicated a whole new philosophy towards 20th-century car design in which low price and utility played unprecedented roles.

The uniqueness of the 2CV derived from the combination of people who worked on it and the way in which their skills combined at a particular moment in a particular way. The car's manufacturer, Citroën, was itself a leader. Formed relatively late – in 1919 – the company, led by André Citroën, was from the outset committed to

mass-producing cars as efficiently as possible using American tools and techniques. The first car to come off its lines in 1948, the Model A, was France's equivalent of Ford's Model T, and can be counted as Europe's first truly mass-produced car. André Citroën was progressive in other ways as well. He advocated the use of advertising, for example, and succeeded in getting the company's name illuminated on the side of the Eiffel Tower in Paris. As well as producing cars for private passengers Citroën moved into commercial vehicles and set up a coach company.

BELOW *Citroën's Traction Avant model (front-wheel drive) was in production from 1934 right through to 1967. This model, an 11B Familiale dating from 1953, extends the length of the earlier version but retains the same low, long, road-hugging body silhouette.*

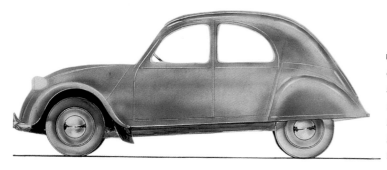

LEFT *Drawings of Citroën's "people's car" show the curved lines of its simple, utilitarian profile. Flaminio Bertoni's design emphasized the rounded radiator grille, the flowing line of the front mudguard, and the teardrop rear mudguard.*

PROGRESSIVE CAR DESIGN

Where car manufacture was concerned André Citroën brought in pressed-steel bodies in 1924. His famous streamlined Traction Avant model, launched in 1934, was the first mass-produced, front-wheel-drive car in Europe as well as boasting a fully-welded monocoque body-shell.

With the Traction Avant, Citroën demonstrated his progressive approach towards automobile design. Its sloping radiator grille made it an immediate icon and the car remained a favourite among French customers for several decades. Unfortunately André Citroën did not live long enough to see his radical car go into full production. At his death in 1936 the Michelin Tyre Company bought the car manufacturer and brought in Pierre Boulanger to be the managing director of the Paris factory.

TOWARDS THE 2CV

Boulanger played a crucial role in the conception of the 2CV. He had a range of useful technical and constructional experiences, having been a pilot in World War I, a draftsman in an architect's office in Seattle from 1908 to 1910, and the designer of a factory building for Michelin in Clermont-Ferrand. Above all, Boulanger's ability to manage a technical and creative team was crucial to the project. It was he who coordinated the work of the engineer Henri Lefèvre, who also knew about aircraft technology, and the stylists Flaminio Bertoni and Jean Muraret, on the production of the 2CV.

Bertoni, who began work on the 2CV project in 1935, was an Italian sculptor who oscillated between working as a fine artist and creating "car sculptures". He had cut his teeth in the workshop of the Carrozzeria Macchi in his home town of Varese in Italy, and was living

RIGHT *A 1939 prototype of what was to become the 2CV after World War II. The exterior line is continuous from the front to the rear bumper and the strength of corrugated steel is used to full effect on the hood. This model only had a single headlight.*

in France when hired by Citroën in 1932. He tended to work in clay, preferring to use models rather than two-dimensional sketches.

The idea of producing a car for French farmers who had not driven before had originally been an idea of André Citroën, but it was picked up by Boulanger when he entered the firm, and he quickly made it his own. His specifications for the car were strict. Famously, it had to be capable of transporting four people, or two farmers with a 50 kg (110 lb) weight of baggage (a bag of potatoes!), across a ploughed field, without breaking the eggs that they carried with them in a basket. It was to have a maximum speed of 65 km/h (40 mph) and a specified level of fuel consumption.

THE VERY SMALL CAR

Work began on the car in 1936 and continued into 1937. Prototypes were made – a wooden mockup being constructed in 1936 – and tested in secret, and in 1939 the factory was ordered to produce 250 metal prototypes. Only a few were produced, however, since the advent of the war put an end to this stage of the project.

The clue to the design of the original 2CV, known as the TPV (*très petite voiture*, or "very small car"), lay in the requirement for lightness, a requirement that resulted in the use of a lightweight magnesium alloy chassis. In addition structural members were perforated, and corrugated metal was used for strength in imitation of the Junkers airplane. Boulanger and Lefèvre's knowledge of aircraft technology also led to the use of mica for the windows and cloth and tubular steel for the seating, which was suspended from the roof frame. If weight was a principal determinant, so too was comfort for the driver and passengers, although everything was realized through minimal means to keep overall costs as low as possible. Clearly, though, Bertoni's sculptural eye ensured that the aesthetic dimension was not ignored but was integrated with all the other requirements so that the car was

ABOVE *Pierre Boulanger took over as managing director of the Citroën factory at the death of the company's founder in 1936. He worked closely with the engineer, Henri Lefèvre, and the stylist, Flaminio Bertoni, on the creation of the 2CV.*

ABOVE *The sculptor Flaminio Bertoni began working with Citroën on the body of the 2CV in 1935. His background included experience in both car body styling and sculpture and he combined the two skills to great effect in his work for Citroën's little "people's car".*

understood not only as a fulfilment of its brief but also as a visual realization of the constraints that had underpinned its design.

The 1939 prototype of the 2CV provided the basis for the postwar version, which was launched at the Paris Automobile Salon of 1948. Inevitably a number of modifications were introduced – the single headlight was replaced by two, steel replaced the magnesium, and the rear wheels were covered. The mica was replaced as they had discovered that it scratched easily. The basic form, level of simplicity, and ethos remained in place, however, and the "Tin Snail" or the "Duck", as the car was soon nicknamed, appealed immediately to the French public and was an overnight success.

THE IRREPLACEABLE "SNAIL"

Although minor improvements were made over the next four decades and the engine size was increased, the basic minimalist appeal of the "very small car", or the "four wheels under an umbrella" as Boulanger had described it back in the 1930s, remained intact right up to 1990, when it finally went out of production.

ABOVE *The interior of the 2CV continued the theme of utility that characterized its exterior. The seats, for example, were made of fabric sewn on to an exposed tubular-steel frame; since the car was conceived as an agricultural vehicle they could be moved to accommodate its load.*

Citroën made an attempt to repeat the same formula with its little Ami 6 car, Bertoni's last design, launched in 1961. Built at Citroën's new factory in Brittany, the model had a 602cc engine. Although its body was much less utilitarian, it failed to capture the popular imagination in the same way as the 2CV. Ironically, the attempt to reach the expanding middle-class market had been achieved more successfully by the basic little "Snail" than by the later exercise in style.

Launched in 1967, the Dyane was Citroën's next attempt at a 2CV replacement. It was positioned between the 2CV and the Ami 6 in market terms and its form was reminiscent of the former car albeit more self-consciously styled. Once again, however, the "Snail" proved to be a more timeless design, capable of inserting itself into the lives and psyches of several generations of car owners.

SIR ALEC ISSIGONIS

PRINCIPAL DESIGNS

1948 *Morris Minor*
1959 *Austin/Morris Mini*
1962 *Austin/Morris 1100*
1964 *Austin/Morris 1800*
1969 *Austin/Morris Maxi*

Like Dante Giacosa in Italy (see pp.98–101), Alec Issigonis (1906–88) was an engineer by training but a car designer by trade. An interest in the whole car, conceived and realized by a single mind, underpinned for him, as it did for Giacosa, the process of design. Although an automobile designer's work is undertaken with a team of people, this does not prevent an individual from taking control of the project and putting his mark on the result. So it was with the designs of Alec Issigonis in the second half of the 20th century: and the success of his two strongest designs, the Morris Minor of 1948 and the Austin/Morris Mini 11 years later, bear witness to it.

EARLY EXPERIENCE

Born in Turkey, Issigonis came to study engineering in Britain, in London's Battersea, just after World War I. His first employment was as a draftsman in the design workshop of Edward Gillett in London, where he acquired enough experience to obtain a job with Humber. His interest in drawing remained with him throughout his career, with sketches for his designs being intrinsic to his method of working. From Humber he moved on to work for Morris Motors at Cowley.

ABOVE *Created to compete with the other European "people's cars", the little Morris Minor of 1948 was Issigonis' first automobile design success. Its monocoque structure was radical and its form was both compact and unified, although the front still retained a vestige of American styling.*

LEFT *Alec Issigonis is shown at his retirement party in 1971, standing next to the first production model of his Austin/Morris Mini. Launched in 1959, the Mini earned him a reputation as one of Britain's leading car designers. By the end of his career, he had become – along with Dante Giacosa of Italy – one of the most notable engineer-designers of the 20th century.*

During the war Issigonis took on the challenge of designing a car that would provide Morris with an equivalent of the Fiat Topolino (see pp.98–101) and the VW Beetle (see pp.94–7), which would be as advanced in its engineering as in its styling and would place Britain at the cutting edge of car design. At this time it would seem that Issigonis was interested in aerodynamic styling as well as in the metal grille designs that were emerging on the other side of the Atlantic. His sketches for the Morris Minor show his interest in the teardrop wheel fenders and the metal "teeth" of the radiator grille, but the end version shows a softening of these forms to create an integrated body-shell with a residual hint of streamlining showing in the fenders and the curved back of the car. In production terms its monocoque structure was radical and pointed the way ahead for the European car industry.

POPULAR SUCCESS

The Minor was Britain's "people's car", intended to allow a family to travel in reasonable comfort in a space- and fuel-efficient motor car; above all it was an automobile with a friendly image and a pleasing appearance. Unlike Volkswagen and Fiat, Morris did not invest heavily in the Minor and the engine was not as powerful as it should have been; the car won the public over on its image alone. The first series offered a two-door version and a convertible, while in 1950 a four-door Minor came on the market. The Traveller model, with its "skeleton on

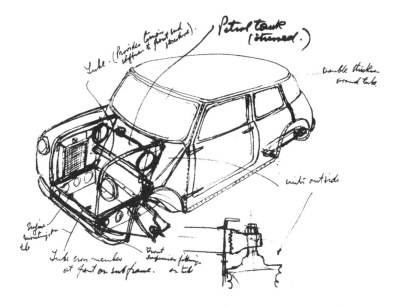

ABOVE *Issigonis used the freehand sketch as a key element in the design process. His early experience as a draftsman in the design office of Edward Gillett helped him to refine his drawing skills, and he used the sketch as a means of problem-solving.*

BELOW *A sectional view of Issigonis' BMC Mini shows how the carefully positioned components, among them the transverse engine, resulted in a compact design that maximized the interior space of this small car. There were no wasted corner spaces in this rational design.*

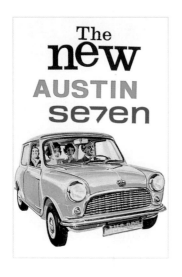

ABOVE *The BMC Mini played a role in sustaining the company's commitment to mass mobility and family travel, which had been established by the Austin Seven (Chummy) back in the 1920s: while the look of its cars changed dramatically, Austin's philosophy of the car did not.*

the outside" ash framing, proved highly popular and outlived the other models, remaining in production until 1971. The Minor went through several facelifts in the 1950s, the split window disppearing in 1956, and its performance improved as larger engines were introduced.

AN ANTI-STYLE ICON

If the Morris Minor found a place in the hearts of the British in the immediate postwar years, Issigonis' subsequent design, the Mini, became a key icon in the 1960s. Issigonis left Morris in 1952 when it merged with Austin to become the British Motor Corporation (BMC), and spent some time with Alvis. He was brought back to BMC by Leonard Lord, the group's managing director, and from 1956 set to work on the design of a new British people's car. This time the stimulus came from the fuel shortages produced by the Suez crisis, and the competition from bubble cars (see pp.112–3).

The challenge was to create the smallest car for four people plus luggage which used the minimum quantity of fuel. Typically Issigonis approached the problem from the inside out, to create as much internal space as possible. He achieved this by laying the engine in a sideways (transverse) position; putting the wheels at the extreme four corners of the "box" and making them two-thirds the usual size; and putting the gearbox in the sump under the engine.

The result was radical. At only 3 metres (10 ft) long, 1.2 metres (4 ft) wide and 1.2 metres (4 ft) high, the Mini was shorter than the Fiat Topolino. Yet four adults could get into it in comfort and pack some luggage in the trunk. The exterior owed its appearance to what might be called "anti-styling". Issigonis was not influenced by fashion, nor was he interested in the accoutrements of status. He sought a timeless design that was the direct result of engineering decisions. Thus the car had no extras and no overt styling features. It was essentially a box, and all the utilitarian requirements to make it a working car – headlights, door handles, radiator grille – were given a minimal treatment. There was no overt streamlining as there had been in the Minor. The monocoque body-shell of the Mini was no more than a casing to protect the passengers and the components inside. Nothing was included that could not be justified either by function or by cost.

A CULT FOLLOWING

The design of the Mini was dramatically different from the styling exercises of the Americans from the 1930s onward, moving towards a new approach that had more in common with the principles of product design. The result, ironically, was a cult object which, despite Issigonis' dislike of marketing and advertising, became an icon of popular culture. Linked with the names of models, pop stars, and fashion designers, including Twiggy, the Beatles, and Mary Quant, the styleless Mini (the name itself was invented by the British public) became a lifestyle appendage *par excellence*.

Nineteen sixty-one saw the advent of the Mini Cooper, a racing version made possible by the intervention of John Cooper. This provided a more masculine version of what had become to some extent a woman's car, as a result of its ease of handling and lightness. Above all, however, the Mini was linked with the concepts of youth and fun. Ever popular, it remained in production until October 2000.

Although Sir Alec Issigonis (as he became in 1967) was responsible for many more designs fo Morris and Austin, he retired soon after British Leyland took over BMC in 1968. His retirement saw the end of a period of experimentation and radicalism in the arena of the British small car that has not been surpassed.

LEFT *Renault launched its first "people's car", the 4CV, in 1946. It was characterized by its rounded forms and the three wavy chromed metal strips across its front. These gave the car a friendly appearance which no doubt played a part in its remaining in production until 1961.*

RENAULT'S "PEOPLE'S CARS"

During World War II Louis Renault kept his factory open to supply the needs of the German army, a decision that led to his imprisonment as a collaborator in 1944 and the takeover of his factory by the French government. However, it also allowed him to work in secret, before his imprisonment, on a project that was close to his heart, the design of a Renault "people's car".

"THE FLEA" IS BORN

The Renault 4CV was launched in 1946, two years after Louis Renault's death. The first model was shown painted in sand yellow, a colour that had been created for military purposes for action in the desert. Swiftly nicknamed "the flea" because of its colour and shape, it was an immediate popular success. In design terms the little rear-engined car, with its rounded forms and continuous body lines, owed something to the VW Beetle (see pp.94–7) and the Fiat Topolino (see pp.98–101) but it had its own unambiguous character. While an early prototype had had a rounded front that came right down to the bumper, in imitation of the Volkswagen, later models reintroduced a straight hood, which gave it a more conservative but also a more friendly appearance. This sense of friendliness was enhanced by the

wavy horizontal radiator grille, suggestive of whiskers or a smile; the little bump of the hood immediately above, resembling a nose, reinforced it still further. This marked the beginning of Renault's interest in "character cars", a trend that reached its apogee in Patrick Le Quément's little Twingo, launched in the 1990s (see pp.224–7). Marketed as "the little car for all", the 4CV quickly found a place in French everyday life and remained in production until 1961, when it was replaced by the Renault 4.

Pierre Lefaucheux, who took over when the company was nationalized in 1945, began to think about a successor to the 4CV. It was clear to him that French consumers were beginning to have more disposable income to spend on cars and the logical direction, he believed, would be to create a new, more spacious, more comfortable, and safer version of the Renault 4CV, ideally using the same engine. He asked Robert Barthaud, the head of styling, to do a few preliminary sketches and in 1950 announced the commencement of Project 109, which was to end up, in 1956, with what came to be called the Dauphine. The name appeared by accident in a press statement that called the 4CV the "queen of the market" and which suggested that the new model should be called the "dauphine" (that

is, the daughter of the queen). The name stuck. The first prototypes came out of Renault's technical centre in 1952. Unhappy with the form proposed by the company's in-house designer, Lefaucheux was impelled to consult the Italian body stylist Ghia, whose input into the appearance of the Dauphine was crucial.

In 1954 Lefaucheux was killed in an accident and tragically failed to see his project realized. When it appeared in 1956, like the 4CV before it the Dauphine appealed strongly to the French public. It was much more sophisticated but it maintained the same friendly image as the earlier car. Visually it was less American and more European in inspiration. The chrome grille of the 4CV had disappeared and the fenders were much more integrated into the main body of the car. Renault marketed it as a fashion accessory for women, available in a range of attractive colours, including lime green and pale yellow.

OTHER CHARACTERFUL CARS

Nineteen sixty-one saw the launch of the Renault 4, which was seen as the company's competitor to Citroën's 2CV. A basic utility vehicle in essence, the Renault 4 had a few more luxury details than the 2CV, and stayed in production until 1992. Some years later, in 1972, Renault capitalized on this earlier success with the launch of its Renault 5, which has been described as the first of the modern "superminis". Once again it managed to hit a nerve, providing the car-buying public with just the right combination of character, comfort, performance, and low price.

ABOVE *The Renault Dauphine of 1956 began its life six years earlier as Project 109. This stylish little car, designed with input from the Italian coachbuilder Ghia, was a huge popular success in France. Like the 4CV, it was a rear-engined car.*

BELOW *A prototype for what became the Renault 5, which replaced the Renault 4 in 1972. This was a revolutionary car for the company and was a simple, elegant design, capable of holding four people in comfort despite its small size.*

BUBBLE CARS

The 1950s saw the introduction of a number of very small, three-wheeled cars that became known as "bubble cars" because of their rounded forms and curved-glass windows. Their attraction lay in their low price and low fuel consumption – and in the fact that their owners did not have to pay the full car tax on them. They were also easy to park and represented the next step up, in car ownership terms, from a motorcycle and sidecar. In spite of their miniature proportions parents could squeeze a couple of children into several of the models and they became an attractive second car for many families, comfortable enough for a trip to the library.

THE GERMAN MESSERSCHMITT

The first bubble cars were products of Germany and Italy. In 1953 the little Messerschmitt 175 arrived, the creation of a German aeronautical engineer, Fritz Fend, who had served in the Luftwaffe. It grew from the idea of an invalid carriage into a car proper and was put into production by the former aircraft manufacturer as a means of getting going in peacetime. The links with aircraft were strong, the vehicle itself looking somewhat like the cockpit of an airplane on wheels. Plexiglass was used for the canopy. Entrance was by lifting the entire roof, and later versions incorporated a pivoting front seat to make getting in and out easier. The teardrop-shaped Messerschmitt had two wheels at the front and one at the rear and its small body-shell featured streamlined bulges at the front and over the two front wheels, giving a visual unity to the whole car. The windshield was curved. In a 1955 version this curve was extended, an electric wiper was added,

ABOVE *The Isetta bubble car was first produced in Italy by the Iso company, but the German firm BMW took over its manufacture in 1954 and kept it in production for a decade. This model dates from 1958. The Isetta was the most compact and stylish of the postwar bubble cars.*

LEFT *A 1964 catalogue for the Isetta emphasizes its economical role in everyday life. The image shows the way in which the front opened for ease of entrance. The elegant form of this little car confirmed Italian style as a world leader at this time.*

and the quality of the interior was improved. The little car could accommodate an adult and a child. As the decade progressed, more details were added to subsequent models and soft-top and four-wheeled versions were also introduced.

THE ITALIAN ISETTA

Following fast on the heels of the Messerschmitt the Isetta, produced in the first instance by the Italian company Iso, was a slightly different vehicle. Still retaining the two front wheels, it came in two versions, one with a single back wheel and another with two back wheels positioned closely next to each other. It was more overtly bubble- or egg-shaped than the Messerschmitt, with its wheels placed more directly under the cabin itself and with fewer excrescences. The German car manufacturer BMW took over production of the Isetta in 1954, a year after its introduction in Italy, and kept it going until 1964, by which time 160,000 cars had been made.

Unlike the Messerschmitt, entrance into the Isetta was through the front but a larger door made entry easier. The steering wheel was designed to pivot when the door was opened. Again, different versions were available, including one with a "bubble" rear window and another with a sliding side window; a convertible also made an appearance. In 1957 BMW launched its four-wheeled 600 model which was an Isetta but which clearly borrowed a significant

amount from the earlier three-wheeled version. The 600 had a door at the front, like the Isetta, but also another on one side which allowed access to a back seat.

The Heinkel, or Trojan as it was named when it was launched in Britain, also owed much to the Isetta although its monocoque body construction made it considerably lighter. Once again its roots were in the German aircraft industry. Production ceased in 1958.

THE BUBBLE'S ENDURING APPEAL

The appeal of the bubble cars expanded through the 1950s and countless small companies entered the field. Britain, for example, could list many names, among them the Petite, the Clipper, the Frisky, and the Scootacar. It was a fad that came and went, mainly owing to the increasing availability of inexpensive "proper" cars as well as the hazards of driving the unstable three-wheelers. However, with the advent of Japanese microcars in the 1990s, it is clear that the attraction of the very small car has not entirely disappeared, and the need to lower fuel consumption makes them very appealing once again.

BELOW *The Messerschmitt bubble car, launched in 1953, was the creation of Fritz Fend, a German aeronautical engineer, and its form recalls that of an airplane cockpit. Although the original only had three wheels (one at the rear) later versions had four wheels.*

UTILITY VEHICLES

Several of the landmark car designs of the 20th century had their origins outside the consumer marketplace. Vehicles designed for military and agricultural use, expeditions and other specific functions, occasionally, through their very "stylelessness" and overt functionality, "hit the button" where design was concerned. Many of them were visually stable for long periods and, as a result, became classics. Often they moved sideways from their original destination as utility artifacts to become cult consumer objects.

THE FIRST JEEP

The most obvious example of this kind of transformation is the American Jeep. This began life as a four-wheel-drive "general-purpose" vehicle (hence the name, derived from "GP") created by the Bantam Car company, the manufacturing outfit formed in 1929 when Henry Austin had attempted to produce an American version of his little Austin Seven (see pp.92–3). Bantam's GP vehicle was taken up by the American army in 1941. Its utilitarian appearance, rugged character, and strong performance features were ideally suited to a military context. During the war, the Willys-Overland company was better equipped than the Bantam Car company to undertake the large-scale production of the Jeep that was needed and, with the help of the Ford Motor Company, it took over production of the military vehicle. In 1951, when the Jeep was selected to be one of the eight automobiles included in an exhibition at New York's Museum of Modern Art, the curator described it as "a sturdy sardine can on wheels", so basic and utilitarian was its form.

OPPOSITE *The British Land Rover, designed by the chief designer at Rover, owed much to the American Jeep. The prototype, created in 1947, was built, in fact, on a Jeep chassis. Although it was conceived as an agricultural vehicle it quickly moved into the general marketplace.*

LEFT *The rugged and utilitarian appearance of the Willys Jeep, which was adopted by the American army in 1941, led to its becoming a timeless design classic. As a mark of recognition one was included in an exhibition held at New York's Museum of Modern Art in 1951.*

When the war ended Willys-Overland decided to keep producing the Jeep for the civilian market, starting production of its CJ (Civilian Jeep) line in 1945. The industrial designer Brooks Stevens was brought in to create a Jeep station wagon – the Wagoneer (the first all-metal station-wagon) – in 1946, a Jeep truck in 1947, and a convertible, the Jeepster, in 1948. All three depended heavily on the rugged aesthetic of the utility vehicle. The Jeepster combined the front end of the Willys station-wagon with the rear fenders of the Jeep truck. It was a striking vehicle and its flat-topped fenders remained a key characteristic of all its versions. Unfortunately it was not publicized adequately and only just under 20,000 had been manufactured by the time it went out of production in 1950.

In essence the Jeep and its variants became part of the American landscape from the mid-1940s onward, appearing in a range of guises but always retaining its original identity as a utility vehicle transformed into a consumer object. In 1974 Stevens designed the Cherokee, the first of the sports utility vehicles (SUVs), showing a strong continuity with his Jeeps of the 1940s. Kaiser took over Willys-Overland in 1953 but Willys wagons and trucks continued to be produced until 1965. The company subsequently went into the hands of American Motors (1970) and then Chrysler (1986).

FROM JEEP TO LAND ROVER

Another seminal utility vehicle to reach international cult status was the British-designed Land Rover, which owed a huge debt to the American Jeep. Maurice Wilks, the chief designer at Rover at the end of World War II, is said to have been using an ex-army Jeep on his estate and was conscious that he would need a replacement when the car wore out. He had several Jeeps taken apart at the Rover factory to see how they were built, and used what he found to create an agriculturally oriented four-wheel-drive vehicle for the postwar British market. Because of the restrictions on steel, which was only being used for the export market, the body of the Land Rover was made from aluminium alloy. The car was developed at the Rover plant by Wilks: a prototype, built on a Jeep chassis, was created in 1947, and the final model was launched at the Amsterdam motor show in 1948. It was an immediate hit among British farmers and gradually moved into a more general market as well.

The original Land Rover, the Series 1, was a very basic automobile with no concessions made to physical comfort. Visually it was characterized by the positioning of its headlights behind its mesh grille and of the sidelights on the bulkhead below the windshield. Like that of the Jeep before it, the body-shell, made out of flat panels, showed no signs of the bulbous streamlined forms that were so fashionable at this time in mass consumer automobiles. Its appeal was down to its utilitarian qualities and its off-road capabilities. The 1954 version exhibited a few styling modifications but essentially the basic format remained unchanged.

Meanwhile the Rover company was also producing a number of road-going sedans that were proving successful in the British marketplace, including the Rover 75, modelled on Raymond Loewy's design for the Studebaker Champion (see pp.136–9). In 1965 a marketing man at Rover, Graham Bannock, decided that there was a place for a car that had the utility of the Land Rover in travelling over

rough terrain combined with the comfort and luxury of the sedans. The result, launched in 1970, was the Range Rover, which remained in production, basically unchanged, until 1995.

The Range Rover struck a chord with British people. Its success as a rural car was rapidly joined by its ubiquitousness in an urban setting as well. Its appearance, created by the Rover in-house team, headed by David Bache, demonstrated a softer, smoother, more seamless approach, and the utilitarian look and the "hand-made" aesthetic of the Land Rover were removed to produce a car that was comfortable and performed well in rough terrain.

UTILITY CHIC

Both the American Jeep and the British Land Rover proved highly successful in the consumer marketplace. Although their origins were primarily functional they met a market need that valued the utilitarian both as a practical necessity and as a nostalgic longing. Both of them symbolized a "working" society that used its material goods as tools rather than as display items and, in a world in which car styling was becoming increasingly extravagant, this alternative automobile message had a strong appeal for many people. Both in a rural and in an urban setting, therefore, these utility vehicles served a purpose. By the end of the century that purpose, arguably, was primarily symbolic.

The automobile typology developed by these vehicles was widely emuluated in the 1980s and 1990s. The concept of the "sports utility

The Grand Jeep Wagoneer of 1984 shows how the utility vehicle had, by this decade, become a stylish urban phenomenon. Its combination of ruggedness with interior space and comfort made it a favourite for family outings and a popular car with the middle-class market.

vehicle" developed rapidly and was embraced by manufacturers around the world. Both the Jeep and the Land Rover themselves experienced dramatic rebirths in the consumer context. In the late 1980s Chrysler turned the Jeep into a thoroughly chic urban car. From the early rugged 1940s model it became transformed, its flat fenders, for example, being replaced by a rounded style. Similarly, the story of the Land Rover's progressive transformation into the Discovery, the Defender, and the Freelander demonstrates how a classic design could be repackaged over and over again to create new markets. The British designer Gerry McGovern, a graduate of London's Royal College of Art, worked at Rover as chief designer overseeing the creation of these models.

OFF-ROADERS FROM JAPAN

The Japanese manufacturers, always keen to make the most of the links between automobiles and lifestyle, were quick to pick up the SUV as a typology they could easily exploit, and models such as the Toyota Landcruiser, the Mitsubishi Shogun, the Isuzu Trooper, the Mitsubishi Pajero, and the Mitsubishi Chariot Grandis began to flood the market. The "high-off-the-ground, four-wheel-drive, large-wheels, cow-catcher-grille" look was a winner worldwide and the Japanese were highly successful in giving it a number of different faces. By the end of the 20th century, through their multiple incarnations and imitators, the Jeep and the Land Rover were still very much a part of the international automobile landscape.

DESIGNING
DREAMS

...so nice to come

No, the fighting isn't over. Nor is Buick's war work finished.

But victory in Europe is releasing many fighting men to come home — and permitting the country to turn, at least in part, to the making of things they will find nice to come home to.

To many a fighting man, this will mean such pleasures as an open road, a glorious day — and a bright and lively Buick.

The roads are here. The each rising sun. And th enlivens Buick's factor ready process for getting duction of cars.

We aim to make those turning warriors have cars that from go-treadle fit the stirring pattern citing, forward-movir many millions have foug

DESIGNING DREAMS

*D*epending on your point of view, car design in 1950s America can be seen as the highest or the lowest moment of that creative practice in the 20th century. According to its harshest critics, it was a time when car styling was at its most superficial, preoccupied with decorative surfaces and excessive detailing and aimed at a market interested only in acquiring conspicuous status symbols. Others describe the period as the heroic age of car styling, when imaginations were at their most unfettered and when large-scale manufacturing gave stylists their greatest freedom to create some of the 20th century's most potent icons; symbolism was at its most sophisticated, and the link between automobiles and contemporary popular culture at its peak.

Whatever one's opinion, it was certainly an era that cannot be ignored. To date, most attention has been given to the huge, chrome-laden, gas-guzzling automobiles created by General Motors, Chrysler, and Ford. These elaborate cars competed neck and neck from the mid-1950s, their designers conscious that they had to outdo each other to keep the manufacturers in business. This intense style race lasted for about five years and saw the "Big Three" incrementally adding extras to the basic bodies of their cars in the battle to attract customers. The additions included bigger and better body adornments – chrome, fins, radiator grilles, rear lights – inspired by jet and rocket imagery; technical novelties, including power steering and electric windows; and luxurious interior extras such as beauty accessories, drinks cabinets, and cigarette lighters. They set out to stimulate desire by drawing on a range of pleasure-evoking images, combined with an evocation of technological utopianism that was enormously attractive to a generation living in the early days of space exploration and believing in the redemptive power of modern technology.

BUY MORE WAR BONDS

BUY STILL MORE WAR BONDS

ome to !

This is the 1942 Buick which sets the high standards to be surpassed in new models now being made ready.

WHEN BETTER AUTOMOBILES ARE BUILT

BUICK WILL BUILD THEM

BUICK DIVISION OF GENERAL MOTORS
Every Sunday Afternoon—GENERAL MOTORS SYMPHONY OF THE AIR

The Army-Navy "E" proudly flies over all Buick plants

ne with
that now
he make-
o the pro-

ll that re-
about —
light will
ively, ex-
world so

LEFT *An advertisement for the 1942 Buick. The text accompanying this rendering of this dramatically styled car for the future emphasizes its role in the postwar dreams of home-coming soldiers who had contributed to the war effort.*

While the symbolic potency of these large automobiles cannot be ignored, they were not the only cars to emerge from the United States in the early postwar years. It was not until 1949 that the "Big Three" got their new cars on to the roads in any number, by which time several independents – Kaiser Frazer, Tucker, and Studebaker – had all got going much more quickly and, in design terms, were showing the way forward. These firms worked with consultant designers and succeeded in creating a body of cars that were way ahead of their time. Sadly, neither Kaiser Frazer nor Tucker were able to produce their cars in significant numbers, and Studebaker was compelled to merge with Packard in 1954. Nonetheless, in the story of 20th-century car design, their achievements are landmarks that cannot be ignored.

In addition to the significant styling achievements of a handful of independents it is also important to note that not all

American cars of these years were big and emblazoned with chrome and fins. The creators of America's sports cars of this era, from Ford's Thunderbird to Chevrolet's Corvette to Studebaker's Starline coupé of the early 1950s, were looking closely at Europe and designing cars to compete with the smart imports that were arriving in increasing numbers. These cars were simpler and smaller than the lumpy sedans and they led directly to the cleaner-look cars of the next decade.

For the young car stylists of that era the postwar years in the United States were undoubtedly exciting ones in which to work. Many of them had served in the war, often in aeronautics, which led to the strong use of aircraft and jet imagery in the 1950s. Several had worked alongside Harley Earl in the pre-war years and perpetuated that pioneer's approach to styling to a significant extent. While to some degree this limited the industry to a

BELOW *The Duke and Duchess of Windsor are pictured beside their specially built Buick Estate wagon in Palm Beach in the late 1940s. The Duke played an active role in the design, stressing an emphasis on space and baggage protection.*

RIGHT *This photograph from 1955 shows a styling studio employee spraying a scale model of a prototype car for General Motors. This was the era of the annual model, and intensive work went on within the studio.*

particular in-house model and to a particular process of designing – one that typically moved from the sketch to the creation of a full-size clay model on an aluminium armature – individuals such as Virgil Exner, Bob Bourke, Bill Mitchell, George Walker, Eugene Bordinat, Elwood Engel, Frank Hershey, Howard Darrin, John Reinart, and Alex Tremulis brought their own personal philosophies and tastes to the task, thereby ensuring that the practice of styling remained as individual as any other form of creativity. Most importantly of all, this was the era in which the engineer lost ground to the designer who, for the first time, became one of the most powerful figures in automotive manufacturing.

The automobile was a major factor in the expansion of the suburbs in 1950s America, with the corresponding need for increased mobility. The housewife had to have a car to do the shopping while her husband drove to work on the new motorway

system. Increased affluence made the purchase of a car possible for many people who had never owned one before and, for the first time, the market became fragmented, with husbands, wives, and teenagers targeted separately by the manufacturers. Car advertising proliferated in the press and on television, and the automobile came to be considered as the major purchase of the household, closely followed by the refrigerator. Colour entered the suburbanites' lives in their kitchens and in their cars, and, as Norman Bel Geddes had predicted in the mid-1930s, garages appeared on the fronts of suburban dwellings .

The enthusiasm for automobiles was ubiquitous and remained so through into the 1960s, although by that time the market had fragmented even further and tastes varied enormously. While the baroque cars of the late 1950s and early 1960s gave way to simpler-looking, more individualized cars, the

desire for power and speed was intensified. New kinds of automobiles – compacts, personal luxury cars, and "pony cars" – came to the fore, competing with the large sedans that had dominated the picture in the earlier period.

The first signs that postwar American automobile culture was changing gear came in the late 1950s with the publication of a series of books written by the cultural critic Vance Packard, who attacked conspicuous consumption and what he saw as the manipulative tactics of the manufacturers that were forcing the American public to part with its money. The car industry came under enormous attack, with General Motors singled out for particular attention. Packard's points were reinforced in 1965 by the publication by Ralph Nader of a book entitled *Unsafe at any Speed* which, by pointing out how dangerous American cars actually were, put the first real nail in the coffin of the exuberant

automobile culture. Once again General Motors came out of the attack very badly. The growing safety lobby led to the passing of the National Traffic and Motor Vehicle Safety Act in 1968 and by the end of the decade it was clear that American consumers had lost their confidence in automobile culture and that they sought protection from the large manufacturers.

This crisis of consumer confidence was compounded by the oil crisis and the environmental lobby of the early 1970s which put an end to the era of the gas-guzzlers once and for all. The car ceased to signify the good life and started, instead, to become a threat to the future well-being of the human race. At the same time the careers of the second generation of car stylists began to draw to a close and a new, specialist breed of car designers set out on their careers in a climate that had very little in common with that which had prevailed only two decades earlier.

RIGHT *Harley Earl's dream car of 1951 named the LeSabre after the Sabre jet fighter. Earl used one of these dramatically styled cars for his own personal transportation, so close was it to his ideal car. Its design details clearly derive from jet airplanes.*

THE AGE OF THE JET

By the end of the 1930s, American car design had succeeded in combining the expressive aesthetic of aerodynamic streamlining with the more conservative demands of the marketplace to retain such familiar components as the hood, fenders, windshield, and radiator grille. Although the pure teardrop form had appeared only in a few experimental models, its smooth surfaces had infiltrated the everyday automobile to a significant extent. The cars of the late 1930s and early 1940s were large, bulky objects, the headlights integrated into the massive wings, the aggressive chrome radiator grilles shining and showing their teeth, the bumpers curved sinuously around the bodies.

EVER BIGGER, EVER BETTER

While it looked as if the modern motor car had finally arrived, and the American automobile had taken display as far as it could go, there was still more to come. The war years proved to be a testing ground, providing a second wind for the established car stylists (and breeding a new generation as well) who went on to move beyond the influence of sailboats, dolphins, airships, and World War I airplanes, to attempt to incorporate imagery derived from more contemporary items of progressive military technology and transportation: the fighter jet and the space rocket.

The cars that America produced from the late 1940s to the early 1960s were without precedent. The "Big Three" manufacturers – General Motors, Chrysler, and Ford – led the way, producing cars on an annual basis, like fashion goods, in their attempts to outdo each other. These incremental "improvements" led to a situation in which "bigger and better" were the bywords and, in their enthusiasm to dominate the marketplace and stimulate consumer desire, designers strove to push automotive display to new levels of ostentation and elaboration. Performance became less important than showiness; comfort and style more significant than utility. The resulting cars were, in essence, a modern form of mass-market luxury which offered something entirely different from the exotic woods and leather of the up-market custom car of a couple of decades earlier.

FINS

Nowhere was this sharp competition more visible than in the application of fins to the rear ends of cars. The trend had been initiated by Harley Earl (see pp.22–5) who, at the beginninng of the war, was given the task of differentiating the Cadillac from the other General Motors marks. To create the required level of difference Earl incorporated some small fins on the rear of the car. The effect was

RIGHT *The Lockheed P-38 Lightning aircraft, designed by Clarence Johnson, was a source of inspiration for General Motors' Harley Earl. Its rear fins, in particular, found their way into a number of postwar car designs from his studio.*

immediate. Combined with the absorption of the front fenders into the side of the car to create a "slab side", and the use of curved glass on the front windshield, the fins introduced a whole new look into American car design.

JET BECOMES CAR

Earl had been thinking about fins for some time, not specifically for the Cadillac but for a later car, the LeSabre of 1951, named after the F-86 Sabre fighter jet. In 1947 he had seen a Lockheed P-38 Lightning fighter plane; designed by Clarence Johnson, it had three fuselages and aerodynamic tailfins. Impressed, Earl resolved to introduce its dramatic look into car design. The resulting Cadillac Sedanet of 1948 showed the way forward. Other manufacturers followed General Motors' lead and by the mid-1950s tailfins had become a familiar appendage on many American mass-market cars.

Fins were not the only iconographic reference to jets. The curved windshield was inspired by the cockpit of planes, and several cars of the late 1940s had "bullet noses" that were reminiscent of aircraft. Numerous other visual references abounded. The message was clear. Cars no longer looked to the past for their inspiration. Gone were the references to aristocratic values and the days of the "horseless carriage". The car now belonged unequivocally to the second half of the 20th century. Even the concepts of comfort and display, so crucial to these cars' *raison d'être*, were couched in a new language, one that borrowed from contemporary interior decor and the feminine worlds of fashion and beauty. A new palette of colours – pink, pale green, lemon

BELOW *Harley Earl with Firebird II (left) of 1956 and Firebird I created two years earlier. The forms of these pioneering gas turbine dream cars were heavily influenced by those of jet fighters, especially the rear fins.*

yellow – appeared to seduce consumers into purchasing mode. Labour-saving devices, such as power steering and electric windows, were also extremely popular in these years of modern luxury, enticing customers to participate in the new automotive culture.

THE FINS WARS

The lush interiors were directed at female consumers; the jet fighter imagery of the exterior was overtly masculine. The fins war hotted up in the mid-1950s, by which time General Motors had introduced them on all their cars. Chrysler joined the fray with their 1955 range, designed by Virgil Exner. The next half decade saw each company attempting to outdo the other by making its fins rise to ever greater heights. The Chrysler Imperial had particularly exaggerated tailfins from 1955 onward: by 1961 its chrome pods contained headlights set into them. Chrysler claimed that its fins had aerodynamic properties that improved performance, but it was unlikely anyone was listening.

Earl's *pièce de résistance* was his Cadillac Eldorado. The 1959 model, made during his last year at GM, had the largest fins so far, with "rocket" tail lights set into them. By the end of the decade, cars took their lead less from jets and more from comic-book depictions of rockets and space vehicles. The fantasies depicted in such images were becoming realities on the roads of the United States.

The Eldorado Brougham took luxury to its limits. Based on a show car that Earl had designed in 1954 and shown at the Motorama of that year it came equipped with everything a passenger could require, including built-in powder compacts and drinks containers. Earl's idea that "getting into a car should feel like going on holiday" was fully realized in this extravagant automobile. His ideal was not restricted to the Cadillac, however, but was reflected in the design of the cheaper cars as well. His philosophy penetrated the whole of General Motors' thinking at this time and, because of the company's strong position in the marketplace, also significantly influenced car design in general.

LEFT *A drawing of a fantasy finned space rocket depicted on one of a series of four 1950s collector's cards. Numerous car designs from the same period bore a striking resemblance to this imagined form of futuristic transportation.*

PROVIDERS OF DREAMS

In the United States the 1950s were dominated, for consumers, by the "dreams that money can buy". The postwar economic boom brought the automobile within the reach of more people than ever before. This new generation looked forward rather than back; craved the luxury they had been deprived of; and, above all, needed to impress and outdo their neighbours. Cars represented the ultimate material product and the car stylists were ready to cater for all these urgent needs As a result styling dominated engineering and the car stylist was revered as a popular hero, the provider of the dreams that had become so crucial in the lives of so many people.

This was an era of excess in car design, which, because of its incremental exaggeration and its emphasis on style above all else, had to come to an end. When it did, by the mid-1960s, car designers would be left to rethink the image of the private car and to try once again to construct a meaning for it which the market could buy into.

HOWARD DARRIN

In the context of American car design Howard Darrin (or "Dutch" as he was usually called because of his country of origin) was a rare individual because he never really settled with a single manufacturer. He operated more as a traditional coachbuilder than as a car stylist but succeeded, particularly towards the end of his career, in creating cars that were worthy of the most progressive of in-house stylists.

CUSTOM CARS IN EUROPE

Although he had an engineering background, Darrin acquired most of his skills on the job. He began his career as a coachbuilder working in partnership with Tom Hibbard. In the 1920s the two men had gone to Paris, home of modern custom-car styling, initially contracted to the Belgian company Minerva. By 1927 they had branched out and were building bodies for a wide range of companies, among them Bugatti (see pp.50–53), Rolls-Royce (see pp.54–5), and Hispano Suiza (see pp.68–9). Darrin and Hibbard acquired a reputation as solid as the more established European coachbuilders and were kept in work by the requirements of, among others, American customers in Paris.

When Hibbard returned to the United States to work with Harley Earl (see pp.22–5) at General Motors in the 1930s, Darrin stayed on. He returned a little later and, like Earl before him, spent a period working in Los Angeles, designing custom-car bodies for Hollywood stars. He would successfully draw on this background of experience in luxury custom cars when he moved into designing production cars.

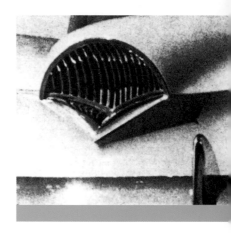

ABOVE *A detail of the Kaiser Darrin sports car, showing the dramatically different form of its radiator grille. The innovative form of this progressive car confirmed Darrin as a leading stylist of the day.*

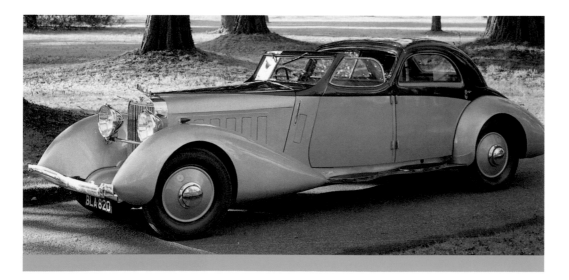

LEFT *This 1934 Hispano Suiza K6 sedanca coupé boasted bodywork designed by the coachbuilders Fernandez & Darrin. It is typical of the progressive work undertaken by Darrin during his time in Paris.*

ABOVE RIGHT *The Kaiser Frazer DKF-161 of 1953. This car, with its plastic body, was designed by Darrin but only produced in limited numbers. Its elegant profile marked it out as special in the context of American automobile styling of this era which was in general much more extravagant.*

As it did so many others of his generation, World War II moved Darrin in a new direction. Based at a flight-training school in Nevada, he experienced a closeness to planes that clearly influenced his car designs. Nowhere was this more apparent than in his design for a car that the Kaiser Frazer company set out to launch in the early 1950s.

A PROGRESSIVE DESIGN

Josef Frazer had a background in the Willys and Graham-Paige car companies and Henry Kaiser was a ship-builder. They had seen the financial opportunities offered by moving into the postwar automobile market. While most companies went back to their pre-war models after 1945 in an attempt to meet the huge consumer demand for cars, these two industrialists saw a chance to create a progressive car that would be far more appealing. Very few independent companies were either interested or able to compete with the "Big Three" manufacturers. Frazer and Kaiser called on Darrin to create a prototype, which he did

in his own workshop. The car he created, later to become the Kaiser Darrin 161, was selected over its in-house alternatives.

The Kaiser Darrin was a radically different-looking car which owed more to British and European sports car design that it did to contemporary American gas-guzzlers. Its fibreglass body boasted subtle curves, integrated front fenders, a dramatically sloping windshield, and integrated headlights. Special features included a sliding door and an idiosyncratically shaped radiator grille. In its American context it was way ahead of its time. However, owing to funding difficulties, only just over 400 cars were produced, most of them in 1954, and it never made the full impact it deserved. Darrin himself acquired 50 of them and sold them to his Hollywood customers.

In spite of the strikingly progressive design of the Kaiser Darrin, after its demise Darrin continued working as an independent designer, finding projects here and there with manufacturers of luxury cars. Yet he never surpassed his work with the Kaiser Frazer company.

RIGHT *A sketch for an Auto Union 1000 coupé from the mid-1950s.*

ALEX TREMULIS

PRINCIPAL DESIGNS

1941 *Chrysler Thunderbolt*
1948 *Tucker Torpedo*

Like Howard Darrin (see pp.126–7), Alex Sarantos Tremulis (1914–94) achieved renown primarily as the designer of a single postwar car, namely the Tucker Torpedo of 1948. Also like Darrin he had a pedigree background in the world of car styling: Tremulis had worked with Gordon Buehrig (see pp.34–5) on the Cord 812, having taken over from him in 1936, and, the following year, he spent some time in the Oldsmobile division at General Motors before moving on to design the Thunderbolt for the coachbuilders Briggs. He drew heavily on this last experience during a period spent in Beverly Hills creating car bodies for wealthy clients. His deeply rooted knowledge of what people wanted from their cars undoubtedly proved an advantage in the postwar years when the concept of cars as a form of modern luxury became so widespread.

FUTURISTIC DESIGN SKILLS

Before World War II, therefore, Tremulis was in a strong position to meet the needs of the postwar car-buying public. His skills embraced futuristic design as well as the ability to work with engineers to get cars produced. Tremulis' final apprenticeship, before Tucker found him, took place during the war when, from 1941 onward, he was employed by the airforce to work on advanced aircraft concepts. Such proximity to the imagery of future aircraft was without doubt the perfect training ground for postwar car design. In the airforce Tremulis worked on a

RIGHT *Jeff Bridges as Preston Tucker in the film* Tucker the Man and his Dream *(1988) featuring a fleet of Tucker Torpedos designed in 1948. The shape of this car was highly distinctive and it was among the most progressive of its era.*

BELOW *A model of the Ford Mexico concept car which Tremulis worked on during his time in the Ford Advanced Styling Section, where he worked between 1952 and 1963. It was among the most remarkable of the cars to emerge from that studio.*

new space vehicle concept, later to be called the Dyna-Soar, and he visualized a number of forms that have been described as resembling flying saucers. His fertile imagination was clearly geared to space-age images and it aligned him with much of the thinking in postwar car design. The car he designed for Tucker had more than a little of a "Dan Dare" quality to it.

THE TUCKER TORPEDO

In 1946 Preston Thomas Tucker, who had worked on B29 engines during the war, set up the Tucker Corporation with a view to creating a progressive postwar car. Like Kaiser Frazer (see p.129), he represented the dying breed of independent car-makers, and he had huge financial difficulties in getting his project going. Several people had a go at designing a car for him but in December 1946 he approached Tremulis, giving him 100 days in which to create a prototype.

Unable to get hold of any clay, Tremulis created a model from sheet iron. As a result his first hand-made version of the car was

dubbed the "Tin Goose". It was a remarkably original car, characterized by its triple headlights – the central one swivelling when the driver turned the wheel – and a front compartment to duck into in case of an accident. It was described by newspaper reviewers as "the first completely new car in 50 years" and featured many innovations. The interior was designed by Audrey Moore Hodges. The Tucker was shown to the public in June 1947 and was received with tumultuous applause. Fifty-one cars were produced the following year but Tucker's financial problems were such that the factory was forced to close in January 1949.

Tremulis spent the rest of his car-styling years working on a range of futuristic projects. For a while he was involved with Kaiser Frazer working on a speculative sports car, and in 1952 he entered the Ford Advanced Styling Section, where he remained until 1963 collaborating on, among other projects, the Ford Mexico concept. Later he moved on to Subaru in California, where he designed the Brat. Yet nothing he designed was ever as revolutionary as the thwarted Tucker of 1948.

CONCEPT CARS

In 1950s America, showing the public cars that were ahead of their time served both to acclimatize consumers to stylistic and technological changes on the way, and also as valuable market research. Harley Earl (see pp.22–5) was the prime mover in developing this strategy. In 1952 Earl instigated Motorama, an annual event, which grew out of the lunches that Alfred P. Sloan Jr, erstwhile chief executive of General Motors, held in New York during the National Automobile Show, which toured key metropolitan centres. General Motors used Motorama to show its most fantastic automobile visions of the future, and it quickly became the most popular car event of the year.

Earl had already shown an interest in "concept cars"; he had created the Buick Y Job in 1938 with the explicit aim of designing an automobile the sole function of which was to show the way ahead. It featured an electric roof that was concealed inside a metal cover when not in use and a long, low, wide streamlined body.

HARLEY EARL'S DREAM CARS

After the war Earl continued to create "dream cars" as a means of letting his imagination run riot. His LeSabre of 1951, the nearest a car had come by that date to resembling a jet fighter on the ground, had a roof that could sense when it was raining and lower itself accordingly, as well as heated seats. Its body was made of cast magnesium. A few production models were made but its primary function was as a focus for styling ideas that were picked up in subsequent GM models.

The Motoramas reached their peak in 1956 when GM parted with a million dollars to put on a fantasy show for the eager public. The star was the Firebird II automobile. Made of titanium, it was even more of a jet on the ground than the LeSabre had been. Its glass canopy, through which passengers entered, was cockpit-like and its huge rear fin made it look ready for takeoff. Firebird III, two years later, was even more futuristic, and demonstrated the shift that took place in Earl's

ABOVE *Harley Earl's Y Job of 1938 was the first "dream car", created to give the public a sense of the "car of the future". It exaggerated current tendencies, such as sensuous, sculptural form and the use of chrome trim to evoke speed, to elicit a response from the audiences to whom it was presented.*

LEFT *George Walker, vice-president and head of styling at Ford, is pictured with Ford's first true dream car, the X-100 of 1953. Ford, slower than the competition at first, pursued the idea of concept cars enthusiastically in the mid-1950s.*

imagination, from working from a basis in reality to achieving a new level of fantasy inspired by science fiction. Together the LeSabre and the three Firebirds can be seen as the purest expression of Earl's styling. Freed from the constraints of production and the marketplace they showed how far he was able to envisage a car that had moved completely away from all the features inherited from the "horseless carriage", towards an utterly novel concept dependent on those fastest, most streamlined and technologically advanced objects of 20th-century transportation, the jet fighter and the moon rocket.

The remainder of the 1950s saw a multitude of GM fantasy cars emerge to enthrall the public, from the Pontiac Bonneville Special,

BELOW *American concept cars borrowed heavily from science fiction. This fantasy depiction of cars of the future features an amphibious automobile that is as at home in the sea as on one of the raised highways envisaged for the future.*

with its "jet-style" rear lights, to the Oldsmobile Golden Rocket. The company's campaign to woo its customers in this way proved highly successful and was the envy of its competitors, Chrysler and Ford.

CHRYSLER'S DREAM CARS

Chrysler had not been far behind GM, however, in developing the notion of the concept car. In 1941 the Thunderbolt of Alex Tremulis (see pp.130–31) had been used by the company as a model of future design. After the war it developed a number of automotive proposals aimed to give the company a forward-looking profile. The two models it created with Ghia – the Plymouth XX 500 and the Chrysler X-310 – were both indications of Chrysler's awareness of Earl's work and their determination to keep up with GM.

One of the first tasks of Virgil Exner (see pp.140–41) when he entered Chrysler was to develop a series of "dream cars" that would

move the company on in the eyes of consumers. Since the failure of the Airflow (see pp.32–3), Chrysler had been cautious about letting styling take the lead over engineering but now the company's attitude changed dramatically. Exner's Firearrow series of 1953–4, the DeSoto Adventurer of the following year, and the Norseman of 1956, were all exercises in futurity. Nineteen fifty-six saw the emergence of the Chrysler Dart, which had huge tailfins and, like Earl's Buick Y Job, featured a roof that slid back into a metal compartment. In 1957 the Plymouth Special encapsulated Exner's visualizing skills at their strongest, its huge side panels joining the rear and front fenders into a single sculptural form. Exner's cars all had a European feel to them and lacked the raw "Americanness" of Earl's creations. While this gave them a greater sense of visual sophistication they also lacked something of the unbridled fantasy of GM's equivalents.

FORD'S DREAM CARS

Given the "anti-styling" approach of Henry Ford (see pp.20–21) in the early century it is perhaps not surprising that of the "Big Three" the Ford Motor Company was the last to enter into the creation of "dream cars". But in 1953 it showed its X-100 model to a style-hungry audience as part of its fiftieth anniversary celebrations. The car's torpedo form was to become familiar in Ford sports cars over the next decade. It featured a list of innovative, technically advanced features, among them a power-opening roof, an electric shaver, and a dictaphone.

Ford went on to create a number of other futuristic cars, among them the Mexico and the Mystere of 1956. Its greatest claim to fame was William Schmidt's design for the Lincoln Futura, a dream car that

ABOVE *George Walker with Ford's Levacar of the 1950s. This car-cum-spaceship epitomizes the futuristic utopianism of the era. Walker, head of styling at Ford, was responsible for ensuring that the company did not get left behind in the highly competitive automobile world of the early postwar years.*

RIGHT *George Barris' concept car with its elegant fins, elongated body, and curved windshield is best known as the Batmobile, which featured in the* Batman *television series. This icon of popular culture brought the idea of the car as a marker of the future to the attention of many people.*

became reality in that it provided the basis for the Batmobile, a much-loved American television icon of the 1960s created by George Barris.

By the late 1950s the practice of showing cars that were unlikely to become production vehicles but which displayed new design and mechanical innovations that would feature in other cars of the near future had become widespread. The practice relied on the public believing in the automobile as a symbol of modernity and futurity, and on a vision of a future ruled by technology. That shared dream was at its strongest in the mid- to late 1950s, fading not long afterwards.

The dream car also belonged to the heroic era of the American car stylist. By the mid-1950s most manufacturers had established a styling section along the lines of that at General Motors. In addition the large companies also had advanced styling sections headed by the most imaginative and forward-looking designers.

The second generation of designers who led the way in the 1950s were still car enthusiasts rather than the products of the new specialist training centres such the Pratt Institute in New York and the Art Center School in Los Angeles. Many of them had had some kind of contact with Earl's studio and they all understood the approach towards styling that had made GM the company it was. Their imaginations made the 1950s concept car a key phenomenon in automotive culture of the period.

RAYMOND LOEWY

PRINCIPAL DESIGNS

1934 *Hupmobile*

1947 *Studebaker Champion*

1950 *Studebaker Landcruiser*

1953 *Starliner coupé*

1962 *Studebaker Avanti*

1972 *Fairchild-Hiller Safety car*

1975 *Studebaker Avanti II*

He may be better known as the designer of the Lucky Strike cigarette packet, the Coldspot refrigerator, a group of locomotives for the Pennsylvania Railroad Company, and the Gestetner duplicator, but through his long career the pioneer industrial designer Raymond Loewy (1893–1986) was also involved with automobile styling. He arrived in the United States from his native France in 1919 and, before turning his hand to products, worked in the advertising, magazine, and fashion industries. The success that came from his redesign for Sigmund Gestetner led to an approach, in 1931, by the Hupmobile company, which retained him as a consultant for four years.

FIRST CAR DESIGNS

During those four years Loewy persuaded the conservative company to radicalize its cars by integrating their headlights and spare wheel into the outline form, unifying the body-shell, and introducing streamlining. Loewy financed a full-scale clay model himself before Hupmobile was convinced of his recommendations and even then they only implemented some of them into their 1934 model.

His work with the Hupmobile company fuelled Loewy's interest in automotive design, although his design for them only remained in

ABOVE LEFT *Raymond Loewy poses in front of the cab of the Pennsylvania Railroad locomotive that he designed. The train's streamlined form brought this futuristic imagery to the attention of the public in a dramatic way.*

LEFT *One of Loewy's first automotive commissions was the design of Hupmobile's sedan of 1934. Its sloping radiator grille, continuous body line, and integrated headlights helped to modernize the car's appearance.*

production until 1936. Two years later he was approached by the Studebaker Company, based in South Bend, Indiana, to work with them as a consultant, and in 1938 he started putting together a team that would plan a new range of automobiles. World War II put things on hold, as Studebaker went over to manufacturing military trucks. Although the company's status as an automotive manufacturer independent of the "Big Three" put pressure on it not to take too many financial risks, its wartime activity meant that it could resume business quickly after the end of the war.

LOEWY'S FIRST STUDEBAKERS

In 1947 the first postwar Studebakers rolled off the production lines. Virgil Exner (see pp.140–41) had played a significant role in their development but had fallen out with Loewy in a dispute regarding his input. Whoever was personally responsible for the new cars – the Champion, and subsequently the Commander and the Landcruiser – they were stunningly different and made a huge impact with their new elegant forms. Their surfaces were much less emblazoned with chrome highlights than the vehicles of their competitors, which Loewy called "jukeboxes on wheels". The 1947 Champion's rear tapered subtly and its fenders and doors merged into a single sculptural form in a way that was reminiscent of contemporary European cars. Loewy's approach was labelled "overall design" and it pointed the way towards what came to be called the "pontoon style".

The next few years saw a number of cars emerge from Studebaker that took Loewy's innovations forward, among them the bullet-nosed Landcruiser, introduced in 1950, which was inspired by jet fighters. In 1953 the designer executed his next breakthrough, the Starliner coupé. Just as Exner had played a role in the 1947 designs so the coupé owed a great deal to Bob Bourke, a member of the Loewy team based at South Bend. He had been taken on by Studebaker in 1940,

ABOVE *A Coldspot refrigerator from the mid-1930s designed by Loewy and manufactured by Sears Roebuck. The sleek lines were a direct result of the object being made from curved metal panels like a car. The recessed door handle was also modelled on that of the automobile.*

The New Studebaker for 1950

entered the Loewy team in 1944 and worked on the 1947 series; with Exner's departure to Chrysler, Bourke had taken over the reins.

Loewy used a subtle salesman's strategy to convince Studebaker's executives to produce his car, presenting them first with a more conservative sedan model and only showing them the much more radical coupé, kept under wraps during the initial presentation, when pressed to do so. Inevitably they opted for the more interesting car.

THE STARLINER COUPÉ

The Starliner coupé pushed forward all the 1947 innovations, taking the sculptural form of the body-shell to new heights. Dubbed "the American car with the European looks", it was even more obviously influenced by Europe, Italy in particular, than the Champion. Loewy was aware of the growing importance of imported European sports cars and, with this elegant little car, he had created a competitor. The emphasis was on lightness, with broad expanses of wraparound window being used, and every effort was made to make the car lower and wider than anything that had come before. Once again chrome was

used sparingly and the radiator was highly restrained, far removed from the monstrous cow-catcher grilles that adorned the fronts of many contemporary American cars. Above all the rear tapered away and there were no signs of fins. The Loewy coupé, as it was called, received several accolades in its day, being dubbed "a work of art" by New York's Museum of Modern Art and appearing on the front cover of *Time* magazine. It was one of the first sports cars to be produced in the United States, and it formed the basis of Studebaker's successful Speedster model of a couple of years later. However, Loewy's success with his 1953 design did nothing to help Studebaker's failing finances, and the company merged with Packard in 1954. The merger gave it a little more time but by 1966 the last Studebaker had been produced.

This did not happen without one more attempt by Loewy to turn things around through design. Although he had left Studebaker in 1955, six years later he was called back by the company's new president, Sherwood H. Egbert, to work on a new automobile. The result was the Avanti of 1962, a mass-produced, high-performance sports car. Given the urgency of Studebaker's financial situation the

LEFT *The new Studebaker of 1950, designed by Loewy's office. The jet-derived styling of the radiator grille was in keeping with American automobile styling in these years but the designer combined it with a new, European-derived, elegance.*

RIGHT *This chart, compiled by Loewy, shows the evolution of automobile design up to the mid-1930s. His careful drawings demonstrate all the key visual changes that had occurred since the late 19th century.*

BELOW *Loewy's Studebaker Avanti II of 1975, based on the original model launched in 1962, shows the designer's commitment to the subtleties of European styling. This elegant automobile emphasized the sculptural approach to car design.*

car was produced very quickly; Loewy worked on the first concepts by himself before bringing in the team, and a full-size scale model was presented in a matter of weeks. The Avanti was a radically different-looking car: its smooth, sculptural body was a fully-integrated form and few visible seams interrupted the flow of its lines. Its long hood evoked the speed of which it was capable and its neat rear emphasized its aerodynamic properties. Although the car was too late to save Studebaker the rights to produce the Avanti were bought from Studebaker and the car survived the death of the company.

PERSONAL DESIGN CREDO

Throughout his involvement with car design over half a century, Loewy was critical of America's prevailing attitude towards car styling. He called the swollen cars of the 1940s examples of the "jelly mould" school of styling, and he described most 1950s American cars as "gaudy merchandise". Although he spent all his working life in the United States he retained an interest in design in Europe, merging the best of each culture into a unique "Loewy" formula.

In 1971–2 Loewy created the Fairchild-Hiller Safety Car, used by the US Department of Transport for testing. Combining aerospace technology with orthodox production techniques, it was intended to be copied by commercial manufacturers which could thereby benefit from its safety features, including roll-cage construction, a periscopic rear-view mirror, and energy-absorbing safety glass. In those days of increased awareness of the safety requirements of automobiles Loewy was able to offer his design skills to the industry as a whole.

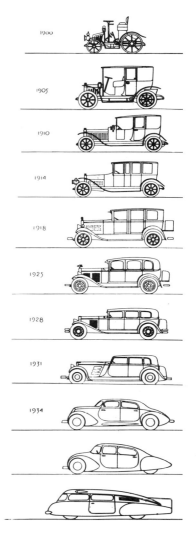

VIRGIL EXNER

Yet another of the 20th century's leading figures of the automobile world to come out of Harley Earl's stable at General Motors (see pp.22–5) was the car stylist Virgil Exner (1909–73). In 1933 Exner was appointed styling chief of the Pontiac division. Four years later he moved to Raymond Loewy's office (see pp.136–9), and in 1939 Loewy moved him to Studebaker at South Bend, Indiana. Five years later Exner was fired by Loewy over the design for the 1947 model: Loewy was incensed by the fact that, he believed, Exner had been working on a model by himself and was putting it forward for consideration. Studebaker hired Exner back as an independent consultant.

CHRYSLER

In 1948 Exner was appointed by K.T. Keller to the Chrysler company, which incorporated the marques of Plymouth, Dodge, De Soto, and Imperial, had no new postwar models, and was suffering from the competition of GM and Ford. Chrysler had become an engineering-led company and did not value styling as much as the other firms. Exner was to provide an antidote to this conservative approach. In 1953 he was promoted to director of styling.

The work Exner undertook with Chrysler from 1948 to 1962 has been well documented. He moved the company away from its engineering emphasis to become the manufacturer of some of the most

RIGHT *The Firearrow was an "ideas car" from the early 1950s in which Exner began to experiment with new styling concepts in order to promote Chrysler's design image. Features such as the wraparound rear window and the embryonic fins marked his cars out in these years.*

BELOW *The Chrysler d'Elegance, an "ideas car" from the early 1950s, closely resembled the K310 of the same period. Their strongly European, sculptural appearance marked a new phase for car design at Chrysler and earned Exner a reputation as a progressive designer.*

stylish American production cars of the late 1950s. He was committed to the Italian approach to car styling which saw the car as an abstract sculpture. When he launched his "ideas cars" in the early 1950s – the K310, the De Soto Adventurer, the Dodge Firearrow, the Chrysler d'Elegance – he turned to Ghia to hand-make his show models.

A NEW IMAGE

Nineteen fifty-five saw the launch of Exner's first full range of Chrysler cars. It was clear that he was proposing a new image for the company's automobiles. Christened the "Forward Look", his automotive aesthetic was characterized by the way in which his low, wedge-shaped cars with their soaring tailfins looked as if they were just about to take off at high speed. The first Chrysler 300 was launched in this year. The Imperial boasted stunning "microphone" tail-lights.

In 1957 an even more confident range of Chrysler cars designed by Exner was launched. He used his earlier "ideas cars" for inspiration and these automobiles, with their long hoods and short rear decks, represented strong competition for GM. The Imperial of this year was the first car to use curved glass for the side windows, and the tailfins were higher than ever. The war with General Motors was on.

As a tribute to his successful work for the company, in 1957 Exner was made a vice-president of design at Chrysler. This was a huge accolade from a company that only a decade earlier had not had any significant designers associated with it. Although Exner planned yet another design coup for 1963 it was not to be; political moves within the company meant that his designs were modified. He left Chrysler in the early 1960s and spent the rest of his career as a car stylist, a freelance consultant, and designing pleasure boats.

RIGHT *The small rear fin of Chrysler's New York Deluxe model was a sign of things to come. The way in which Exner neatly incorporated the rear headlights inside the fin and used chrome to finish off the detail was a mark of his highly developed sculptural skills.*

DESIGN AT FORD

During World War II a number of key management changes took place at the Ford Motor Company (see pp.20–21). Henry Ford's son Edsel, who had done so much to make the company design-conscious in the inter-war years, died in 1943. A power struggle ensued but it was finally agreed that his eldest son, Henry II, should take over the reins. The new head of Ford was immediately confronted by the problem of post-war production. The company's models were looking distinctly outdated and there was a desperate need for a new injection of style.

FIRST ATTEMPTS

At first E.T. Gregorie (see pp.40–41), who had worked so closely with Edsel Ford, was given the task of coming up with an innovative solution. His proposal for what was intended to become the 1949 Ford was a heavy, bulbous model which was of its time but not overly original. In an attempt to find a better solution the company also asked George W. Walker, an independent product designer who had been supplying Ford with component designs for several years, to come up with a design. This was a new strategy, which served to give the top

LEFT Designers work on a clay model in the Ford styling studio in the mid-1950s. Under George Walker, who became head of styling at that time, Ford moved into stronger competition with GM and Chrysler. By the end of the decade the "style wars" were raging.

executives a high level of control over the styling of its automobiles. By introducing a level of competition they aimed to "divide and rule".

Walker's proposal for the 1949 car was considered superior to the in-house version proposed by Gregorie and his team, and production went ahead of what was a radically new automotive proposal, much cleaner and leaner that Gregorie's swollen alternative. It was heavily inspired by aeronautics, especially through the inclusion of a circular, propeller-like motif at the centre of its chromed radiator grille. The lines of the car were taut and sleek and there were no surface embellishments, a characteristic that ultimately brought about its downfall when Harley Earl (see pp.22–5) brought in his more baroque automobiles a few years later.

CONSIDERATIONS OF STYLE

The 1949 Ford took the company forward into the post-war era, however, and Walker worked closely with Ford from that year onward, claiming responsibility for the 1950 Lincoln, the 1951 Mercury, and the 1952 Ford. The last car featured distinctive circular headlights, which were to become part of the company's new brand image.

The stylists at Ford had none of the autonomy of their General Motors equivalents, however, and styling remained largely subservient to engineering and marketing. The situation was revised to some extent when Walker was made vice-president in charge of styling in 1955. At the same time the department was restructured along GM lines. Five discrete departments were created, namely Car and Truck, headed by Robert Maguire; Special Products, headed by Roy Brown; Mercury, headed by Eugene Bordinat (later to become Walker's successor); Lincoln, headed by John Najjar; and Advanced Styling, led by Alex Tremulis (see pp.130–31). For the first time the Ford company began to address the question of styling in a proactive

manner and prepared to take on GM and Chrysler on their own terms in what were to become the "style wars" of the later 1950s.

Bordinat and Najjar, as well as Elwood Engel (later to become vice-president of styling at Chrysler) and Joseph Oros, were all young designers who had worked with Walker. By the 1950s Walker had established himself firmly at Ford with a strong team around him. Although this consultant designer has never acquired the same level of mythology around him as Harley Earl he was, nonetheless, an equally charismatic, larger-than-life figure. Like Earl he had a working-

class background and subscribed to an overtly masculine culture. And like Earl, again, he was as style-conscious about his own appearance as he was about the cars he designed, and was known for his extravagant clothes and sumptuously designed office. Walker had trained as a designer at Cleveland School of Art and later at the Otis Art Institute of Parsons School of Design in Los Angeles. By 1957 he had a team at Ford made up of 650 staff, but his department remained style-oriented and never acquired the same level of marketing power as Earl's at General Motors.

THUNDERBIRD AND EDSEL

Without doubt the first significant styling achievement was the work undertaken for the Ford Thunderbird, launched in 1955. This was followed by the Ford Edsel of two years later. These two cars were, in sharp contrast with each other, a resounding success and a colossal failure respectively. The Thunderbird, a small, "fun" sports car conceived along European lines, was created to compete with GM's Corvette of 1953. Designed by Bill Burnett, William F. Boyer, and Franklyn Quick Hershey, its modest form and restrained fins made it a

precursor of the "personal luxury car" that was to increase in importance in the following decade. The Edsel, by contrast, was an extravagant car, developed over two years with input from market researchers and psychologists. Aimed at the middle-income family, it set out to provide it with size, status, and difference. Unlike its competitors it had horizontal gull-wing fins, a distinctive horse-collar, vertical grille (which some critics claimed was modelled on the female sex organ), two-tone paintwork, and lots of chrome. In spite of all the efforts that went into its production, the public dramatically rejected the car, thereby demonstrating that intuitive styling was more effective than this exercise in consumer engineering.

Ford's Lincoln division was more successful. The Mark II Continental of 1956, designed by John Reinart, showed that the public still had confidence in this mark. The luxury Mercurys were also revitalized in this decade.

In essence Ford competed openly with GM and Chrysler through the second half of the 1960s, adopting the same strategy of creating bigger, longer, wider cars with increasing amounts of elaboration to meet the needs of the ever-expanding ranks of automobile consumers. The Thunderbird went through several transformations, with the addition of two seats in 1957 and another facelift in the following year. Elwood Engel remodelled it again in 1959.

THE MUSTANG AND BEYOND

In 1961 Eugene Bordinat took over from Walker. The first great achievement of his new regime was the creation of the Ford Mustang. This "muscle car" (see pp.150–51) had been the brainchild of the young vice-president, Lee Iacocca, who had wanted to create a car to compete with European sports cars. The design task was given to Bordinat's team and the Ford division, headed by Joseph Oros, won the day. The Mustang was developed over the next couple of years and launched in 1964 at the opening of the World's Fair in New York. By 1966, just two years later, a million Mustangs had been sold.

Bordinat served as Ford's head of styling right up until 1980, when he was superseded by Jack Telnack, who brought the Europe-inspired "aero" look into the company.

ABOVE LEFT *In 1956 the Mark II Lincoln Continental was launched showing yet another side of the Ford Company's new interest in sophisticated styling. This luxury car, designed under the leadership of John Reinart who had taken over from Eugene Gregorie, was a flagship for the company.*

LEFT *The extravagant styling on Ford's unsuccessful Edsel model was not appreciated by the general public. The front radiator grille, in particular, was much derided.*

RIGHT *Production at the Ford plant in Detroit in the early 1960s. By that time the visual excesses of the late 1950s had been replaced by a new "neoclassical" look which was pioneered, at Ford, by Eugene Bordinat, who liked a "clean" look.*

BILL MITCHELL

PRINCIPAL DESIGNS

1938 *Cadillac 60 Special*
1959 *Cadillac Eldorado (with Earl)*
1959 *Chevrolet Corvair*
1962 *Corvette Sting Ray*
1963 *Buick Riviera*
1967 *Chevrolet Camaro*
1967 *Pontiac Firebird*

Bill Mitchell (1912–88) was a classic example of the second generation of car enthusiast American car stylists. He studied mechanical engineering, and then took evening art classes at New York's Art Students League while he was employed at the Barron Colliers advertising agency. Throughout his career, the sketch played an important role in his personal automotive design process.

This basic training by no means equipped him with all the necessary skills to make him a car stylist when he submitted some sketches to Harley Earl (see pp.22–5) at General Motors in the mid-1930s. It was, rather, his enthusiasm for cars (his father had run a Buick agency) that impelled him to take this initiative.

By the age of 23 Mitchell was working with Earl, who had hired him on the basis of his sketches alone. From 1935 he worked in General Motors' Cadillac division, becoming head of studio three years later. Earl was an enormous influence on Mitchell and he inherited from him a love of cars that went deep. Right from the start Mitchell had a feel for cars, as did Earl, that derived from the direct sensation

BELOW *Chevrolet's original Corvette of 1953, below, was designed before Mitchell took over from Earl as head of the Styling Section at GM. From 1959 onward, he created a number of updated versions of this little sports car, among them a study of 1962 named the Corvette Shark.*

of driving them. He spoke eloquently about the effect of being behind the wheel of a powerful, beautiful car and the accompanying feeling of power and status. Mitchell's was a very masculine approach to car design which stressed the emotive power of the car as an extension of the body, and his designs expressed the idea of the car as something that imbues its user with an instant sense of identity.

DESIGNING CADILLACS

As head of the Cadillac studio Mitchell's first essay in car design came with the Cadillac 60 Special of 1938, a car that was ahead of its time in many ways. Although it featured the typically streamlined body of its era, it did not yet have its headlights integrated into its fenders. The use of chrome as a decorative feature on the radiator grille and on the air outlets along the sides of the hood was handled deftly and with confidence. The subtle detailing extended to the interior.

The 1940s saw Mitchell working on a number of new ideas for Cadillac concept cars. A model of 1940 showed an early use of space-age imagery which gave the car a very progressive feel. Mitchell began to develop an approach that depended more on sculptural form and less on chrome for its impact. During this decade he began to define his philosophy of automobile design which moved away from the conservatism of Detroit styling and sought a more radical way forward.

After the war Earl set up an independent design office focusing on products rather than automobiles and asked Mitchell to head it. The two men, although very different in temperament, made a good team. Mitchell spent five years working in Earl's firm, before returning to General Motors. Unlike many of his peers, he was not involved with aircraft during the war but served instead for a short time in the navy. As a result his work is less overtly jet-inspired than that of several other successful stylists. He sought a look for cars that was inspired by their own inner potential and that belonged to them and them alone.

Mitchell remained Earl's right-hand man through the 1950s, working with him on the notorious 1959 Cadillac Eldorado (see

ABOVE *A General Motors concept car of the 1960s designed by Mitchell. The designer created a range of cars on this visual idiom inspired by the forms of sharks and other natural forms. The intention was to remove all excrescences and create a single torpedo-shaped form.*

BELOW *Bill Mitchell is seen here in 1963, at the peak of the period of time that he spent with the General Motors Company, discussing Corvette styling ideas with Irv Rybick, head of the Chevrolet Styling Studio, and Bill Tochman, a studio engineer.*

p.126). When the big man stepped down in that year Mitchell took over. Earl was a hard act to follow but Mitchell blossomed quickly, recognizing that an era – and an automotive styling approach – had burned itself out and that another one must take its place.

CARS FOR DRIVING

Mitchell's years as vice-president of design at General Motors, which ended in 1977, represented the flowering of his personal philosophy. From the outset he set about designing a new kind of car which moved beyond the fins and chrome of the previous era. One of his most successful cars to reach production was the Chevrolet Corvair, a car with an integral body/frame construction and clean lines. In 1954 Earl had created the Chevrolet Corvette, arguably the first American sports car, which had revived the rather dull appearance of that brand. Mitchell's Corvair represented a break with tradition and a shift into the "cleaner" style of the 1960s. It was the first of a generation of cars that Mitchell was to create that were less mobile parlours and more cars for driving. Visually they were characterized by a sculptural sense of line and form with few decorative additions. His was a more minimalist approach which responded to the changing needs of the 1960s market but which also stemmed from personal preference.

Among the numerous cars that marked out Mitchell's reign at GM are the Buick Riviera – which he described as "somewhere between a comfortable sedan and a sports car" – the Corvette Sting Ray of 1963, the Chevrolet Camaro with its classic "Coke-bottle" styling, the Oldsmobile Toronado of 1966, and the Pontiac Firebird of 1967. In 1962 he drew inspiration from the shark for a series of concept cars, including the Mako Shark which evolved from the Stingray. A sharp ridge around its waist gave it a dramatic appearance while its nose evoked that of the fish that had inspired it.

SCULPTURAL BEAUTY

A Stingray coupé had been created in 1959, which Mitchell used as his personal car, giving a clear indication of where the later production car would go. Both models had curved backs, extended thrusting hoods, and exaggerated side air outlets that evoked power and speed. The hardtop had a split rear window. Like Earl before him Mitchell was a master of the highlight, using lines, ridges, pleats, and curves to

BELOW AND BOTTOM *The Chevrolet Corvette Sting Ray, designed by Mitchell in the early 1960s, seen from the rear and from inside. The low, flat appearance of this model was inspired by the form of the creature after which it is named.*

create shadows and light areas on the metal body-shell to give cars their sculptural appeal. It was an art that Mitchell took to a high level of sophistication. Rather than depending on chrome detailing to create display, he let the car's body, with its own sculptural qualities inspired by the world of nature, speak for itself.

The Firebird was aimed at a young market and offered the requisite level of power. As in several other designs Mitchell used the shallow front end, the "snout", with its split radiator grille and built-in headlights, to evoke this sense of power. With a minimal means of expression at his disposal he used the language of the car's basic components to get across the message he wanted to communicate. The long hoods and truncated rears said it all. As Mitchell told his colleagues, their role was to make a car "look like it'll do something".

Above all Mitchell was committed to the idea of formal beauty in cars, which meant considering every visual feature with enormous care, being aware that each one contributed to the expression of the whole. The key to his contribution to 20th-century car design lies in his application of his skill as a fine artist and his ability not only to draw a powerful and attractive car but also to turn it into a reality.

US MUSCLE CARS

The mid-1950s had seen the emergence of the "fun" sports car, such as the Corvette, the Thunderbird, and the Starliner coupé. During the decade the car market had fragmented such that wives chose large station-wagons, husbands selected comfortable sedans, and their sons and daughters opted for sports cars. By the end of the decade the concept of the "personal luxury car" had emerged – the car, that is, with no room for passengers or luggage, which individuals drove for themselves, for the sheer pleasure of driving. The increasing homogeneity of the marques produced by the "Big Three" led eventually to a thirst for individualism that could not be met by the chrome-laden monsters.

INDIVIDUALISM AND THE YOUTH MARKET

From the 1930s onward many young people – men in particular – had opted out of mainstream car consumption, constructing and racing their own "hot rods" and subsequently "custom cars", and that sense of needing something special was, by the early 1960s, beginning to permeate through to the mass market.

Simultaneously young people became a significant market for the first time for car manufacturers and they began to seek ways of accommodating the spirit of rebellion, of "anti-Detroitism", that was infecting the market and swinging the pendulum away from the big, bulky 1950s cars that were differentiated only by the positioning of their chrome and the size of their fins. This new mood led to the emergence of the "muscle cars" and "pony cars" that represented a dramatic change in American car styling, even though they lasted for less than a decade. Muscle cars, fast and aggressive, literally had "muscles" – curves and bulges on their body surfaces.

The first muscle car was the Pontiac GTO (the letters were borrowed from the classic Ferrari). Designed for the postwar baby boomers, its appeal lay in its ability to achieve 160 km/h (100 mph) in a straight line. John De Lorean took over as head of engineering at Pontiac in 1965 and was responsible for many of the powerful cars that emerged in the late 1960s and early 1970s, among them the Firebird and its Trans Am version. Among GM's other contenders for the title of muscle car was the Mitchell-designed Chevrolet Camaro. Since he had created the Buick Riviera in 1963 to compete with the Thunderbird, Mitchell (see pp.146–9) had worked on a number of cars for the youth market, imbuing them all with his characteristic "razor-edge sculpting" style.

ABOVE RIGHT *An AC Mark II 289 Cobra that was launched on the market in 1962, based on the AC Ace, an elegant British sports car, The curved, "muscly" forms of its front area provide a sense of enormous power while the "surly" grille is highly distinctive.*

LEFT *A photograph of the 1965 Ford Mustang shows the way in which this high-performance car looked in action. The sleek form was designed to ensure that the car could travel at high speed and look good while doing so.*

Ford's Mustang of 1964, with its look of a muscly horse, gave rise to the term "pony car". Created by Lee Iacocca, the Mustang stood out because of its pared-down look which made reference to hot rods. While the basic model was very simple and had no frills, it had a sporty presence that could be enhanced through the addition of a wide range of accessories. Its body was very close to the ground and it evoked a sense of raw masculinity. More significantly, perhaps, it was inexpensive, and quickly became a market success.

A PASSING CRAZE

Many other muscle and pony cars followed, including the Ford Fairlane GT of 1966, the Dodge Charger (advertised as "a car you can buy when you decide you don't want to be like everyone else"), American Motors' AMX, the Buick Skylark GS, also of 1966, and the Chrysler Barracuda of 1967 which gave away its visual inspiration in its name. All boasted the same long hoods, short decks, and gaping mouths and looked as if they were about to leap into action.

By the early 1970s the craze for muscle and pony cars had faded. What had been light, innovative cars had become bigger and heavier and, more importantly, had started to look like each other, thus losing the individualism that had been their *raison d'être* in the first place.

FROM FUNCTION TO STYLE

FROM FUNCTION TO STYLE

*T*he most significant shift in the story of European car design after 1945 was the demise of the coachbuilding tradition in practically every country except Italy. Only in that country did the trade find a way of adapting itself to the changed conditions of automobile production and consumption in those years, to the extent that it not only flourished locally but provided skilled car designers for the rest of the world as well.

Many reasons for the emergence of Italy as a leader in the field of car design have been offered. They include the changing car markets in countries such as Britain and France which lost their aristocratic and middle-class markets for luxury cars in these years; the increased taxation on luxury cars that was levied in France; and the spread of car ownership. Added to these market-oriented changes were others deriving from technological shifts in car manufacture, especially the widespread impact of the mass-produced unitary car, which saw the chassis and the body as part of a single unit designed as a totality rather than as two separate entities that came together at a late stage of manufacture.

The shift in thinking that necessarily came with this reconceptualization of the automobile was grasped and exploited by the numerous talented Italians who rose to this new challenge. They succeeded in evolving a new approach to car design which embraced both special models and production cars. Both were perceived as sculptural opportunities just waiting to be imbued with the spirit of modernity. Italians brought a sculptural approach to car design, a contribution that may be explained by the words of one writer who has noted that "the historical Italian genius is for sculpture, as the French is for romantic poetry and the British is for poetic drama." It was a skill that was certainly manifested in car design in the decades after World War II.

LEFT *A wooden maquette of Bertone's Alfa Romeo Giulietta Sprint, one of the seminal designs to emerge from postwar Italy. Stylists created full-size models so that they could have direct experience of their designs "in the round".*

The Italians did not operate in isolation. They drew heavily on German developments in aerodynamics, an expertise evident in cars such as BMW's stunning 328 of the inter-war years, made by Touring of Italy. They were also dependent on American styling innovations of the 1930s and 1940s, incorporating long, low bodies and unified, streamlined automobile forms with integrated wings into their repertoire. Unlike the Americans, however, the Italians resisted the temptation to cover their models with excessive chrome trim and other unnecessary excrescences, maintaining instead a more minimalist approach to the aero-dynamically inspired car form. This resistance to elaboration was also visible in static streamlined product designs of the period emanating from Italy, among them Marcello Nizzoli's body-shell for Olivetti's Lexicon 80 typewriter of 1948, which exposed the seams between its metal castings, making them a visual feature.

By the late 1950s and 1960s Italy's achievement in car design had impacted on several other car-manufacturing countries and a number of fruitful collaborations had emerged, including those between Ghia and Chrysler, and Zagato and Aston Martin, and of Pininfarina with Austin and Peugeot, Michelotti with Triumph and BMW, Touring with Bristol, Bertone with NSU, and Boano with Renault.

Other things were also happening to postwar European car design outside Italy, albeit with less consistently dramatic results. The emergence of what became known as the "Italian line", characterized by long, low lines, unelaborated aerodynamic form, flowing curves, and integrated features, provided a benchmark for other Europeans either to emulate or to ignore. British sports cars, for example, were strongly influenced by this manifestation of high stylishness and several British designers, such as Gerald Palmer

who created forms for the MG company, openly acknowledged their debt to the Mediterranean country. Other British car firms, including Ford of Britain, Hillman, Humber, and Vauxhall, looked to the United States for inspiration instead, incorporating such familiar American styling features as wraparound windshields and fins into their designs. At Vauxhall the London Royal College of Art sculpture graduate David Jones was responsible for all the designs that emerged from that company's studios from the late 1930s right through to 1971.

As well as operating on an international platform, car design also offered an opportunity for individual countries to define their national identities. The growth of the economies in the main countries of western Europe at this time required each nation to distinguish itself both as a means of consolidating a modern identity for its own people and so that it could show a distinctive

face to the rest of the world. France took a lead in this respect and developed a number of cars that were unmistakably "French" in character. Citroën and Renault led the way, with cars such as the Citroën DS showing that the country that had pioneered luxury car styling before the war could make the transition into the world of production cars with equal aplomb.

Germany also demonstrated that it understood the important link between a sense of national identity and car design in the postwar years and it used its strongly engineered cars and distinctive marques – especially those of Mercedes-Benz and BMW – to show that it saw itself as a leader in the arena of advanced technological applications and automotive brand development. In order to emphasize continuity with its pre-war pre-eminence in progressive modern design Germany developed a simple, functionalist product aesthetic which embraced both its

FAR LEFT *Two production models from the Swedish car manufacturer Saab, from the postwar years. The model on the left, the 9-5, was preceded by that on the right, the Saab 92. Both cars owe much to the fighter, the Saab J21, which represented the company's wartime production.*

LEFT *The Italian company Piaggio launched its streamlined little motor-scooter, the Vespa ("wasp"), in 1946. It represented one of the first instances of popular modern design in Italy. Pictured here is a version manufactured by Douglas in 1949.*

cars and its household goods. Porsche, which originated in Austria, conformed to this rigorous Germanic image of "form following function", thereby consolidating the third aesthetic model of postwar production-car design, alongside those of American fantasy styling and Italian "flair". The German example came into its own in the 1970s and 1980s, by which time it had come to embody the concept of good car design.

Another strong European national identity established through car design came from Sweden, which had developed a pre-war design philosophy that had a strong social program contained within it. Conscious of the particular needs of Sweden's population, the Volvo and Saab companies aimed to create Swedish cars for Swedish people. As with many other national identities, however, it proved as attractive outside the country as within, and both firms quickly acquired an international following

of those who admired the quirky character and the strong reliability and safety features of Swedish cars.

Eastern Europe also moved into car manufacture in these years, producing a number of idiosyncratic designs, created by firms such as Russia's Moskvitch and Volga, and Czechoslovakia's Skoda and Tatra, many of which emulated American and British models. From 1945 until the 1970s all these European countries were trying to develop cars that provided their owners with a modern lifestyle accessory, which allowed them access to the world of mass modernity. This in turn confirmed them as modern nations. Whether through the purchase of a "people's car", a sports car, or a family saloon the majority of the populations of many of these countries was able to participate for the first time in a modern postwar Europe that was significantly defined by the mobility and social status offered by the modern automobile.

ITALIAN STYLE

RIGHT *A Ferrari 250 GTO from the early 1960s. One of Italy's most stylish brands, largely thanks to a long-lasting collaboration with Pininfarina, Ferrari has captured the combination of sculpture, power, and excitement that characterizes postwar Italian automotive design.*

The years after World War II saw a blossoming of car design in Europe. Nowhere was this more evident than in Italy, where pre-war coachbuilding traditions were updated to meet the changes in manufacturing techniques that had transformed the international automobile industry. The ability of coachbuilders such as Pininfarina (see pp.162–5), Bertone (see pp.166–9), and Zagato to adapt to the new climate ensured Italy world leadership in the field of progressive car styling. From their beginnings supplying single car bodies to exclusive makers they learned to design across a spectrum, from one-offs to production cars, and, in some cases, even to manufacture cars themselves. Stylistically they learned quickly from pre-war advances made both in the United States and in Europe, combining them to create a stunning new aesthetic hybrid which, characterized by its long, low, racy, sleek, sculptural forms, came to be known as "Italian style".

ITALY AS DESIGN LEADER

The advances made in postwar Italian car design were part of a bigger picture. By the late 1940s it was clear that Italy was to become the design leader of Europe. Eager to cast off the memory of fascism, to create a modern national identity, and to get industry back on its feet, the country's few large manufacturing companies, such as Olivetti and Fiat, and its larger number of small ones, such as the furniture manufacturers Cassina, Artemide, and Artifort, and the coachbuilding firms, embraced the concept of modern design. The little Vespa motor-scooter of 1947, produced by Piaggio, acquired an iconic status in the new, liberated Italy; by the end of the 1950s it had been superseded by Fiat's little 600 and 500 models (see pp.98–101).

The flexible mass-production systems adopted by the small furniture and product firms were the key to their success, permitting

them to create products in batches rather than in large-scale, standardized runs. This was equally true of the car manufacturers who came to the fore at this time. Alfa Romeo, Maserati, Lancia, Ferrari, and Lamborghini aimed their cars at a luxury, style-conscious market and produced expensive cars which appealed on the level of their performance and, significantly, on their stunning good looks. The "supercars" of this era were a result of these companies' ability to straddle the boundary between racing cars and road cars and to bring the thrill and excitement of the former to the latter. It was, in many ways, an old formula, which had been implemented by Bugatti (see pp.50–53) and others at an earlier date, but the postwar Italian movement took it a step nearer to the mass market.

LANCIA AND ALFA ROMEO

Lancia and Alfa Romeo were the oldest of these innovative Italian manufacturers. The former had been established by Vincenzo Lancia in 1907, who had typically moved from racing into car production. His cars from the 1930s had pioneered monocoque construction and were visually advanced. After the war, he went on to create a series of practical sports cars calling on the skills of Pininfarina, among others,

to style his elegant machines. Alfa Romeo had begun its manufacturing back in 1910. The interwar years had been mostly dedicated to racing and, from the early 1930s onward, support from Mussolini made possible the designs by the racing drivers Vittorio Jano and Enzo Ferrari who gave the company many victories on the track as well as a number of high-performance cars. It was not until after the war that Alfa created its first production car, the Giulietta; like Lancia, it went on to create several highly successful and stylish sports cars with the help of the eminent coachbuilders of the day.

MASERATI, FERRARI AND LAMBORGHINI

The Maserati and Ferrari companies were products of the inter-war years, the first formed in 1926 and the second in 1938. Once again racing dominated these companies' stories. The Maserati brothers had raced other people's cars before deciding to create their own, and it was not until the late 1950s that their first road car, the 3500 GT, burst on the scene, showing the way in which the spirit of the track could be transferred to the road with enormous success. Ferrari's story was similar. By the mid-1950s it was manufacturing dramatically styled sports cars which challenged America's Thunderbird and

LEFT *Pininfarina's elegant Cisitalia (fourth from left) stands out among other stylish automobiles at Milan's first postwar Triennale exhibition in 1947. It epitomized the restrained streamlining that featured in many of Italy's postwar products.*

RIGHT *Olivetti's Lettera 22 typewriter of the early 1950s, designed by Marcello Nizzoli, exhibited the same subtle curves and unadorned streamlining that typified Italy's contribution to automotive styling in these years.*

Corvette and which set the seal on Italy's lead in this area. A little later the Daytona and Dino models, by Pininfarina's Leonardi Fioravanti, and the stunning Testarossa, turned the name of Ferrari into a legend.

Lamborghini was a product of the 1960s, created to outdo Ferrari in the supercar arena. Its cars also quickly became legends, taking the Italian sports car to its stylistic limits. As with all these successes of the 1950s, 1960s, and 1970s, Lamborghini's cars were the result of a collaboration with an external designer, in this instance Marcello Gandini of the Bertone studio.

CONSULTANTS AND DESIGNER-COACHBUILDERS

The Italian manufacturers all understood that collaborating with a designer not only ensured them a more interesting visual solution but also, importantly, provided a form of added value in the marketplace for their cars. They were participating in the growing "designer culture" that was emerging in postwar Italy which provided them with a means of taking their cars beyond the everyday into the world of art. As a strategy this model of car design had been initiated with exclusive

one-off automobiles but, in the postwar era, it began to penetrate batch-produced and even mass-produced cars as well.

Most importantly, the coachbuilders of the pre-war years transformed themselves into consultant designers in order to provide this service. Although a few failed to make the transition, such as Castagna which closed its doors in 1952, the majority found a way of adapting to the new context. Pininfarina, who had been operating both as a manufacturer and as a designer since 1930, worked closely with Ferrari in the postwar years while Ghia, one of the oldest of the Italian coachbuilders, established in 1915, moved seamlessly into the postwar period, creating bodies for a number of manufacturers, including Maserati, both inside and outside Italy. Ghia's successes of the postwar period included Luigi Segre's special body for the Volkswagen Beetle (see pp.94–7) of 1953, known as the Karmann Ghia, which helped to introduce Italian style to the world at large. The company also made a significant impact in the United States, working closely with Chrysler through the 1950s and 1960s. By the 1970s it was designing cars for Ford as well. Touring also managed to keep

RIGHT *Automobiles such as Fiat's little Balilla sports car pictured here, a track car that participated in many races in the inter-war years, were the backdrop to the Italian foray into road-going vehicles in the postwar years. Many of the most successful cars began life on the track.*

going. Working with Ferrari, Alfa Romeo, and the British company Bristol, it also made its mark on postwar sports-car styling.

Vignale and La Zagato were formed in the postwar period, in 1948 and 1945 respectively, although their founders, Alfredo Vignale and Ugo Zagato, had had apprenticeships in the Italian coachbuilding trade of the pre-war years, the former with Stabilimenti Farina and the latter through his own car-body firm. Their services were immediately sought after and they supplied bodies to a range of manufacturers. Vignale's clients included Ferrari, Maserati, and Lancia, while La Zagato created special bodies for Fiat in the 1940s and 1950s as well as collaborating with Alfa Romeo, Lancia, Maserati, and Ferrari.

The collaborations between the manufacturers and the designers employed by the coachbuilders-turned-design-consultants proved an unbeatable formula. Combined with Italian design's general emphasis on the sculptural potential of objects and a commitment to creating high-quality goods for a discerning audience it resulted in a movement in car design that was not matched by any other country at the time. The experience of both designing and making winning racing cars underpinned the Italians' strong sense of what made cars appealing to the "man in the street". However, by the last decades of the century, the shape of the Italian car industry had changed dramatically and the movement of the 1950s and 1960s had all but disappeared.

PININFARINA

PRODUCTION HISTORY

1932 *DiLambda*

1935 *Alfa Romeo 6C 2300*

1937 *Lancia Aprilia*

1939 *Lancia Astura*

1947 *Cisitalia 202 coupé*

1955 *Peugeot 403 Berlina*

1956 *Ferrari 250 GT*

1956 *Alfa Romeo Giulietta Spider 1300*

1966 *Alfa Romeo Duetto Spider*

1968 *Ferrari Daytona*

1984 *Ferrari Testarossa*

N oone embodied the sculptural approach to car design more than the Turin-born designer Battista "Pinin" Farina (1893–1966). Part of the renowned Farina family of coachbuilders (see pp.70–73), Pininfarina gained his nickname for being the youngest of ten children, and never lost it. He contributed to the world of 20th-century automobiles as an industrialist, as a car body-maker, and as a designer.

BEGINNINGS

From an early age he observed the shift into mass manufacture at first hand in his brother's Turin workshop and he applied his knowledge in his own enterprise from 1930 onward. His war experience with manufacturing propellers, and a visit to Detroit to see Ford's factory, helped to crystallize his approach to mass automobile manufacture which involved all-metal pressings and advanced production techniques. By the postwar years he had extended this initiative by designing cars for Italy's leading car manufacturers, Lancia, Alfa Romeo, Maserati, and Ferrari, as well as supplying bodies, and in many cases production cars as well, for companies in the United States, France, and Britain.

As a designer Pininfarina succeeded in developing a new automobile aesthetic which brought together European developments and

ABOVE *The mark of the Pininfarina coachbuilding company which was led by Sergio Pininfarina from 1930. The company worked with leading Italian automobile manufacturers, notably Alfa Romeo and Ferrari.*

RIGHT *The body of the little Alfa Romeo Giulia Spider sports car of 1962 was designed by Pininfarina. Its low, pointed radiator air-intake with its two horizontal flanking intakes made it distinctive, as did its simple, sculptural body-shell.*

American ideas. The 1930s saw him move in the direction that was to earn him a reputation as Italy's leading stylist. This was particularly apparent in his commitment to streamlining, expressed by the tapered rears of some of his designs, and in the creation of two seminal cars: the Alfa Romeo 6C 2300 B aerodynamic berlinetta of 1935, and the even more dramatic Lancia Aprilia of 1937. It was already evident that, unlike American stylists who exalted in the amount of decoration they could add to their streamlined cars, the Italian's approach towards this flowing, unified visual idiom did not involve the addition of chrome to highlight surface details. The Aprilia boasted a simple aerodynamic shell in which the front fenders had all but disappeared while the rear ones were just in evidence. The only surface details were perforations in the metal for ventilation at the front and in the rear fenders to achieve lightness. Three-dimensional sculptural form was allowed to speak for

itself. In contrast, also, to the fashionable French cars of the inter-war years which were becoming more and more ostentatious, Pininfarina sought simplicity and clarity in his designs of these years.

A WORK OF ART

The achievements of the pre-war years led directly into what many consider Pininfarina's most significant car design, the 1947 Cisitalia 202 sports berlinetta. Although it was in production only until 1952, the car's seminal importance was recognized with its inclusion in the 1951 exhibition *Eight Automobiles* in New York's Museum of Modern Art. The show's message was that cars can be seen as art objects as well as machines and that they can be as beautiful as more conventional works of art. The Cisitalia was the nearest Pininfarina came to creating a piece of automobile art: "With this car," he said, "Dusio and

I were playing the poet." Dusio was the owner of the Cisitalia company, set up after the war to create innovative sports cars. With Dante Giacosa (see pp.98–101) before he went to Fiat, his company created several striking automobiles. The collaboration with Pininfarina was inspired, but the car was a greater hit as an artwork than a racer and, owing to its high cost and its lack of success on the racetrack, very few were produced. Visually, however, Pininfarina's design broke new ground. It made the fenders smaller and used the horizontal radiator grille to good effect. The result was a car that was an unadorned sculptural form. Pininfarina explained, "The automobile's lines must be pure, smooth, essential; we could no longer use the habitual symbols that looked like so much plumbing work."

INTERNATIONAL PARTNERS

In the early 1950s Pininfarina expanded his factory production and his coachbuilding operation. In 1951 he entered into a collaboration with Nash Kelvinator, thus becoming one of the first European body-makers to work with a Detroit company. The results of their work included the Ambassador and Healey models. Later in the decade another American partnership resulted in the creation of a limited edition Cadillac Brougham. The British company BMC was equally keen to "Italianize" its production and, from 1955, Pininfarina created a number of cars for it, including the little Austin A40 and the Morris 1100. France was quicker off the mark, and Pininfarina and Peugeot joined hands in 1951, the start of a relationship that proved fruitful for several decades. The 403 sedan of 1955 was an early success story and many others were to follow, including the 406 coupé which was produced in its entirety at the Pininfarina works at Grugliasco.

ABOVE *Battista Pininfarina (on the left of the photograph) is seen in the Alfa Romeo factory at Arese, inspecting the quality of the production of one of his cars. He combined the roles of businessman and designer very effectively.*

LEFT *The little Austin A40 Farina of 1962 represented one of the few occasions in which Pininfarina worked with a British manufacturer. The result was an elegant automobile. The Italian designer also styled the Morris 1100.*

ITALIAN PARTNERS

The most significant relationships Pininfarina entered into were with Italian car manufacturers. Before World War II he worked with Lancia, and in 1952 he began his association with Enzo Ferrari. Ferrari had been in business for as long as Pininfarina and had resisted close links with a body-maker; such was Pininfarina's international success that he changed his mind. The first result was the 212 Inter Cabriolet which took forward the advances achieved in the Cisitalia. It was characterized by its curved, bulging front, which featured in later models, and combined aerodynamics with aesthetics in an effective union. The 1950s and 1960s saw a sequence of ever more stunning Ferraris touched by Pininfarina's transforming hand, including the 342 American coupé of 1953, the 250 GT Spyder of 1957, the 1959 250 Testarossa racing Spyder, the 1963 250 GT, the Dino 206 GT of the mid-1960s, and the Daytona of 1968. The last, produced two years after the death of Battista Pininfarina, was styled by in-house designer Leonardo Fioravanti, who went on to draft Ferrari's Berlinetta Boxer.

The late 1950s and early 1960s saw new developments for Pininfarina as well, including a shift in his Florida series for Lancia, from 1955 onward, from ovoid forms to flat surfaces, edges, and angles – a direction that was to become much more widespread in the 1970s. He also ventured into the world of experimental cars, once again influenced by the United States, creating his dramatic X model in 1960 and his Y model a couple of years later. On the racetrack his Fiat Abarth cars of the late 1950s won countless prizes.

In 1966 Battista Pininfarina was succeeded by his son Sergio (b.1926), who had worked with him since the mid-1950s. The younger man, an effective industrialist, has sustained the reputation of the company up to the present day. The early 1970s saw the installation of a wind tunnel in the factory and the cars produced for Lancia and Ferrari reaped the benefits of this reinforced interest in the aesthetic implications of aerodynamics. The company continued along the same lines through the 1980s and 1990s, expanding its sphere of interest to include Japan and China and continuing, with the help of a granddaughter and two grandsons of Battista Pininfarina, to respond to such demands as the need for compact, energy-efficient vehicles while at the same time creating timeless, beautiful cars that carried forward the mission of the company's innovative founder.

NUCCIO BERTONE

Bertone is practically synonymous with Italian car design in the second half of the 20th century. Some of the most memorable cars of that epoque – the Lamborghini Miura and the Alfa Romeo Giulietta Sprint to mention but two – came out of the Bertone stable and are indelibly linked with that name. This is despite the fact that neither of the Bertones – father Giuseppe (1884–1972) and son Nuccio (1914–97) – were themselves designers. Instead both were inspired businessmen; more importantly, they both knew a good designer when they saw one.

Bertone senior had set up his coachbuilding firm in Turin in 1912. Very quickly he established a business supplying car bodies to Fiat and other Italian manufacturers of the day. By the inter-war years he was working with Alfa Romeo creating bodies for a range of its chassis, among them the Tipo 6C 2300. In 1933 Nuccio completed his studies in accountancy and joined the family firm. He was fascinated by cars and quickly became committed to the importance of styling. Unlike Pininfarina (see pp.162–5), Bertone had not ventured into manufacturing by this date: that was to come in the postwar years.

Nuccio Bertone took over his father's firm in 1952. Over the next five decades he was to create a coachbuilding and car production

BELOW *Car production at the Bertone plant. Nuccio Bertone worked in his father's coachbuilding firm before setting up his own business in postwar Turin; he eventually moved into production as well as body design. This image shows the painting plant.*

RIGHT *Bertone's Alfa Romeo 2000 Sportiva of 1954. The subtle curves of this luxurious Italian sports car typified the sculptural approach towards car body design Bertone encouraged in the mid-1950s.*

business that employed the leading designers of the day and worked with a wide range of Italian (including Alfa Romeo, Fiat, Lamborghini, Maserati, and Lancia) and international manufacturers (including Citroën, BMW, Jaguar, Aston Martin, Volvo, Opel, Skoda, NSU, and Chevrolet) to create some of the era's most classic cars. The sequence of outstanding designers who worked for Bertone included Franco Scaglione, who was employed from 1952 to 1959; Giorgetto Giugiaro (see pp.178–81), between 1959 and 1965; and Marcello Gandini (see pp.176–7), from 1965 to 1980.

A LEAP OF FAITH

Nineteen fifty-two was a difficult year to set up in business in Italy. Nuccio Bertone had no orders, so he took an initiative which involved speculatively building some bodies, created by Scaglione, for two MG TD frames. He exhibited them at the Turin Autoshow of that year and received an order from S.H. Arnolt, an American automobile distributor, for 100 of each car. This piece of luck would prove crucial to the future well-being of the company. The cars, which combined the qualities of a family car with the sportiness of a racer, were the first examples of a formula that was to prove highly successful.

FRANCO SCAGLIONE AND GIORGETTO GIUGIARO

From the outset Scaglione succeeded in creating striking concept cars, which provided a source of inspiration for his production models. His Abarth coupé of 1952, also shown at Turin, was a futuristic creation with three headlamps, clearly inspired by jet planes. He took his interest in fantasy cars further with his three BAT (Berlina Aerodinamica Tecnica) proposals of 1953, 1954, and 1955. The curved fins rising up from the sides of the front windshield on the middle model, BAT 7, showed the full extent of his sculptural skills. Yet he was equally capable of holding back from such extravagances and achieving very simple, unostentatious forms that depended for their impact on their attention to visual detail. Nowhere, perhaps, was this more evident than in his design for the Giulietta Sprint of 1954.

Alfa Romeo had been told by the Italian government that it was to produce a small family car for the postwar market, and the Giulietta was its response. The saloon model was unremarkable in appearance but Bertone was charged with creating a sports version, which was offered as a prize for a lottery that Alfa Romeo organized to raise funds to mass-produce the Giulietta. It was Bertone's first real success: the company ended up not only designing the sports car but producing it

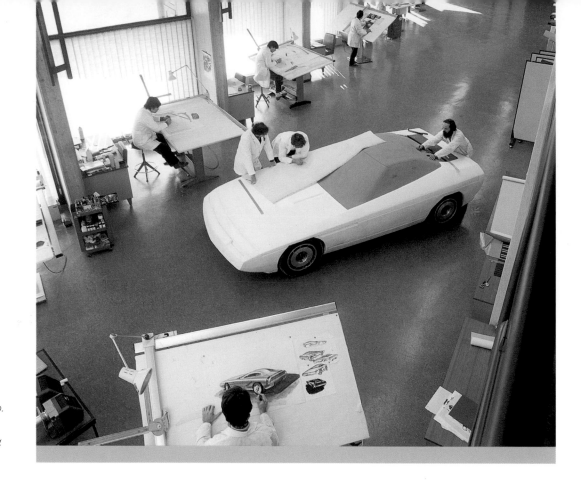

RIGHT *A view inside the Bertone styling studio in the 1960s. The image shows the two main stages of car design at Bertone: drawing-board sketch and full-size mockup. The stylists are seen here wearing white coats as if they were working in a scientific laboratory.*

as well. Scaglione's design had transformed a banal car into a supremely stylish one. By 1962, when production ceased, well over 30,000 Giuliettas had been made. A little later Scaglione created a Sprint Speciale version which incorporated futuristic styling.

Among other projects for Bertone Scaglione worked on prototypes for Aston Martin (see pp.62–3), Bentley (see pp.56–7), and Jaguar (see pp.58–61). One of Italy's most interesting designers, he had studied engineering before working for Pininfarina and moving on to

Bertone in the early 1950s. When he left his post as design director in 1959 he worked as a freelancer for a short period, but in the late 1960s he vanished without trace.

His replacement was Giorgetto Giugiaro, who had been working in Fiat's styling studio. Giugiaro's first project was for the German company NSU, for which he created the Sport Prinz. Giugiaro stayed with Bertone for only six years but in that time he created some highly successful designs, including the Giulia 105 series GT coupés that

RIGHT *One of the many futuristic concept cars to emerge from the Bertone studio. From the 1950s the firm employed designers – from Scaglione to Giugiaro to Gandini – who were able to work on striking space-age-inspired fantasy cars as well as on production models.*

were in production from 1962 to 1967, and the Fiat 850 Spyder of the mid-1960s. He was also responsible for the Iso Grifo of 1964, the Chevrolet Corvair Testudo of 1963, and the Ferrari 250 GT coupé of 1961. In keeping with Bertone's commitment to one-off body designs and production cars Giugiaro worked across a spectrum. His ability to create practical cars for mass manufacture was as strong as his talent for sleek sports cars with innovative "sci-fi-inspired" features, such as the huge front-hinged canopy on the top of his Testudo that allowed the driver his or her only entrance into the vehicle.

MARCELLO GANDINI AND BEYOND

Marcello Gandini followed Giugiaro and took Bertone design in an even more glamorous direction through his work with Lamborghini, from the Miura to the Espada to the Countach, innovative sports cars that set a new international standard. Gandini followed these with a concept car for Alfa Romeo, the Carabo, and went on to create a car that proved one of Bertone's most successful of all, the Fiat X1/9. This little wedge-shaped sports car (which has been called a "baby Ferrrari") was especially popular in the United States and brought the sports car within reach of many who hitherto had not had access to it.

After Gandini's departure in 1980, Bertone continued to develop, creating production cars as well as one-offs and special models; in 1982 it entered into a relationship with Citroën. The BX of 1984 was the first fruit of this union, followed by the body for the XM of 1989 and the Xantia of 1993. Through this collaboration Citroën entered a new phase, once again producing cars that had a strong image and identity. Other projects included the Opel Astra cabriolet and the convertible Fiat Punto, both designed and made by Bertone. In addition Bertone's concept cars continue to impress. From the Nivola of 1990 to the Blitz electric sports car of 1992 to the 1994 Karisma, the company has remained at the leading edge of car design, showing that the name of Bertone is still synonymous with innovative styling.

BELOW *A series of cars designed by Scaglione for Bertone, including one of the series of three fantasy cars that he envisaged for Berlina Aerodinamica Tecnica in the mid-1950s.*

MICHELOTTI

In the important transition in Italian postwar car styling from the coachbuilder to the design consultant the name of Michelotti (1921–80) stands out. He was among the first independent designers and he established the practice of collaborating both with the large body-making firms and with car manufacturers themselves. It was a way of working that caused him to remain anonymous to a certain extent, but his contribution to postwar Italian car styling is now fully recognized.

TRADITIONAL BACKGROUND

Michelotti's background lay in the traditional world of coachbuilding: at the age of 16 he began in the workshop of the Stabilimenti Farina, rising from jack-of-all-trades to chief designer by 1939. After World War II he decided to leave Farina and, in 1949, set up on his own, working at first from his bedroom. From that year onward Michelotti created vast numbers of car designs for the leading body-makers of the day, including Vignale, Bertone (see pp.166–9), Ghia, and Allemano, rarely getting his name credited for the innovative proposals he put forward. He was a highly prolific designer, able to work from preliminary free sketch to technical drawings and eventually to full-scale wooden models. Among his triumphs of the early 1950s were the Ferrari 212 Export berlinetta credited to Vignale and the Bristol 404 undertaken for Bertone. Many of Vignale's designs for Ferrari of these years were the creations of Michelotti as well.

ABOVE *A detail of Triumph's Spitfire Mk IV showing Michelotti's sculptural skill in the way in which he embedded the headlight into the body of the car. His work was characterized by such attention to detail combined with a grasp of the car as a single formal entity.*

RIGHT *A sketch by Michelotti for a car for the British Standard Motor Company. The "Zobo" of 1957 never left the drawing-board as such but its lines appeared in the Triumph Herald that emerged two years later. The vestigial fin was a hallmark of that particular design.*

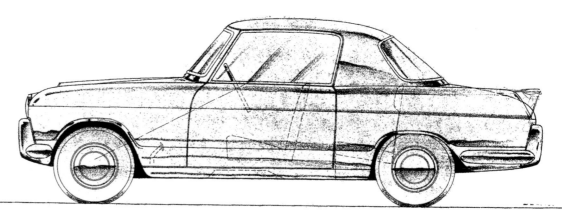

AN ITALIAN TRIUMPH

Some of Michelotti's most lasting work came through his collaboration, from 1957, with the British manufacturer Triumph. A shift in taste was occurring in Britain towards a more European aesthetic and Triumph brought in Michelotti to work on a number of their models. The Herald, launched in 1959, was the first car to show the Italian input. The TR4 sports car also demonstrated how the new stylistic approach could transform the company's cars: it was wider and lower than its predecessors and its uncluttered body featured a single line that ran, parallel to the ground, from front to rear. Its unified, well-proportioned form brought a new, sleek stylishness to the British sports car.

After the success of the Herald and TR4 Michelotti went on to create several other Triumph cars, including the Spitfire, the 1300, the 1500, the 2000, the Toledo, the Dolomite, and the Stag, imbuing them all with a simple stylishness that quickly became the hallmark of the company. All his designs had a distinctive feel to them characterized by the use of straight parallel lines and the attention devoted to details such as the lights, windshields, grilles, and badges all of which were positioned with precision to create a sense of balance and harmony.

Triumph was not the only company to benefit from Michelotti's involvement. In the early 1960s his design for BMW's 1800, for which he styled the reverse-sloping grille, had a crucial effect on the continuing success of the German company. Other designs for BMW were the 700 and the 2002 models. Michelotti also collaborated with other international big names, from the French company Renault (creating the Alpine A106), the Dutch firm Daf (for which he designed the 55 model), and the Japanese company Hino (he designed the Contessa).

By the early 1970s Triumph had been absorbed into British Leyland and Michelotti found it increasingly hard to get work. He died in 1980. The name of Michelotti survived through the widespread admiration for his work. Many of the cars he created, the Triumphs in particular, have become collectors' items.

ERCOLE SPADA

The Zagato coachbuilding firm established a reputation for high-quality car design in the 1960s, mainly due to its chief stylist Ercole Spada (b.1938). Self-taught, Spada entered the firm at the age of 22, and immediately made an impact with his stylish design for the Aston Martin DB4 GT. Nineteen chassis were supplied and all were transformed into the sleek, sculptural, aerodynamic automobiles that made the world aware of the young Italian's design work. Launched at the London Motor Show in 1960 the DB4, with its low beltline, tapering rear, Perspex windows, and triple-bubble bonnet, was one of the show's most memorable cars.

SOPHISTICATED STREAMLINING

As the 1960s progressed other equally sophisticated cars emerged from the Zagato studio bearing Spada's signature, including the Alfa Romeo Giulietta SZ of 1963 and two racing cars for the company, the TZ1 and the TZ2. Increasingly the science of aerodynamics inspired his work and enabled his cars to move at speed with minimum air turbulence. Unlike those of the inter-war American pioneers, Spada's streamlined automobiles resisted the need to evoke speed through added decorative details such as chrome trim. His was a more

BELOW *The Aston Martin DB4 GT of 1960. Spada's design for Zagato displays the characteristic "panoramic look", a name referring to the way in which the windows curved into the shape of the roof to create a single form. The rear "Kamm tail" was also a typical feature of the designer's work.*

RIGHT *Seen from the rear, Spada's cars displayed a number of features that became hallmarks of his designs for Zagato of the 1960s. The aerodynamic form and "Kamm tail", in conjunction with their light weight, meant that these were high-performance cars.*

sculpturally oriented aerodynamism which depended on reduction of form to its bare essentials, although this is not to say that Spada was unaware of the evocative power of his forms and their ability to thrill.

SPEED WITH STYLE

Spada's design for Lamborghini of the mid-decade, the 3500 GTZ, exploited his skill in seducing his audience through a heightened awareness of the impact of form. The car, of which only a couple were produced, featured the characteristic long, low body with a protruding bonnet and nose and high wheel arches. The rear window, integrated into the line flowing from roof to rear end, was almost horizontal while the back was sharply truncated to create a "Kamm tail", which contributed to the aerodynamic performance of this dramatic piece of automobile art. Perhaps Spada's *pièce de résistance* for Zagato was his more compact Alfa Romeo Junior Z of 1969, aimed at a younger

market keen to participate in the world of style and speed. Again an absence of chrome and a cut-off tail contributed to the strong form of this car. Its striking profile combined a front wedge, a low, straight beltline, and a subtly tapering back ending in a cut-off rear.

Lancia also benefited through its contact with Zagato, particularly with Spada, and the Fulvio Sport and the Flaminio 3C were two of the results. By the end of the 1960s Spada had made Zagato one of Italy's leading design consultancies. In 1969 he left the company, to try his hand as a solo designer. Over the next eight years he worked for Ford, among others, creating the GT70 and a number of other impressive vehicles. From 1977 to 1983 he devoted his attention to BMW's series 5 and 7. From 1983 onward he worked with the Italian design consultancy the I.D.E.A. Institute, a design studio led by Franco Mantegazza, where he continued to refine his eye and to work with a range of manufacturers, including Lancia, Alfa Romeo, and Fiat.

RIGHT *Seen from the front, Spada's designs were characterized by their curved extended bonnets, their integrated headlights, and their raked windscreens. The Lancia Fulvia of the 1960s, seen here, manifested all these features.*

PIETRO FRUA

Pietro Frua (1913–83) is among the most significant and least documented of Italy's postwar car designers. He played a vital role in the creation of a number of key automobiles, often alongside others. He worked as an independent stylist for much of his 50-year career, which spanned the inter-war and postwar years. Together with a handful of other "grand old men" of Italian design, he witnessed, and played some part in, the dramatic changes of the mid-century.

EARLY DESIGNS

Frua undertook an apprenticeship at Fiat and cut his teeth at Stabilimenti Farina, where he rose from junior designer to general manager in less than a decade. A couple of years before the war, he decided to go it alone and turned his hand to product design as a way of making ends meet. It has been suggested that he created the first design for what became the Vespa motor-scooter at this time. In 1944 he bought a bombed factory, with the intention of moving into car manufacture. In the late 1940s a series of one-off designs by Frua emerged, among them a wooden-bodied Lancia Aprilia, but it was not until the mid-1950s that success began to come his way, when a deal with Ghia resulted in him working exclusively for that prestigious

ABOVE *A chrome trim detail covering an air vent on the Maserati 3500 GT, one of Frua's designs for Maserati. Frua paid great attention to detail in his body designs.*

BELOW *The Maserati Mistral of 1965 was one of Frua's most eloquent creations and marked him out as a designer of great sophistication.*

coachbuilding company. The relationship lasted for about five years, during which he created some designs for Maserati and the Renault Floride. The collaboration with Ghia ended acrimoniously, however, and Frua once again launched himself as an independent designer.

INDEPENDENT ITALIAN STYLE

The late 1950s and early 1960s saw new relationships with the Swiss coachbuilding company Ghia-Aigle and the German firms Borgward and Glas. Frua also retained links with Maserati and, in 1962, created the 3500 GT, three models of which were built. He also had a part to play in the creation of the famous Volvo P1800. His cars of the 1960s were characterized by a typically Italian sculptural elegance. He went beyond many of his peers by removing the vestigial fenders that featured in so many Italian cars of this era, thereby achieving more simple and unified body-shells. His Maserati 2000 GT Spyder and his Glas 1300 GT Coupé both boasted simple, unadorned aerodynamic forms that were widely admired. The Maserati Mistral, the Glas 2600,

and the AC 428 also date from this time, when Frua worked independently in a small studio in Turin. In the production of his prototypes he relied on the network of small workshops that existed in that city.

The mid-1960s was a prolific time for Frua, in which he created a series of cars for Glas and developed various one-off modifications for standard models. The latter included a coupé version of the Citroën DS and a reworked Jaguar E Type of 1966. From 1968 onward he concentrated on one-off designs and abandoned the idea of manufacturing. His achievements included the stunning Rolls-Royce Phantom VI of 1971, which represented the first link between the prestigious British company (see pp.54–5) and an Italian designer. The car was characterized by its long, low, unified body which subtly tapered at the front and rear. Frua coloured his car lime green and used top-quality leather for the interior in true Rolls-Royce style. He completely eliminated all signs of the fenders to enhance the unified look of the vehicle. Apart from some work for the De Tomaso company, this car represented the end of Frua's career, and he died a decade later.

ABOVE *Frua played a role in the design of Volvo's famous P1800 of the early 1960s. The car is probably best known for being driven by Roger Moore in the television series* The Saint. *Frua was undoubtedly partly responsible for the subtle lines of the car but the Swede Pelle Petterson also played an important role in the creation of this stunning automobile.*

RIGHT *Frua in his later years working on a large-scale drawing of his design for the Rolls Royce Phantom VI, which he created in the early 1970s. He succeeded in combining the traditional look of this high-status car with a new sense of elegance in its body silhouette.*

MARCELLO GANDINI

The baroque automobiles that Marcello Gandini (b.1938) created for Lamborghini and others from the 1960s to the 1990s represent Italian car styling at its most dramatic and aggressive. The sense of drama and aggression was achieved through the designer pushing his imagination to its limits in envisaging the future. In his cars for Lamborghini and others Gandini blurred the distinction between the racetrack and the road and established the concept of the postwar "supercar".

THE FIRST SUPERCARS

It was in 1965 that Gandini, the son of an orchestral conductor, gave up working as an independent designer and began to work for the Bertone coachbuilding company (see pp.166–9), replacing Giugiaro (see pp.178–81) who had just left. Within a year he had set out on the path that he was to follow for the next few decades. The Lamborghini Miura of 1966, designed by Gandini in the Bertone styling studio and aptly named after a Spanish fighting bull, was the first of the supercars. In formulating this vision of the future he looked to the Ford GT40 as a model and created an incredibly low car – the roof was only 1005 mm (39½ in) above the ground – the most striking feature of

ABOVE *A detail of the front headlight of Gandini's Alfa Romeo Montreal. The emphasis on horizontality and the attention to visual balance are characteristic of his work.*

which was the way the doors swung up at the front and rear to allow passengers entry and exit. The Miura was intended for only two people, had very litle luggage space, and rejected practicality in favour of the thrill of sitting just off the ground in a cockpit-like space and travelling at high speed with the front of the car tapering away into the distance. The V12 engine was mid-mounted to allow Gandini to create the form he desired.

The Lamborghini company was very young, having created its first car in 1963. It was formed, so the story goes, by a tractor manufacturer, Ferruccino Lamborghini, who was displeased with the performance of his Ferrari and wanted to show that he could do better. The Miura was followed by a number of other striking, mostly concept, cars created for other Italian manufacturers by Gandini in the Bertone studio, including the Alfa Romeo Montreal of 1967, the Autobianchi A112 Runabout of 1969, and the Lancia Stratos of 1971. The Autobianchi provided the basis for the highly successful little Fiat X1/9 of 1972 intended to replace Giugiaro's 850 Spider, which was created for the American market and which came to be known as the "baby Ferrari". Perhaps most successful of all was Gandini's second design for Lamborghini, the Countach.

CONCEPTS OF LUXURY

After Gandini left the Bertone studio in 1980 to try his hand as an independent consultant he continued to work on a handful of production cars but excelled as ever in the area of concept cars. The Citroën BX of 1982 exemplified the former, while the 1989 Chizeta Morodor, an attempt by two Italians to produce the most extravagant "rich man's daydream" ever, was a super sports car along Lamborghini lines. This set out to offer an unprecedented level of luxury, both in the sensuousness of the form and in the comfort of the interior.

Nineteen ninety saw Gandini's first design for Lamborghini undertaken as an independent. This was a dramatic automobile which took all the rehearsed visual themes several stages further. In 1991 he was approached to work on a new Bugatti, the EB110, and in the same year he created the Iso Grifo. By the mid-1990s Gandini was working with Maserati, designing the Shamal and showing that his visual language could work equally well across a range of different cars. He remains committed to the dramatic rather than the functional, to the power of form to excite, and to the thrill of the fast car. It was a formula that worked for more than four decades, and that still stands at one end of the spectrum of car design in the 21st century.

GIORGIO GIUGIARO

PRINCIPAL DESIGNS

The impact of the Italian coachbuilders who had set up in business before World War II and who, after 1945, carried on for a couple of decades, had begun to diminish by the time of the fuel crisis in the early 1970s. The small, batch-production manufacturers were nearly all coming under the control of Fiat and the mass-produced car was the stylists' main challenge. Giorgetto Giugiaro (b.1938) filled the gap that was left by the earlier generation of stylists. Having been trained by them (five years at Bertone followed by two at Ghia) he understood the working practices of the Italian coachbuilders and the way in which they had been transformed into design consultants. He saw the need for a fundamentally new approach to the discipline of car design. In pioneering that approach he earned an international reputation.

ART AND SCIENCE

Giugiaro's contribution lay in the way he combined art with science, or more specifically sculpture with engineering. He had a background in both areas, having studied at a fine art academy and a technical school. In addition his father and grandfather had been painters and fresco-makers and the young Giugiaro was steeped in the world of artistic practice. At the age of 17 he took his two skills to the workshop

ABOVE *The Maserati Boomerang, a two-seater coupé dream car, was shown in prototype form at the Turin motor show in 1972. Its low lines and razor edges evoked power and speed. The front came to a dramatic point, dramatically reinforcing this overall image.*

LEFT *The Maserati Ghibli of 1966, created by Giugiaro, marked a phase in his career in which lines were subtly curved but also very tense. The length of this car, which was produced in a limited series, was reinforced by the flatness of the bonnet.*

RIGHT *Giugiaro's Alfa Romeo 2600 Sprint, produced in a series in 1960, was an early design created when the designer was working with Bertone. It was conceived as a status car and Giugiaro gave it an appropriate elegance of line.*

of Dante Giacosa (see pp.98–101) at Fiat and absorbed that great automobile designer's ability to create beautiful cars on the basis of an understanding of the engineering and practical constraints involved.

Giugiaro first showed his hand at Bertone (see pp.166–9), where he played a strong role in the creation of the Alfa Romeo 2600, the Asa 1000, the Ferrari 250 GT, the Simca 1000, and the Fiat 850 Spyder, while his imagination was let loose on a series of stunning concept cars that emerged from the Bertone studio, among them the Corvair Testudo – Giugiaro's first "dream car" – which manifested the characteristic clean, sculptural curves of those years and featured a dramatically curved front windshield.

INTERNATIONAL ACCLAIM

It was while he was working for Ghia that international attention was first focused on Giugiaro. Two of his designs were exhibited at the Turin Automobile Show of 1966, the Maserati Ghibli and the De Tomaso Mongoose. They both impressed visitors with their clear-cut lines and minimal curves. The flat bonnet of the Ghibli showed a new emphasis in Giugiaro's work on simplicity of form while the vehicle's length sustained his commitment to automobile drama.

Around this time Giugiaro began to move towards a new way of thinking about car design which went beyond the concept of a body joined to a pre-existing chassis and towards a need to understand and grapple with the car as a single unit. In 1968 he left Ghia and set up his own company, Italdesign, based initially in the centre of Turin. From the outset he realized that automobile design required a multi-disciplinary team of experts and he took with him two men with whom he had built up a strong working relationship: engineering designer Aldo Mantovani, and business manager Luciano Bosio. Together they provided a formidable team capable of creating whole cars for clients.

At Italdesign Giugiaro continued to work on both concept and production cars, the ideas developed in the former fuelling the latter. His unique aesthetic approach reached its full flowering over the next decade, with such classics as the Alfasud, the Volkswagen Golf, the Fiat Panda, the Lancia Delta, and the Fiat Punto. In essence he subordinated features such as the grille to an overall design approach that focused on the "problem-solving" aspects of reconciling the realities of aerodynamics with sculpture and the tensions between the space and comfort of the interior with the constraints of the exterior. Each project was an exercise in applying logic to the solution of these

ABOVE *A drawing of what is perhaps Giugiaro's most successful car. Launched in 1974, the VW Golf was a radically new design with straight, angled lines. It was intended as a successor to the classic Beetle which had been in production since the 1940s.*

problems and letting the car evolve as the problems were resolved one by one. Giugiaro concentrated on issues such as the amount of glass used, the way the lines moved into each other, the thickness of the metal, the readability of the dashboard, and the minimal comfort requirement. As the fuel crisis bit deeper he became preoccupied with the functionality of the car and the economy and technology of manufacture, aware that designing was not a matter of merely creating an image but of specifying the means of manufacture as well.

Giugiaro's 1970s cars introduced a straight-line look and focused on the aerodynamics of the wedge front. In his show cars, including

BELOW *A drawing for Fiat's Panda, which was launched in 1980. This small utilitarian car was characterized by its straight lines and its versatile interior. Giugiaro was catering for those who wanted to combine utility with style.*

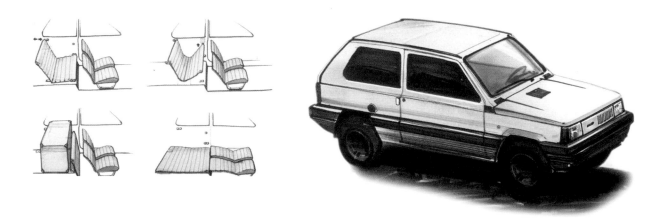

the Alfa Romeo Caiman and the Maserati Boomerang, he decreased the angle of the windshields so that the cars acquired a dramatically pointed front end and sat extremely low on the ground. In his Alfasud of 1971, his first project as an independent designer, he combined aerodynamics with comfort, in a masterpiece of rational design in which every inch counted. In the VW Golf, commissioned by the German company to replace the highly popular Beetle, launched in 1974 (the same year as the VW Scirocco, which he also designed), he brought together the strategies he had developed over the previous few years, in the context of designing for a mass audience. The sharp lines of the slanted hood, windshield, roof, and rear window combined to create a balanced profile, while parallel horizontal lines along the sides united the two volumes into a single unit. Although a small saloon, with its cut-off rear end it retained the feel of a sports car.

CONTINUAL INNOVATION

From his huge success with the Golf Giugiaro went on to create a series of production cars all of which resulted from meeting head on the challenges of the briefs set by his clients. In the Fiat Panda, for example, he created an inexpensive, functional car that met the basic requirements of comfort for first-car buyers. In addition to the striking profile, which derived from a use of straight lines and flat glass, much of the ingenuity invested in this design focused on the interior, which combined minimal yet comfortable upholstery with a flexible and movable seating arrangement capable of turning the car into a utility vehicle as required. Giugiaro's commitment to resolving the tensions

between comfort and compactness had been demonstrated, prior to his work on the Panda, in his design for a New York taxi, a project initiated by the Museum of Modern Art. It had emerged again in his Megagamma, created specially for the Turin motor show of 1978. His decision to create extra space by raising the height of the automobile pointed the way forward to many of the designs for MPVs (multi-purpose vehicles) of the 1990s, showing how far ahead in his thinking Giugiaro was and how influential his innovations have been.

By the late 1970s the demands made by the fuel shortages on aerodynamic efficiency were such that Giugiaro abandoned faceted forms for more rounded shapes. The Fiat Uno of 1983 bore witness to this new trend, as did the Punto of a decade later. The 1980s and 1990s also saw Italdesign work on many visionary projects with international clients, from the Lancia Marlin and the Ford Maya to the Bugatti ID 90 and the BMW Nazca. In the spirit of the earlier coachbuilders, one of his roles has been to show possible ways forward. In 1997 he worked with his son Fabrizio to create a prototype for the little mini MPV, the Daewoo Matiz, which depended strongly on his earlier (1992) concept developed for the Lucciola. In the early 21st century Giugiaro continues to draw on his enormous repertoire of concepts to take the automobile still further into the future.

BELOW *The 1995 Lamborghini Carla pictured here was a concept proposed by Italdesign. Its futuristic form and dramatic rear spoiler show the design firm's continued commitment to new automotive solutions which evoke the qualities of power and speed.*

BRITISH SPORTS CARS

Postwar Britain saw a growth of interest in the sports car. As a typology this car had its roots in European automobile racing and its appeal was primarily to the expanding middle-class market of the postwar years. The British middle classes extended their sporting traditions into driving open-topped sports cars. Unlike their Italian and American counterparts, the British sports cars of this period were, with a few notable exceptions, both small and relatively inexpensive.

This was especially the case with MG's little sports cars, which made a huge impact internationally in the 1950s and 1960s. The brand had been established as an offshoot of the car company set up by William Richard Morris (MG stands for Morris Garages). It was led by Cecil Kimber, who formed the MG Car Company in 1928. Through the inter-war years MG developed the diminutive Midget, which was just big enough for two people. This was followed by a series of racing models which competed at Brooklands in England, as well as at the Italian Mille Miglia, winning numerous victories at both events.

MG SPORTS CARS

Kimber died in 1945 when the company was about to launch itself into the sports car market on a significant scale. The postwar TC Midget quickly became a cult car but it was followed by an even more successful model, at least in design terms. The TF, launched in 1953,

ABOVE *Triumph's TR3 model from the 1950s combined elegance of line with high performance. Following on from the TR2 of 1953, it was one of Triumph's first inexpensive sports cars, manufactured in the hope of appealing to the American market.*

LEFT *Jaguar XK120s in a still from the 1954 British film* Fast and Furious *featuring John Ireland and Dorothy Malone. So deeply embedded was the symbolism of the sports car in 1950s Britain that it could be the subject of a feature film.*

was created by one of England's leading car stylists of the era, Gerald Palmer. It was strongly Italianate in appearance with an extended bonnet, flowing fenders, and two-tone bodywork. Palmer had worked in the MG design office at Cowley in the pre-war years before moving, in 1942, to a company called Jowett where he created a remarkable streamlined saloon car, the Jowett Javelin, launched in 1946. He was taken back as an MG designer in 1949, where he went on to create a new range of MGs, Rileys, and Wolseleys that were inspired by the work of the Italian designers of the period.

ICONS AND LEGENDS

Palmer helped to turn MG into a design-conscious company and its sports cars of the 1960s – the MGB of 1962 and its popular variant the MGB GT coupé of 1965 – bore witness to its ability to create small, stylish models with enormous appeal. The MG factory closed in 1980 but the mid-1990s saw an attempt to recreate the spirit of MG with the RV8 model of 1993 (which sold mostly in Japan) and, two years later, an MGF roadster, designed by Gerry McGovern. By then the MG sports car had become a legend and, above all, an icon of Britishness.

The other British sports car to acquire the status of a legend in the postwar years was the Lotus. Once again the company's roots were in

BELOW *The Austin-Healey Sprite II of 1964, a small, two-seater sports car with a neat body-shell and simple styling features, shared its body with the MG Midget. Its continuous waist-line and lack of extraneous features made it a very appealing little car.*

racing, but the 1950s and 1960s saw a growth in the production of sports cars for a burgeoning market, which have since become classics. The name of Colin Chapman is inseparable from that of Lotus. Combining designing with racing and entrepreneurial activity, he was responsible for the emergence of several memorable cars.

LOTUS: RACERS AND ROADSTERS

Chapman's preoccupation was with designing cars to win races, and he borrowed ideas from aircraft construction to create light cars that would perform well. He had acquired his knowledge in the RAF and at the British Aluminium Company after the war. Like his fellow designer Alec Issigonis (see pp.106–9), Chapman was as interested in the engine as he was in the bodywork of his cars and applied his engineer's expertise to the whole vehicle. By 1952 he had created the Lotus Mark 6 racing

car. The priority was speed but Chapman gave it a streamlined aluminium body with a sloping nose and rear tailfins, an intervention worthy of any car stylist of the day. By 1956 Chapman's future as a designer rather than as a racer was confirmed. The following year saw the emergence of the Lotus 7, available in kit form, followed in the same year by the Lotus Elite, the company's first closed passenger car, which made its appearance at the Earl's Court Motor Show.

The production of a road car was central to Chapmans' ambitions of expansion but funds did not permit a metal body. The compromise was the construction of a fibreglass shell, the shape of which was designed by a friend, Peter Kirwan-Taylor: the result was the first production car with an all-plastic structure. More successful than the Elite was the Lotus Elan of 1962. Chapman's racetrack successes had also expanded by this time and the two-seater sports car he created in this

LEFT *The Lotus Elise of 1996, one of the marque's more recent models. It is a monocoque design made from aluminium and as a result is extremely lightweight, a factor that significantly enhances performance.*

year provided the financial backing he needed for the Elan, his second attempt at a road-going car. Sporting a fibreglass body once again and featuring pop-up headlights, the Elan rapidly also became a legend.

Over the next decade and a half Lotus created a number of memorable production cars that sat alongside its victories on the track. The Europa of 1967, with its cut-away rear fins, was followed by the Elan Sprint of 1970. In 1975 Giorgetto Giugiaro (see pp.178–81) designed a prototype for the Esprit the final version of which was rendered a classic by its appearance in the James Bond film *The Spy Who Loved Me*. In 1984, two years after Chapman's death, Giugiaro worked with Lotus again, this time on the Etna model. In 1989 a new Elan was launched. In 1995 the Elise, introduced at the Frankfurt motor show, showed that the legend that was Lotus was alive and well.

OTHER POSTWAR LEGENDS

Between them the MG and Lotus companies formed a British sports car movement that acknowledged styling advances made in Italy but that grew, in essence, out of the British racing tradition adapted for a postwar market. Other firms contributed to the movement in the 1950s. The Morgan company, for example, adopted a different strategy from the other two, more forward-looking firms, deciding that

it was more likely to stay in business if it celebrated its past and used its pre-war traditions to create a brand image for itself in the 1970s. It was a strategy that was highly effective.

At the expensive, luxury end of the British sports car spectrum the Alvis company, formed in 1920, employed the Swiss coachbuilder Graber to create bodies for several of its models, among them a drophead coupé of 1959 and the TF21 of 1964. The sleek lines of these cars showed the public what British sports cars could look like at their most sophisticated. The Sunbeam company, in operation since 1901, created a stunning little sports car, named the Alpine, in 1959, which showed the British sports car at its most progressive.

Other names, such as those of Austin-Healey, Riley, Aston Martin, Lagonda, Fraser Nash, and Bristol evoke the heyday of postwar British motoring when the sports car represented a distinctly British achievement, based on past traditions but forward-looking and optimistic. By the 1970s it was a modern tradition that was in decline, however, destroyed by the take-overs of those years and the absorption of small firms into large ones. In spite of the attempts made to revive the MG and the Lotus in the 1990s there can be little doubt that historians will look back at the British sports car as primarily a phenomenon of the 1950s and 1960s.

FRENCH STYLE

*B*y the middle of the 20th century, primarily as a result of taxes brought in by the French government that curtailed their viability, the link between France and the *grands routiers* of the inter-war years – the products of Bugatti, Lago-Talbot, Delahaye, Hotchkiss, and others – was fading from view. Only a handful of small-scale manufacturers attempted to sustain the tradition. Between the mid-1950s and the 1960s, for instance, Facel Vega made a brave effort to launch a series of highly styled luxury cars on to the French market. The FVS, launched at the 1954 Paris motor show, and styled by Monsieur Brasseur, was an elegant automobile with a modern, flowing appearance. It was followed by a number of other striking models, the Facellia sports car among them, but by 1964 the company had to admit defeat in the face of overwhelming odds.

Other French manufacturers depended on mass production for their survival. Simca and Peugeot thrived in the postwar years but were not especially style-conscious. Exceptionally, Simca's Aronde

model of 1951 had an Italianate feel to it (the firm had built Fiat's cars in France between the wars) and was a success until it went out of production in 1962, while Peugeot's 203 of 1948, the first model to be launched after the devastation the company had suffered during the war, introduced bulbous American styling to France. Yet neither company was able to create anything that might have been described as "French style". That particular challenge was left to the two giant French automobile producers Citroën and Renault.

IDIOSYNCRACY AND INVENTIVENESS

By 1950 both Citroën and Renault had made their mark in the arena of small cars, creating highly original and somewhat idiosyncratic designs, which resembled nothing that was being produced elsewhere. Together the two companies exhibited a level of inventiveness that was beginning to single out French automobiles. The combination of utility and visual originality that characterized

RIGHT *Citroën's little Ami 6, seen as the successor to the 2CV, was in production between 1961 and 1969. It had a quirky appearance, made especially so by the inclusion of the backward-sloping rear window.*

LEFT *The DS 19, a styling master-piece from the hands of Flaminio Bertoni, was undoubtedly Citroën's most impressive and lasting design from the 1950s. Its science-fiction looks and sculptural lines combined with innovative automotive technology to create one of the century's automotive icons.*

both the Citroën 2CV (see pp.102–5) and the Renault 4CV (see pp.110–11) set in train a radical approach towards car design that both companies were to develop over the next five decades.

CITROËN'S CHALLENGE

In the early 1950s Citroën's challenge to itself was to move on from the creation of two automobile legends, the Traction Avant of the 1930s and the 2CV of 1948. Remarkably it managed to exceed both of these achievements with the launch, in 1955, of the DS 19. The Déesse ("goddess") is one of the few cars that have inspired writers outside the field of automobile criticism to extol their virtues. The French cultural critic Roland Barthes described it as "a purely magical object", which excited interest "less by its substance than by the junction of its components". The form of the smooth body-shell of the DS, created, like the 2CV before it, by the Italian sculptor Flaminio Bertoni – this time assisted by Pierre Franchiset – was like nothing

else that had been seen in automotive design up to that moment. It was aerodynamically shaped, and the fact that front-wheel drive allowed the front and rear axles to be far apart meant that the wheels had plenty of space between them. This gave a sense of solidity to the way in which the car sat on the ground. Most radically of all, the DS had no front radiator grille, and the bonnet sloped dramatically right down almost to the floor giving the car a special profile and providing a strong visual feature. The glass in the rear window was cleverly curved in such a way as to prevent raindrops from staying on the window. In addition to its innovative styling features that gave it a startlingly new appearance, the DS also broke new ground on the technological front with its hydro-pneumatic suspension. So strong was the appeal of this new car to the French public that 12,000 orders were taken on the first day of its launch.

Before his death in 1964 Bertoni designed one more car for Citroën which, also, was novel in appearance. The little Ami 6 of

RIGHT *The Renault 5, launched in 1973, has been described as one of the first "superminis". Combining compactness with comfort and reliability, it appealed strongly to a young urban market keen to participate in automotive culture.*

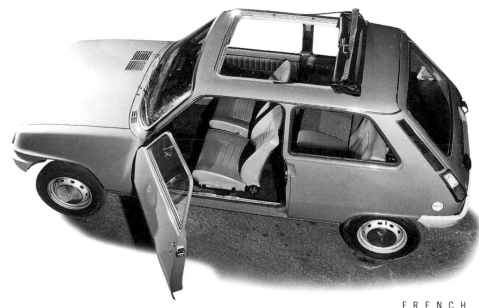

1961 may not have been as impressive as the DS, but its backward-slanting rear window endowed it with an undoubted uniqueness of character and, once again, confirmed Citroën as an avant-garde company that certainly had no need to look to other countries for a lead in design. Bertoni's place at Citroën was taken by the American Robert Opron, who had been working with the company before being promoted to head of styling, and therefore understood the culture that it was his job to sustain.

The Dyane of 1967 was intended to be a modernized 2CV, although in the end it would be outlived by the older model. It was created by the team at Panhard that had been taken over by Citroën. Opron's principal achievements came later, and were linked with the large saloon cars that Citroën launched from 1970 onward. The SM, which followed the Dyane, was a dramatic-looking car with sleek lines and an emphasis on what has been described as its "glasshouse of lights" at the front. The GS of 1970 was a flagship, high-performance

ABOVE *A headlamp on the Citroën Maserati that turns with the steering. This sort of ingenious detailing characterizes the approach to design at the Citroën company.*

car, while the CX of 1974 carried forward the interest in aerodynamics that had been the hallmark of the legendary DS. That year was also the one in which Citroën was bought by Peugeot, as a result of the high development costs of the CX. Although this by no means spelled the end of Citroën as a company linked with the idea of design innovation – as demonstrated by the little Visa, the Xantia, and the Saxo – nonetheless, in terms of cult status, nothing has yet superseded the cars of the 1950s and 1960s. In 2000 the designer Jean-Pierre Ploué, previously a member of Renault's design team, became Citroën's director of styling, charged with the task of taking the company into the new century.

RENAULT STYLE

The Renault company took a little longer than Citroën to become a style pacesetter. It suffered a number of financial setbacks in the 1960s, although the upmarket Renault 16 of 1964 can be seen as the first of its *voitures à vivre* ("cars for living in") models. However, the early 1970s saw Renault make a dramatic comeback with the little Renault 5, which has been described as the first of the "superminis". Back in the 1940s the company had shown its awareness that designing a novel car was not merely a question of innovative form and visual detailing but rather of arriving at a new car concept that fitted with socio-cultural shifts in the marketplace. The Renault 5

maintained that tradition, providing a lifestyle accessory for a young, sophisticated, urban market in somewhat the same way as Alec Issigonis' Mini (see pp.106–9) had in the previous decade – although the neat, stylish, and up-to-date appearance of the Renault 5 took it into a new league.

The breakthrough for Renault achieved by the 5 was repeated 13 years later by the arrival of the Espace, the first monospace "people-mover", or MPV (multi-purpose vehicle), which was very swiftly emulated by nearly all the other major car manufacturers. This radically new concept was, once again, lifestyle-driven, and showed how it was possible to fundamentally rethink the look of a car by revitalizing its function. The idea of family travel, hitherto largely unprovided for as a specialist activity in itself, had inspired a car that was recognized as a "first" and one, moreover, that put Renault back on the design map in a dramatic way.

With the subsequent emergence of the 19, the Clio, the Twingo, and the Mégane Scénic, among others, by the year 2000 Renault had become a design force to be reckoned with.

By that year also, although its pre-war reputation as a producer of large, stylish, luxury cars had come to an end, France's role was fully confirmed as a country in which innovative, radical, and sophisticated design – in terms both of new concepts and of new aesthetic languages – could flourish.

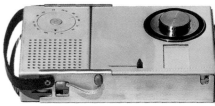

THE GERMAN MACHINE AESTHETIC

German cars have long been associated with advanced engineering and the traits of solidity, durability, and reliability. In addition Germany has a strong tradition of functional modern design, from the 1920s Bauhaus school onward.

MERCEDES-BENZ

The products of the Mercedes-Benz company are rooted in the inventions of Karl Benz and Gottfried Daimler, on the basis of whose discoveries Daimler-Benz created cars in the inter-war years with an emphasis on high performance and engineering prowess. Both racing and road-going cars, including the W25, the 500K, and the 540K, emerged from Daimler-Benz, all marked with the same brand identity, recognized by the three-pointed star and the familiar radiator grille.

In the mid-1950s the manufacturer began to realize the importance of design in the marketplace. The name of Karl Wilfert belongs to this era, the first named body-designer to work with the company's huge team of engineers. He was responsible for several cars produced in the mid-1950s – the 180 of 1953 (the first to position the radiator beneath the hood), the fantastic 300L, and the more popular 190SL.

These began to acknowledge that cars not only had to be efficient, they also had to show that they were, by the form chosen for them.

The company's interest in brand identity and continuity became a fully-fledged design philosophy. The man who pushed this philosophy the furthest, thus helping to create a Germanic car aesthetic, was the Italian Bruno Sacco. He worked for Daimler-Benz for almost four decades, becoming head of the styling centre in 1975. In the early years he worked on the 220 of 1959, the huge 600, the elegant 230SL, the ESV (experimental safety vehicle), and the experimental C111 series. He was also responsible for the design of the S class of 1979 in which chrome was replaced by plastic mouldings, the 190 series of 1982, the E class of 1984, the new S class of 1991, the C class of 1993, and the SLK convertible of 1996. He created a design ethic and aesthetic that gave the illusion that Mercedes cars hardly changed.

BMW AUTOMOBILES

The strong-shouldered, geometric, solid, reliable look of the German automotive machine aesthetic was shared by the country's other key car manufacturer of the 20th century, BMW. Unlike with Mercedes

RIGHT *From the 1950s Mercedes developed a highly masculine aesthetic for its cars which implied technological sophistication, solid construction, and upper-class sophistication. It quickly became associated with the concept of rational German style. Seen here is the 220SE coupé of 1964.*

this look was already apparent in the pre-war years, as manifested by the stunningly futuristic designs of Peter Schimanowski, the creator, probably, of BMW's famous double grille, first used in the 303 model.

In the early 1950s the subtle forms of the pre-war models were replaced by those of the much more sturdy 500 series cars which were nicknamed the "Baroque Angels". After an interlude during which the company took over production of the Italian Isetta it moved into the 700 series, which was designed by the Italian Giovanni Michelotti (see pp.170–71), of Triumph fame. This marked a rekindling of interest in design for BMW and from that moment onward it became, like its competitor Mercedes, increasingly conscious of the evolution of its brand identity.

Through the 1960s, 1970s, and 1980s BMW worked on its evolving image, conscious of Mercedes' parallel developments. Its

blue and white emblem, signifying a rotating airplane propeller, became the equivalent of the three-pointed star. BMW's was a design formula that appealed to the head rather than to the heart but which marked out Germany as *the* producer of quality production cars.

By the last years of the century, however, Japan had begun to apply the same formula, highly successfully, to some of its cars and had become a real contender. In response Mercedes-Benz opened an advanced design studio in Japan, led by the French designer Olivier Boulay, and both Mercedes and BMW had to begin to develop other strategies and approaches towards the design of their cars.

BELOW *With its propeller-inspired badge, its split radiator grille ,and its double headlights, the front end of the postwar BMW – in this instance the BMW 635 CSI – became a marker of a brand that stood for status and quality.*

PORSCHE

As a creator of classic design icons Porsche stands out from almost all others in the postwar years. While it is linked with certain timeless automobile models – such as the 356, the 911, the 904, the 924, the 928, the 959, and the Boxster – the essential Porsche design concept consists of variations on a single theme, that of a classic, aerodynamic, beautifully yet minimally styled sports car in which appearance has been subordinated to utility, form to function.

THE EARLY PORSCHES

The first car to bear the Porsche name – the aluminium-bodied 356 – was created after the war by Ferry Porsche, the son of Ferdinand who had worked on what became the VW Beetle (see pp.94–7). When the elder man died in 1951, his son took on the mantle of the prestigious Porsche name. By 1950 he was creating all-steel 356s in significant numbers at Stuttgart, their striking bodies made by the craftsmen at the Reutter coachworks. The car exhibited all the features that were to become the basis of the Porsche brand for the next five decades, including a sleek, streamlined body made up of curves that flowed seamlessly into each other, an elegant profile, an absence of unnecessary details, and a sitting position close to the ground.

Part of Porsche's success lay in its erosion of the distinction between the racing and the sports car. All its models were fast and aerodynamically efficient, and what is more, they looked as if they were. The Carrera model, launched in 1955, was named after the

LEFT *Ferdinand Alexander Porsche pictured with his father Dr Ferry Porsche.*

ABOVE *The Porsche 928 of 1978 was designed by Tony Lapine's in-house team. This late model is rooted in all the earlier developments of the 1950s and 1960s and the only real refinements are under the bonnet.*

Spanish word for "race" but was equally at home on the road. By the mid-1950s Porsche cars had acquired cult status. The young actor James Dean was killed while driving a Porsche 500, an event that served further to fan the flames of the myth.

NEW MODELS, SAME STYLE

By the late 1950s the company was looking for a 356 replacement and a new racing model. Both of the cars that emerged, the 911 and the 904, came from the hand of F.A. Porsche, known as "Butzi", a third-generation member of the family. The first Porsche to study design, after graduation he worked in the body section under Erwin Komenda, the engineer who had styled the company's cars from the early 1930s.

The search for a 356 replacement was also being undertaken by Heinrich Klie, who had set up the Porsche modelling department in 1951, working with American stylist Albert Goertz. Butzi's proposal for a car with two front seats and two smaller ones in the back won the day, however, and it was launched at Frankfurt in 1963, as the 901. The 911, as it became, was Porsche's definitive postwar car and many of the company's later models were reworkings and updates of this classic design. It re-utilized all the visual and functional strategies that had made the 356 such a roaring success.

From the mid-1960s until the late 1990s the company suffered financial ups and downs, but its design strength remained constant, moving from the hands of Butzi Porsche to those of Tony Lapine, who was responsible for the 924 of 1976, the 928 of 1978, and the 959 of 1983; and, in 1988, to those of Harm Lagaay (see pp.234–5) who created the stunningly different Boxster model launched in 1996. In 1997 Lagaay oversaw the creation of a new 911, once again showing Porsche to be essentially a single-idea company that knew how to develop that idea so as to make it seem new every time it re-emerged.

RIGHT *A Porsche 911S from 1967. The simple, aerodynamic body-shell created by Butzi for the 911 remained essentially unchanged through all the versions of this high-performance automobile. Its simple functionality helped create the firm's reputation for quality cars.*

LEFT *The Porsche 356 Speedster was the first car to be made by the Porsche company after the war. It was designed by Ferry Porsche to be manufactured in aluminium in the first instance; this later model, of 1955, was made of steel.*

SCANDINAVIAN SANITY

Sweden was the only Scandinavian country to develop its own car culture in the 20th century. Together the manufacturers Volvo and Saab were responsible for the development of a specifically Swedish approach to automobile design where the emphasis was less on eye-appeal and more on the principles of strength, safety, and longevity. Saab made sure that its cars were "moose-proof"; Volvo developed car bodies that would withstand the effects of road accidents and give drivers a sense of security and confidence behind the wheel.

VOLVO: A SWEDISH CAR FOR SWEDEN

Volvo was established in 1924 by the economist Assar Gabrielsson and the engineer Gustav Larson, who together set out to create a Swedish car for Swedish roads. From the production of its first car, the OV4 of 1927, Volvo stood by a basic manufacturing principle, which involved designing all its components in-house as a means of maintaining its high standards. In design terms its cars of the 1930s and 1940s looked to the United States for inspiration and featured bulbous, streamlined forms. The PV444, launched at the end of the war, became Sweden's first "people's car". Known affectionately as the Volvo Amazon, it made the country a car-driving nation for the first time. Its sturdy, muscular form showed the company the way forward.

In 1950 Volvo established a styling office, run by a 20-year-old ex-applied arts student, Jans Wilsgaard. For the first few years he was the only exterior designer employed by Volvo and he worked alongside the firm's only interior designer, Rustang Lange, in a very modest design studio. The fruits of their labour were revealed by the launch, in 1957, of the 120 series, the replacement for the PV444. In its various guises the Volvo 120 series remained in production until 1970 and represented the mainstay of Volvo's production through those years. Visually – it belonged to the so-called "pontoon" school of vehicle design – it was an elegant vehicle, drawing on American and Italian influences to create a specifically Swedish car.

In 1959 Volvo launched its sporty P1800, a car designed by the Italian stylist Pietro Frua (see pp.174–5) who was subcontracted by

RIGHT *A wooden model of what became Sixten Sason's little Saab 92. This aerodynamic car was conceived at the end of World War II by Saab's engineers but it took a technical illustrator to give it a form. It clearly owed a lot to developments in streamlining from the pre-war years.*

Ghia, with input from Pelle Petterson, the son of a boat designer who did some consultancy work with Volvo. It earned the company a new reputation for sophistication and stylishness and became a design icon – partly thanks to its use by the actor Roger Moore in the 1960s television series *The Saint*. But Volvo's mainstream reputation derived from its sturdy sedans of the 1960s, 1970s, 1980s, and 1990s. The square, "shoebox" shape of these solid machines was first visible in the 140 series designed by Wilsgaard and his team, launched in

1966. Based on the earlier Amazon, this model was more modern-looking, roomier, and above all safer.

Perhaps more than anything else Volvo's cars have a reputation for being designed for safety. All the 140 series models, including the 1967 Estate, had strong side panels and collapsible steering columns. From that moment the company prioritized the safety element, a fact that it used extensively in its promotional campaigns. Their cars expressed a progressively stronger image of safety. Over the next three

LEFT *A rendering by Sason made in 1947 of what was to become the Saab 92 (see above). This evocative image shows the designer's illustration skills and conveys the level of futuristic fantasy and stylishness that he brought with him to the Saab project.*

RIGHT *The Volvo 121 saloon of 1956 was popularly known as the Amazon because of its strong, rugged features. It combined American styling and an indigenous Swedish approach, with the result that it quickly became a very popular family car in Sweden. It remained in production until 1970.*

decades Volvo launched a sequence of models, including the 240 series of 1974, the 760 of 1982, the 850 of 1991, and the new 960 of 1994, all of which fine-tuned the language of safety, strength, and longevity. By the turn of the century a new direction was needed, and with the launch of its S60 in 2000 Volvo sought to combine safety with sportiness in an effort to revitalize its somewhat middle-aged image.

SAAB: AERONAUTICAL INSPIRATION

Saab cars, too, developed a reputation for resilience, safety, and durability. This image took a while to emerge, as the first cars to come off the production line of this aircraft-turned-automobile manufacturer, in the early postwar years, were inspired mostly by American streamlining and aeronautics. Sixten Sason's prototype of 1946, which became the bottle-green, small rear-windowed Saab 92 production car of three years later, was designed like an airplane wing. Sason was an industrial designer who worked for a range of

product manufacturers in the manner of American industrial design consultants such as Raymond Loewy (see pp.136–9) and Walter Dorwin Teague. Like them he ranged across a variety of products, which he transformed with the sculptural body-shells he created for them. He worked for Saab on a consultancy basis – an unusual arrangement as most manufacturers employed in-house stylists – and created a series of classic cars that earned the company a special reputation in the context of postwar international automotive design.

Sason's last design for Saab was the company's first large car. The Saab 99, launched in 1967, was decidedly idiosyncratic. It was a solid-looking car with aerodynamic curves. The line of the rear window sloped to join that of the trunk cover in a particular manner and chromed air vents acted as visual highlights on the sides at the back of the car. The turbo version of the 99, launched in 1977, was among the first turbo cars to appear anywhere in the world. The turbocharger was justified as a safety feature, with Saab claiming that

ABOVE *The Volvo 145 De Luxe estate car epitomizes the solid, tank-like appearance of family Volvos through the 1960s, 1970s, and 1980s. This secure image and the car's virtually indestructible mechanics developed into an automobile brand that was interchangeable with the idea of "Swedishness".*

RIGHT *Above all else Volvo established a strong brand image for itself through its commitment to car safety. Seen here is the three-point seatbelt that was fitted in the Amazon. The Volvo company invested large amounts of money in developing this image and providing special safety features.*

it made overtaking much safer. Like Volvo, Saab put its new models through a series of safety tests, one of the most dramatic being that in which its cars encountered the carcass of a moose, an animal that constituted a definite safety hazard on rural Swedish roads.

The hole left at Saab by Sason in 1969 was filled by a young designer who had worked with him, Bjorn Envall. Having been surrounded by Saab culture for several years, he understood its special characteristics. In 1979 the Saab 900 followed the 99 and took the company into a new era. The emphasis was still on solidity, quality, and durability, and the new car had a distinctive appearance much dependent on, although considerably more sophisticated than, that of its predecessor. The turbo 900 appeared five years later. In 1985 Envall's experimental Saab EV-1 came out. By the 1980s Saab cars

had a significant cult following internationally, and what many had considered a rather ugly appearance took on a new meaning. In 1993 the new 900 was launched and in 1998 the level of stylishness achieved by Saab was epitomized by the striking "Monte Carlo yellow" 900 turbo convertible, which quickly became highly covetable.

THE SWEDISH ATTRACTION

The lesson learned by Sweden's contribution to 20th-century car design is that it is not only eye-appeal that makes cars desirable. The psychological relationship between cars and their users is a complex one made more so by the injection of many different meanings into the machine; the designer's role is to make those meanings manifest. Nobody has understood that more clearly than Volvo and Saab.

ABOVE *Saab's 900S Turbo model of 1992. Like Volvo Saab's cars acquired a reputation for solidity, sturdiness, and safety. The aerodynamic shape and its powerful engine combined to make it a high-performance car as well.*

RIGHT *At the end of the century Volvo abandoned the geometric, tank-like appearance in favour of a softer, more up-to-date look, which transformed the company's image, adding stylishness to its list of appealing features.*

CARS AND
LIFESTYLE

CARS AND LIFESTYLE

As far as automobile design was concerned, the last three decades of the 20th century experienced a period of despondency followed by a time of enormous and unexpected exhilaration. Fears about car safety and urban pollution in the 1960s had been followed by the sudden oil crisis of the early 1970s which had served to augment the anxieties of the anti-car lobby. No longer was the car the potent symbol of modernity and progress but rather the enemy, there to be feared and mistrusted rather than adored.

While this turnaround was undoubtedly part of a more widespread loss of belief in the future and a crisis of conscience that was felt across many aspects of contemporary culture, its effects were particularly intense in the arena of car design, which felt its excessive past weighing heavily upon it. The 1950s had been a time when a general optimism had prevailed, manifesting itself substantially through a desire to participate in the future through the acquisition of a house and an automobile. Manufacturers were all too aware that the exuberance of that era had encouraged stylists, endorsed by the public, to go beyond the aesthetic limits. Now, perhaps inevitably, the price of that over-exuberance had to be paid.

Stylistically the effect of this crisis produced a blandness that, with only a few notable exceptions, made one car virtually indistinguishable from another. Designers aligned themselves with the dictates of utility and strove to make their cars as functional as possible. The "razor-edge" style was succeeded by the "aero" aesthetic, instigated primarily for reasons of fuel efficiency. Both styles quickly became a kind of uniform for mass-produced cars, which ignored it at their peril. A high level of pragmatism, seriousness, and caution came to dominate not only the

appearance of, but the very approach to, cars, and designers found themselves working within a kind of strait-jacket of regulations and scientific data, conscious that they could not do anything over-provocative or they would have public opinion down on them like a ton of bricks, or so they believed.

The financial difficulties of the 1980s had the effect of creating a "designer culture" in the area of domestic goods – furniture, interior items, and home electronics – in response to consumers' belief that they could either buy themselves out of the recession or forget about it through the creation of and absorption into their own individual "lifestyle". It did not reach the motor car in that decade, however. When it finally did, in the 1990s, the results were dramatic.

Japan was responsible for re-energizing the arena of car design in the 1990s. Its manufacturers and designers achieved this in two ways: first by introducing the idea of the "retro" car, which, by looking back at the heroic period of the automobile, succeeded in reviving its contemporary culture; and secondly, by realizing that the market for cars was fragmented – as were the lifestyles to which they had to conform – and that the days of the undifferentiated car were over. Not only did Japan create a whole new range of car typologies – from the multi-purpose vehicle (MPV) to the sports utility vehicle (SUV) and beyond – it also recognized that different market sectors required and desired different kinds of car. The increasing number of women and young people driving cars, for example, demanded new modes of design thinking.

The new ideas generated by Japan spread quickly to the United States and Europe. The recognition that the car was no longer an icon of modernity but rather a lifestyle accessory gave

designers a new sense of freedom and they were swift to rise to the challenge. Above all this new approach placed a greater emphasis on design than had hitherto been the case. Designers, in tandem with marketing people, were suddenly the key to the whole process of manufacturing and – more importantly – marketing and sales. By the end of the decade car advertisements were even using the named designer as a front man. While the technologists carried on as they always had, developing the use of new materials, new safety systems, and new forms of in-car communications, the designer became responsible not only for the car's looking different but for its being different.

Brand identity and design went increasingly hand in hand, expressed now not merely by a badge on the bonnet but by the whole essence of the vehicle, from the way it sat on the road, to how it made the driver feel, to the aggressiveness of its appearance or the friendliness of its demeanour. The very process of car designing changed such that multi-disciplinary "project innovation teams" were created to ensure that everyone worked together on the "whole car".

As the car manufacturing industry became increasingly global, so the design profession became more and more international as well. American designers, such as J. Mays and Wayne Cherry, moved to Europe to undertake their apprentice- ships, before going back to transform the production of cars in their own country. By contrast, European designers, Patrick Le Quément among them, travelled to the United States to learn about their way of doing things. American designers, such as Christopher Bangle at BMW, headed European design studios while graduates of London's Royal College of Art, among them Murat Gunak at Mercedes-Benz and subseqently Peugeot and

LEFT *A designer at work on creating a clay model for the Mercedes-Benz' A-class car. Combining compactness with a maximum use of interior space this little family car has a striking appearance enhanced by the lines of the wraparound rear window.*

BELOW *The new Fiat 500 (known as the Cinquecento) from the early 1990s recalls the little Topolino of the inter-war years and serves to sustain Fiat's small-car tradition. Its simple utilitarian appearance was developed with the help of Giorgetto Giugiaro.*

Martin Smith at Audi and then Opel, made their mark on companies across the world. European designers – and Germans in particular, such as Peter Schreyer and Hartmut Warkuss – took the strong luxury brands in new, exciting directions.

Despite the international nature of car design, national trends remained in place as well. The United States, for example, led the way in aggressive, "macho" cars, rooted in its popular heritage of drag racing and car-customizing, while Japan, with its congested cities, went down the minicar route. The character car, based on earlier classics such as the Citroën 2CV, re-emerged in new guises to demonstrate to the public that the car could be a friend as well as an enemy – it could even be a family pet. The classics to end all classics, the Volkswagen Beetle and the BMC Mini, were revived to prove to consumers that the heroic period of automobile design was not dead but merely sleeping.

Cars targeted at women provided them essentially with two options: they could either choose a car that was easy to drive and park or they could become "one of the boys" and select a car that was racy and exhilarating. Women also got to design cars in the 1990s – although not many.

Paradoxically, just at a time when the world was becoming increasingly aware of the motor car's role in destroying civilization as we know it, the object itself, in the hands of skilled designers, experienced a cultural revival. By reinvigorating the public's relationship with the automobile, designers, described by the American automotive designer Freeman Thomas as "cultural architects", showed us that, while scientists, technologists, and politicians were the ones who would have to provide the real answers to the problem of the car, culture can lead the way and show that change is possible.

UWE BAHNSEN

PRINCIPAL DESIGNS

1960 *Ford Taunus*
1981 *Probe III concept car*
1982 *Ford Sierra*

Ford had first established its German company in Berlin in 1925. It moved to Cologne in 1931 and its first car to bear the Taunus name was launched eight years later. The years after World War II saw a sequence of American-inspired cars made by Ford for the European market which were all known by the same name. There was little to distinguish them from one another, but the subtle aerodynamic curves of the 1960 Taunus made it stand out from the others and show that Ford Germany could produce a car that was not simply a clone of its American counterparts. With its oval headlights and rounded forms the car anticipated the "aero" aesthetic of nearly two decades later.

DESIGNS FOR FORD

The man responsible for the 1960 Taunus was a German, Uwe Bahnsen (b.1930), who had been trained at the Hamburg Academy of Fine Arts and who had joined Ford as a young designer. It was the first time that his influence had been felt, but he was to go on to make Ford of Europe an automotive company that put design above engineering. In 1976 Bahnsen was made vice-president in charge of design at Ford of Europe. The fuel crisis of that decade had prioritized the roles of efficiency and economy in automotive manufacture and design and Bahnsen took the message fully on board in his attempt to evolve a

BELOW The Ford Taunus of 1960. The simple aerodynamic shape of this car combined with its light weight provided a new way forward for car design which many were to follow.

ABOVE A full-size studio rendering of a dramatic Sierra derivative. The 1982 Sierra represented such a breakthrough that it set the pace for several design proposals to come. Its curvaceous, aerodynamically inspired form was appropriate to an era in which diminishing resources were increasingly on the agenda.

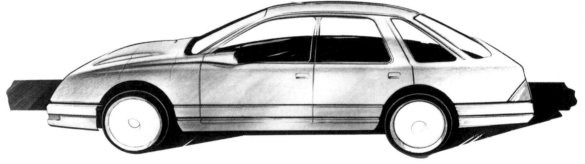

ABOVE *The Probe III concept car was exhibited in Detroit in 1981, to prepare the public for the advent of the startling new Sierra the following year. The new emphasis on aerodynamics was stressed.*

RIGHT *A sketch of the Ford Sierra, designed by Bahnsen and his team.*

new aesthetic that would appeal to the wary car consumers of those difficult years. He was conscious that the showiness of Italian styling had lost its appeal in the new climate and that cars produced in the 1970s should be sending out a different message.

In 1972 Jack Telnack, then head of design at Ford of Germany, had launched the first fully "aero-styled" car: the Fiesta. This new look combined sculptural form with a functional image, the hard intersections between the metal components suggesting a technology-conscious approach. Subsequent designs abandoned this fluid car aesthetic, however, in favour of a sharper style, inspired by the Italians, which became known as the "razor-edge" look.

THE FORD SIERRA

Two of Bahnsen's key designs from the early 1980s, the second-generation Escort and the Ford XR3 Cabrio concept car, were created along these lines, in addition to a number of other cars created under his leadership, the Mark II and Mark III Capri and the Mark IV Cortina, but 1982 saw the launch of a revolutionary design for Ford – the Sierra – which took the aero look into a new incarnation.

From 1976 the Taunus had become identical to the Cortina, the car sold in Britain that combined American with Italian styling and which had become a popular icon meriting a television program about its deep cultural significance. By the early 1980s this car needed replacing, and the Sierra was developed to this end. It began as a concept car, the Probe III, created by Bahnsen's team with the help of Ghia and launched in Frankfurt in 1981. The following year saw an intensive program of development supervised by Bahnsen which included wind-tunnel testing, aesthetic analysis of the curved forms to be used, and extensive consumer research. The final model both looked and was functional. Its sculptural forms spoke the language of fuel efficiency, economy, safety, and quality, and the interior stressed the importance of the driver and provided an ergonomic cabin.

Bahnsen's main achievement with the Sierra was the provision of a car for the moment, whose look symbolized what was needed in the early 1980s – a combination of efficiency, safety, and pleasure. It was a breakthrough for Ford of Europe, showing that this mass-production, globally oriented manufacturer could value the importance of design as highly as any of the Italian firms rooted in coachbuilding traditions.

THE FAR EAST EXPLOSION

Until the last couple of decades, cars created by Japanese and Korean, and latterly Malaysian and Taiwanese, manufacturers have been considered somewhat second-rate in design terms. Although cars from the Far East were linked with advanced manufacturing techniques and affordability their reputation, where their appearance was concerned, was for being derivative, unimaginative, and aesthetically unsophisticated. Whereas Japan managed to call on its unique craft and design traditions in the areas of contemporary architecture and product design, its car designers seemed unable to translate a similar level of sensitivity into that complex object, the automobile.

THE BEGINNINGS OF INNOVATION

Gradually, however, things have changed. The design impact of Far Eastern cars is a fairly recent phenomenon and one initiated by the "retro" movement of the 1980s and 1990s, in which companies such as Nissan, Toyota, and Mazda created a number of highly original cars (among them the Nissan Figaro, the Nissan Pao, and the Mazda Maita) that combined a strong nostalgic feel with a new sensibility. The rash of microcars that came from Japan and Korea in the 1990s,

such as the Suzuki Wagon, the Daihatsu Move, and the Daewoo Matiz, also made Western designers look up and realize that the Far East was making inroads into innovative design.

JAPANESE AUTOMOBILES

The roots of the cars emerging from the Far East lie in a deeper history, however. Japan led the way in automobile manufacture. Several of its leading manufacturers were established in the years between the two world wars. Mitsubishi was producing cars back in the 1920s while Nissan and Toyota both created cars in the 1930s. The Toyota Model AA of 1936, for example, was modelled along the lines of the Chrysler De Soto Airflow (see pp.32–3). When, in 1939 the "Big Three" American manufacturers – Chrysler, Ford, and General Motors – left Japan, having been there since the 1920s, the Japanese car industry took a leap forward. The early 1950s saw the production of a number of mini and three-wheeler cars, Suzuki's Suzulite of 1955 and Fuji's Subaru 360 among them, and Japan quickly became known for producing very small, low-priced cars.

The Japanese "people's car" was a product of the late 1950s and 1960s. Toyota's Publica model of 1961 represented this new

ABOVE *Toyota's Celica 1600 coupé was reminiscent, visually, of Western models. Its main advantage over its competitors was low maintenance costs. When cars such as this flooded the American and European markets in the 1970s they offered reliable cars at an affordable price.*

LEFT *Honda was one of the few Japanese companies to think about the appearance of its cars from an early date. Its Civic model, seen here, was a neat, compact car with clean lines, and it proved popular in an American market on the lookout for smaller cars.*

direction, while Nissan's Datsun Bluebird of a couple of years earlier had been created for similar purposes. In design terms these automobiles echoed American and British models, but their size was particular to the Japanese context. The country soon acquired a reputation for producing small passenger cars and the decade from 1965 to 1975 saw an unprecedented expansion in the manufacture of cars for personal use. The period has come to be called the "my car era" for this reason.

In 1973 Japan suffered considerably from the fuel crisis of that year. However, the crisis had the double effect of slowing down car manufacture but at the same time making the American market aware of the efficiency advantages of Japanese cars over the American gas-guzzlers. This meant that exports increased significantly, and the Japanese car became a global phenomenon in a short period of time. During the 1970s and 1980s Japan extended the level of automation in its factories, bringing in robots to replace human labour. The country was also aware, from an early date, of the implications of pollution, car safety, and recycling, such that they led the field in the ecological aspect of car production, consumption, and use and have continued to do so more recently as well.

A CAR FOR EVERY LIFESTYLE

By the 1980s Japan had become the world's second largest manufacturer of automobiles, after the United States. Design was still not a key issue as very few Japanese cars could be viewed as having any level of sophistication in this area. Among the exceptions were the products of the Honda company, especially the Civic of 1973, which had a distinctive look and was admired by many. The Honda company had been established by Soichiro Honda, one of the very few names associated with car manufacture and design in Japan, and had expanded from motorcycles to personal cars.

The 1980s saw a shift in Japanese car manufacturing as it transferred its energies from production technologies to considering the market, both at home and abroad. A new emphasis on marketing led to a fragmentation of automobile production, so that small passenger cars were joined by larger cars – the Nissan President and the Toyota Century had led the way back in the 1960s – and automobiles for new specific groups of consumers, such as women and young people. Competition from American and European manufacturers lay behind these developments to a certain extent, but the sophistication with which Japan targeted its cars at different

"lifestyles" was based on its deep understanding of the changing market for cars. Before anywhere else did so, Japan understood that the car was, in essence, simply another product that could be marketed alongside fashion goods and hi-fi sets. As a consequence, it launched into the manufacture of a number of new automobile types, including MPVs (multi-purpose vehicles), SUVs (sports utility vehicles), sedans, microcars, and small passenger cars, in the knowledge that each one would fit a different lifestyle. Like North America and Europe, Japan is currently interested in "crossover" vehicles, which mix automobile types and lifestyle scenarios.

CLASSIC REVIVAL

The lifestyle emphasis of the 1980s gave way to the interest in revivalism of the 1990s. Japan had produced no real classic cars of its own so it looked to European examples in creating, for example, its little Nissan S-Cargo (based on the Citroën 2CV). Mazda used the British sports car of the 1950s and 1960s as the inspiration for its revival of the convertible roadster with its Maita and MX5 models. Japanese car designers, in the tradition of the Japanese corporate man, remained anonymous team workers and very few individual's names therefore reached the mass media. One exception to this is

ABOVE *Mazda's MX5 sports car, based on the Lotus Elan, was one of many Japanese cars that sought, in the 1980s and 1990s, to provide new versions of old favourites. Recalling the European sports car of the 1950s and 1960s, Mazda aimed itself at a young international market seeking an affordable "fun" car.*

RIGHT *In pursuit of a "lifestyle" car, the Mitsubishi company produced the Colt Shogun, a sports utility vehicle in a direct line of descent from the Land Rover and the Range Rover. It appealed greatly to both urban and rural dwellers in Europe and the United States.*

Shiro Nakamura, who trained in the West and went back to Japan to head the Nissan design studio. With the development of the Nissan Micra, Nakamura explains, the company was in search of a timeless design that had more in common with the BMC Mini (see pp.106–9) than with transitory lifestyle vehicles. With its more recent Cube, however, Nissan is creating a new trend, following on from the earlier microcars, producing high, square vehicles for city driving and easy parking which maximize their interior space.

Recently there has been a growing trend in naming designers. This goes against the Japanese tendency to emphasize the role of the corporation and underplay the role of the individual. The decision to begin to let car designers' names be visible was a mark of Japan's increasing imitation of practices common in the United States and Europe. By the end of the century a number of Japanese car designers' names had become familiar within the world of automobile styling and they quickly acquired as much cult status as Italian and American designers. One such figure, Honda's Masahito Nakano, has

spoken of the need, in the early 21st century, for Japanese designers to "clear their minds" and move into a state of Zen in which they can be free to be inspired by a wide range of natural sources such as lakes, deserts, or crystals. This is a new attitude and one that suggests that Japanese car designers, like Japanese contemporary architects, have reached a new level of confidence. Nakamura also talks of the need for "clarity and honesty".

BLUEPRINT FOR THE FUTURE

Car design has developed rapidly in Korea as well as in Japan. Like the Japanese manufacturers that have factories and design studios in the West, companies such as Hyundai, Daewoo, and Ssanyong are using Western designers to help them create competitive cars. With their deep aesthetic traditions behind them it is inevitable that, once confident, these countries, together with Taiwan, Malaysia, and eventually China, will develop an automobile design tradition that is bound to influence the rest of the world in a significant way.

LEFT *More than any other country at that time, Japan pushed forward the automated mass production of automobiles in the 1970s and 1980s. In its attempt to capture international markets it refined its production methods and opened factories in host countries where its models were in demand.*

WOMEN AND CARS

Throughout the 20th century car culture was dominated by men as the main drivers, consumers, and designers of automobiles. The self-perpetuating masculine world thus created has tended to exclude women to a significant extent and has encouraged the development of a gendered culture. In turn cars, with their traditional emphasis on speed, power, and advanced engineering, have come to represent the world and values of men.

ELECTRIC CARS AND THE LADIES' AID

This is not, of course, the whole story. Women have had a part to play in the development and design of the modern automobile, although to a large extent at the periphery until recently. During the first decade of the 20th century in the United States and Europe, for example, when motoring was still an upper-class leisure activity and most cars were chauffeur-driven, men and women participated equally in the sport. The availability of the electric car in the first decade of the 20th century gave women their own automobile for use when shopping or visiting friends and manufacturers were eager to make women aware of the easy, clean, and safe properties of this new transportation

object. The decision to use petrol as the main fuel for automobiles rather than electricity represented the first step in the marginalization of women in the world of motoring.

Charles Kettering's invention of the automatic self-starter, known as the "ladies' aid", was an encouragement for women to stay motoring, but it was only the most strong-minded who persevered. Wealthy women, among them the art critic Gertrude Stein, were keen motorists, while the French artist and textile designer Sonia Delaunay decorated her car to match the pattern on her coat.

DECISIONS ON BUYING

World War I brought many women into closer contact with the world of transportation than before, and the number of female drivers increased steadily through the inter-war years, although nothing like as fast as the number of men.

However, those years did see – if the large manufacturers are to be believed – a significant increase in the number of women who made the purchasing decisions about family cars. This stemmed from the shift from utilitarian and economic values as the key ones

determining consumption decisions to an emphasis on notions such as beauty, comfort, and social status as the qualities consumers sought in their automobiles. These "feminine" values were best judged, it was felt, by women themselves, who were much more interested than men in style, colour, and status. As a consequence the car manufacturers turned to targeting women directly and appealed to them in advertisements.

WOMEN IN THE STUDIOS

This "feminization" of car culture persisted into the 1950s, when car aesthetics continued to determine consumer decisions. Both Ford and General Motors employed women in their styling studios in order to better meet the needs of "women's tastes". In 1945 Ford employed two women, increasing the number to six two years later; GM had nine female designers on board by 1958. None of these women was involved with car exteriors, however. Their visualizing talents were confined to car interiors, colours, and accessories. Nineteen fifty-nine saw GM exhibit a number of what it called "Fem show cars" as a mark of what was felt to be the important role of women within car culture.

ABOVE *The 1950s saw several of the large American car manufacturers bringing women into their styling studios, mostly to work on interiors. Pictured here is a designer from the mid-decade surrounded by a multitude of model cars.*

Nevertheless, none of this changed the "macho" atmosphere of Harley Earl's studio (see pp.22–5) or those of the other leading stylists. The commitment to an automotive aesthetic that used jets and space rockets as its source of inspiration (see pp.124–7) showed just how masculine the culture of car design really was in these years.

WOMEN DRIVERS

Notwithstanding the misleading nature of the so-called feminization of car culture in the middle years of the century (in reality it provided a justification for men to show that they appreciated style and colour as much as women did, although they could not admit to it so easily), increasing numbers of women joined the ranks of car drivers through the 1960s, 1970s, and beyond. At first their needs were met by the provision of small cars, the bubble cars (see pp.112–13) and models such as Alec Issigonis' BMC Mini (see pp.106–9) being perceived as ideal for these purposes. Indeed the tradition of the "second car", a means of transport for shopping and picking up the children from school, became a commonly understood phenomenon and many manufacturers moved into this new market.

More recently, models such as the Fiat Punto have been promoted as having plenty of space for shopping bags, as being easy to park, and as seeming "as easy to manoeuvre as a vacuum cleaner". Many

ABOVE *The 1950s saw several of the large American car manufacturers bringing women into their styling studios, mostly to work on interiors. Pictured here is a designer from the mid-decade surrounded by a multitude of model cars.*

cars are advertised in women's magazines, prominent among them the Suzuki Wagon – one of the Japanese microcars that are targeted primarily at women and which has also been described as "a car that's a dream to park" – and the Mercedes SLK, not so much a car for shopping as a fashion accessory in itself and an opportunity for women to show that they have a masculine side and can enjoy driving a stylish, powerful car as much as men. A similar psychology may apply to the increasing numbers of women driving four-wheel drives and big, tough automobiles like Volvos. Another explanation is that women feel very safe in these large "tanks", and it is clear that for many women safety ranks highly as a desirable quality in cars.

WOMEN DESIGN CARS

The involvement of women in automobile purchasing and driving has undoubtedly been more dramatic than their presence in the world of automobile design. While, in the wake of the example set by Ford and General Motors, more and more manufacturers have started to use women in their interior design departments, to date very few have

BELOW *The Mercedes-Benz SLK fulfils the role of a woman's sports car, playing a part in the transformation from women being used to sell cars to women as drivers. Its elegant lines make it a fashion accessory as well as a means of transport.*

RIGHT *The little Nissan Micra of 1998 is one of the many small cars that appeal to women. The use of a car for shopping and taking children to school has increased in recent years and certain cars are targeted at women for these purposes.*

employed female exterior stylists. One notable exception is Renault, which employed the French designer Anne Asensio to work on the concept for the Mégane Scénic and a number of other models. The justification for this may lie in the increasing importance of the notion of the "brand" in car design. As there was in the inter-war years there is still today a silent belief that women are nearer to comprehending the psychology of the marketplace than men and that, therefore, they have an instinctive understanding of what constitutes an effective brand. Asensio has since moved on to General Motors to help it with its brand development.

Although it is impossible to say whether or not men and women design cars differently there are signs that different priorities may affect the way in which the two genders approach car design. While to date the only "feminine" traits of cars have been their emphasis on aesthetics and their strong links with social status, Asensio's decision to interview children to help with the design of the rear seating area of the Scénic (with the result that there is plenty of space in the back, and holders for drinks), shows a new approach to designing which puts the user much more in the foreground.

HOPE FOR THE FUTURE

The increasing participation of women in car culture in the early 21st century compared to the picture a century ago is an indication that the masculine traditions that have been so strong in the story of modern car design may not, as in so many other walks of life, be so dominant in the future.

J. MAYS

PRINCIPAL DESIGNS

1994	*VW Concept 1 (with Freeman Thomas)*
1997	*Mercury MC4 concept car*
1999	*Mercury Cougar concept car*
2000	*Ford 24.7 concept car*

One of the youngest of the designers heading the styling operations of the United States' "Big Three" automobile manufacturers, J. Mays (b.1955) took over the reins from Jack Telnack at Ford in 1997. In the late 1990s Ford was behind General Motors and what had recently become DaimlerChrysler in the styling stakes, and Mays inherited a challenge that he confronted immediately. His was a fresh approach, which focused on the emotional, non-rational meanings of cars and the designer's power to create evocative and distinctive images. For Mays, Ford's "brands" – including Mercury and Lincoln and the European and Far Eastern firms for which the American giant was responsible, Volvo, Jaguar, Aston Martin, and Mazda – needed to be dealt with separately, each one developing its own identity.

CAR CULTURE IN DEPTH

Mays was born in rural Oklahoma and, like so many others of his generation, spent a boyhood dominated by cars, whether drag racing or customizing them. He rejected his first chosen career in journalism to attend the Art Center College in California and from there, after his

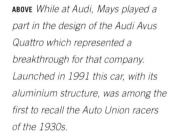

ABOVE *While at Audi, Mays played a part in the design of the Audi Avus Quattro which represented a breakthrough for that company. Launched in 1991 this car, with its aluminium structure, was among the first to recall the Auto Union racers of the 1930s.*

LEFT *The Ford Cougar was one of the company's concept cars developed under the leadership of Mays following his take-over from Telnack in 1997. Its curvaceous, aerodynamic form is combined with crisp edges to create a style that has been dubbed "New Edge" design.*

BELOW *The Mercury MC4 concept car from 1997 was developed while Mays was in charge of Ford's styling. With its rear gull-wing opening and lack of a central pillar between the front and rear doors it proposed a new structure for the family car.*

graduation in 1980, he headed straight for Europe, where he worked for Audi in Germany, with a brief spell at BMW. Audi was an important turning point in Mays' career and he contributed to the design of a number of models, among them the Avus concept car.

In 1989 Mays returned to the United States to become chief designer for Volkswagen in California, where he was responsible for the development of the Concept 1, the precursor of the new Beetle launched later. His partner in the project was Freeman Thomas, the American designer who went on the create the influential Audi TT. Mays' involvement at this time with what might be called a "retro" project (although he prefers the word "heritage" and is adamant that the result was forward- rather than backward-looking, as the Concept 1 was articulated in the language of the late 20th century) would lead to other exercises later, notable among them the revival of Ford's famous Thunderbird and the development of a new design, the Ford Forty-Nine concept car, which looked back to the 1949 model (see pp.142–3) that had taken the manufacturing company successfully into the postwar era.

Following his time with Volkswagen, Mays returned to Audi for a short period in 1993 as design director, but left in the following year to work in a slightly different capacity for a brand identity company called SHR Perceptual Management. Here he was involved less with drawing-board design and more with strategic thinking and branding, and he expanded his skills considerably as a result. In 1997 Jack Telnack asked him to be his successor and his reign at Ford began.

VISUAL MESSAGES AND ON-BOARD COMMUNICATIONS

Mays talks frequently about the influence of movies on his work. He is particularly intrigued by the visual strategies used by directors to engage their audiences and hold their attention. He is also fascinated by the worlds of fashion and architecture and sees both disciplines as having a huge impact on car design and meaning. In the late 20th century both those visual worlds had succeeded, he feels, in learning how to catch people's eye and create powerful, instantly received images and messages.

In the context of Ford he is concerned not to create luxury cars but to engage with concepts for affordable cars that are nonetheless powerful and meaningful. A recent project, the Ford 24.7 concept car, shown in 2000 in wagon, coupé, and pickup versions, manifests a new body language of flat planes and sharp edges (whereas Telnack had promoted a style called "New Edge Design" which combined curves and sharp edges). More than that, however, it also took the idea of in-car communications a step forward, with its link to the Internet and the transformation of its dashboard into a huge monitor.

WAYNE CHERRY

Like J. Mays (see pp.214–15) of Ford and Tom Gale (see pp.222–3) of DaimlerChrysler, Wayne Cherry (b.1938), the man responsible for General Motors' styling turnaround in the 1990s, spent his teenage years drag racing and enjoying America's indigenous automotive culture. His long-standing enthusiasm for that culture underpinned the strongly styled range of vehicles that GM began to launch on the world in the last years of the 20th century. The philosophy guiding the creation of those striking vehicles, the Pontiac Piranha and the Chevrolet Traverse among them, was rooted in Cherry's deeply felt belief in the importance of automotive power and imagery for the American car-buying public. Just as the Chevrolets of the mid-1950s had symbolized the values of a generation of young people at that time, so, believes Cherry, today's cars must have the same potential to be more than merely a means of transportation.

DESIGN TRANSFORMATION

It took some time for Cherry to find a way of transforming GM's cars for the American market. On graduating from the Art Center College of Design in Los Angeles in the early 1960s he went to Europe, working for Vauxhall in England for a decade and a half before transferring to

ABOVE AND BELOW *The all-wheel-drive Chevrolet Traverse is a hybrid concept combining the benefits of a sedan car with those of a truck. It has a state-of-the-art interior (above) with GM's OnStar satellite navigation system and a removable laptop computer.*

Opel in Germany (owned by GM), where he was responsible for all GM's passenger cars in Europe. He returned to the United States in 1991 and was made head of design at GM in the following year, taking over the role from Chuck Jordan.

The early 1990s were difficult years for GM and it took a while for the company to pick itself up and begin to think about design. The revolution in American styling that Chrysler and Ford had initiated had an inevitable impact, and Cherry led the way forward. From the early 1990s he had been setting the scene for a growing diversity of GM cars and for a new approach to styling that focused on the individual identities of the company's numerous brands. The concept of "lifestyle" underpinned Cherry's thinking about new models as much as his commitment to American car culture.

Cherry was particularly interested in the American car buyer's love affair with the functionality of the truck, and he set about thinking about possible "crossover" cars that combined characteristic features of trucks with others derived from cars. The Chevrolet Traverse – a vehicle that looks like a car but functions like a truck – was one result of this new approach. The influence of contemporary sports products offered another means of injecting lifestyle values into vehicles and

the Pontiac Piranha showed how cars could borrow features from mountain bikes and camping tents, transforming them into a new automotive language that spoke to a young market keen to link all its purchases to its preferred way of life.

CREATING BRAND IDENTITIES

Most importantly Cherry's main achievement as vice-president of design was to change the structure of GM's styling section to facilitate new developments, which led to such striking designs as the GMC Terradyne concept car, the nearest an automobile has come to a weapon, the Buick LaCrosse, which owed much to its 1950s predecessors, the Chevrolet SSR, the Opel Zafira, and the Saturn CV1. The unique identities of these models were made possible by Cherry's formation of brand character studios, each of which was led by a key stylist and focused on giving each brand a special quality.

Cherry also increased the number of stylists employed by GM and introduced individuals with extensive experience in Europe, notably Anne Asensio from Renault, who took over responsibility for the brand character studios in 2000. By the end of the century Cherry had put together a formidable team with which to take GM styling forward.

CHARACTER CARS

The fuel crisis of the 1970s precipitated a movement in car design that, from the perspective of the early 21st century, can only be described as bland and lacking in character. The need at that time to emphasize sobriety and to demonstrate a conscientious approach to the world's dwindling resources translated itself into a highly utilitarian approach towards car design that, with only a few exceptions, resulted in a rather lacklustre era of car styling.

A NEW EMOTIONALISM

While the commitment to ecological awareness did not disappear in the 1990s it was joined with a new attitude towards car styling which believed it was possible to be conscientious and fun-loving at the same time. The principal impetus behind the "character car" of the 1990s was the realization, on the part of the manufacturers, that the technological aspect of cars was now so refined that customers could no longer make their purchasing decisions on the basis of it alone.

Furthermore, it had become virtually impossible to distinguish between different models. Manufacturers also perceived that a new emotionalism was entering the world of car purchasing and that consumers were increasingly being led by their hearts rather than their heads in deciding on a car. This was partly a result of the increasing number of women and young people who were making choices about car purchases and requiring cars that were meaningful for them. It meant that the look of the car was becoming paramount and that the symbolic meanings were acquiring a new level of significance. Such a recognition presented a new, exciting challenge to car designers.

THE SEARCH FOR MEANINGS

The search for a new meaning, or set of meanings, for the automobile was given a kick-start by the Japanese "retro" car movement, which was set in motion by Nissan and Mazda. These manufacturers sought

ABOVE *Nissan's little Figaro car of the late 1980s, which recalled a French car of the 1950s, was the first of the retro cars. While its form was highly reminiscent of familiar shapes from the past, its technology belonged to the late 20th century, ensuring that it was also a car of its time.*

LEFT *Fiat's odd-looking Multipla model from the late 1990s, with its distinctive bulge below the front window, brought back the idea, which had been tried many decades earlier, of putting three seats next to each other. The result was a new car concept whose looks were as revolutionary as its format.*

to revive a set of familiar car images, to rework them, and to target them at new markets. In so doing they were creating cars that appealed simultaneously through their references to the past and through their novelty. Gone was the attempt to create ever-newer car objects. Instead the challenge was a more subtle one, that of combining a sense of familiarity with a feeling of excitement.

In the search for automobiles from the past that could bear this level and intensity of reworking, designers looked to cars with strong personalities that could be easily referenced by the public. In this way Nissan's quirky little S-Cargo recalled, although did not reproduce, the French company Citroën's much-loved 2CV (see pp.102–5). Lacking their own classic character cars the Japanese were obliged to look to Europe for their inspiration in this field.

THE CAR AS FRIEND

A defining quality of character cars is their ability to act not as an extension of their driver's body but as their driver's friend. They have to exist, therefore, as characters or images in their own right. As a result they have frequently earned themselves nicknames, often based on animals, suggesting that the car, in this context, becomes a

RIGHT *Ford's Ka of the mid-1990s pioneered the "New Edge" look. Its perky shape, evocative of a finely toned body, combined with the way it "sits" on the road, gives it a strong presence and a character all of its own. With its appeal to men and women alike, it is among the first "androgynous" cars.*

LEFT *The eccentric Nissan S-Cargo of the late 1980s took its cue from the popular little French 2CV launched in the late 1940s. The name of this Japanese car, pronounced like the French word for snail (escargot), makes a direct reference to its source, which was known affectionately as the "Tin Snail".*

kind of pet substitute. Classic examples include the VW Beetle (see pp.94–7), the Citroën 2CV, known affectionately as the Tin Snail, and the little Fiat 500 (see pp.98–101), known as the Topolino (Mickey Mouse). Whether perceived as an animal or a familiar cartoon character, these cars all entered the wider lives of their owners.

EXPRESSIONS OF CHARACTER

The character cars of the 1990s borrowed a great deal from these earlier successes in their attempt to create contemporary images that would last. The design strategies utilized to this end included emphasizing the "face" of the car to provide it deliberately with a level of anthropomorphism. Patrick Le Quément's little Twingo for Renault was particularly successful in this respect (see pp.224–7), its headlights topped with a set of "eyebrows" that gave it a quizzical, friendly appearance. The designers of character cars were not in search of beauty in the classic sense by which Italian stylists of the 1950s and 1960s had understood the term. They aimed, instead, for a level of idiosyncrasy or quirkiness that often seemed nearer to ugliness in the conventional sense of the term.

Character was expressed in a number of ways. While the face of the car was important, the way it sat on the road, on "all fours", was also crucial. Ford's Ka of 1997, a car styled in what was called the

New Edge look – a combination of smooth sculpted surfaces with sharp intersections – sits firmly on its four wheels and seems undeniably to have the presence of a small living organism of indeterminate kind. The strong personality of the Ka derives partly from this sense of presence, partly from its distinctive "nose" when viewed from the side, and partly from the strong integration of its parts which gives it a sense of wholeness.

Where Volkswagen's new Beetle is concerned, character is everything. From its profile resembling a toy car to its nostalgic reference to the original VW classic it exudes personality from every angle. One of its designers, Freeman Thomas, has admitted to working primarily from intuition based on his past experience. In creating the car in VW's Simi Valley studio in California, Thomas and his collaborator, J. Mays (see pp.214–15), explained that they wanted to reduce it to its bare essentials in design terms. The result is a kind of caricature of a car. There is even a small vase on the dashboard, a reference back to an accessory offered for the original Beetle. The new Beetle is described by its publicity as being "unconventional, easy-going, youthful and emotional", all the qualities sought for its user as well.

Inasmuch as they make no claims to be beautiful nor to be powerful extensions of the body, the new tribe of small city cars – the

Suzuki Wagon, the Daihatsu Move, the Nissan Cube, Pininfarina's Metrocubo, and Daimler-Benz's Smart car, can be seen as character cars as well. They are designed above all to be functional, but in the process they have all acquired individual identities that make them personality cars first and foremost. The original character cars, including the 2CV, the Beetle, and the Renault 4, were similarly created with utility in mind and quickly acquired strong personalities, which have lasted. Whether this new generation of cars will stand a similar test of time remains to be seen.

PERSONALITY THROUGH UTILITY

Although it does not fit into the small city car category the Fiat Multipla, with its rows of three seats and bullfrog eyes, also eschews beauty in favour of utility. In this instance it is the utility of interior space that is at stake. Once again, however, this rigorous pursuit of function has meant that the car has ended up with a strong individual identity, expressed through its visual idiosyncrasy and its refusal to adhere to the visual rules of "good design".

As designers increasingly set out to solve problems other than those of where to position the waistline to achieve the maximum amount of elegance and how far apart to position the headlights to achieve the correct visual balance, they will inevitably produce cars with individual identities, which in turn will relate to their users in new and interesting ways. And as car manufacturers continue to raid their pasts and look for visual and cultural references that they can rework to provide a level of familiarity for their customers, the future of personality cars is secure.

ABOVE *The interior of BMW's new Mini, created by the American designer Frank Stephenson, reuses several features of Issigonis' original car from the late 1950s, such as the large, open door-pockets. This model boasts a central speedometer and "aluminium-look" plastic.*

BELOW *Although, with its square frame and round headlights, the new Mini recalls its earlier incarnation it is in many ways a different car, roomier and wider. The form of its bonnet has more in common with contemporary cars than with models from 40 years ago.*

THOMAS GALE

PRINCIPAL DESIGNS

(designed under Gale's leadership)

1987 *Chrysler Portofino*
1991 *Chrysler 300 concept car*
1992 *Chrysler Cirrus*
1992 *Dodge Viper*
1993 *Plymouth Prowler*
1994 *Dodge Ram*
2001 *Chrysler PT Cruiser*

In the 1990s Chrysler was ahead of both General Motors and Ford in moving beyond the bland aerodynamic automotive styling of the previous two decades and bringing design to the forefront. The stylist Tom Gale (b.1943) was single-handedly responsible for that achievement. Unlike his equivalents J. Mays (see pp.214–5) and Wayne Cherry (see pp.216–7), Gale did not come to American car design after experience in Europe but gained his distance from his homeland and its car culture by working with Japanese engineers and stylists at Chrysler's partner at that time, Mitsubishi. It was there that he learned to push new concepts forward and to persuade his superiors of the importance of design to late 20th-century car users.

STRATEGY FOR SUCCESS

Like Mays and Cherry, Gale was born into American car culture and was committed to its continuity. His town of origin – Flint, Michigan – was the home of Buick, and his father had worked for General Motors. Gale studied industrial design at Michigan State University, combining a training in engineering with one in art, and he joined Chrysler in 1967 as a body engineer. In 1985, he took over from Don DeLaRossa as head of design. In the 1970s and early 1980s Chrysler had lost its reputation for advanced styling and experienced financial difficulties.

BELOW *Gale's Dodge Viper was among the first "personality" cars that he created for Chrysler. Recalling racy sports and muscle cars from an earlier age and drawing on his own past for inspiration, Gale brought fun back into driving and helped take Chrysler into a new era.*

Gale managed to persuade the chairman, Lee Iacocca (succeeded by Bob Eaton in 1991) to put design on the level of the other disciplines in the company and to move away from the conservative cars with which it had become associated. The strategy led to Chrysler's re-emergence as one of the world's leading car manufacturers.

DESIGN REVOLUTION

The first new concept cars with a design message began to emerge in the early 1990s featuring a new look that came to be known as "cab-forward design". It was a revolutionary new car architecture that stretched the interior and gave a progressive edge to Chrysler's concept and production cars from then on. The striking images that Gale and his team created for models such as the Dodge Ram pickup truck (1994), the Dodge Viper (1992), and the Plymouth Prowler (1993), made the world notice Chrysler for the first time in years. The Prowler was a modern version of a hot rod born of Gale's enthusiasm for drag racing. Its revolutionary looks were a result of Gale's skill in rooting new designs within American car culture and evoking its heroic past while subtly creating a new image at the same time.

The rest of the decade saw a rapid succession of new concept and production cars emerging from Chrysler, all very image- and lifestyle-conscious. In 2001 it launched the first automobile to be offered simultaneously as a concept and a production car. The PT (Personal Transportation) Cruiser took Gale's thinking to the limit. At once a nostalgic and a progressive car, this family sedan cleverly evoked several different American car traditions, including the hot rod, the 1930s gangster car, and the character automobiles of countless cartoons; details such as its large push-button chrome door handles provide a satisfying memory of what cars used to be like. In spite of its nostalgic associations, the PT Cruiser is also a practical family car for the early 21st century, boasting a large interior space and flexible seating.

Gale's success in re-establishing Chrysler as a car manufacturer that understands the importance of styling has been widely emulated in recent years. He showed how important it had become to present concepts and images that speak to consumers on an emotional level which then offer them the technological sophistication and practicality that they need. After 33 years with Chrysler Gale decided to retire, but his influence will undoubtedly be felt for years.

PATRICK LE QUEMENT

In the early postwar years the French car manufacturer Renault had established itself as a company that valued styling and the individual identity of its small passenger vehicles. Models such as the Renault 4 and the Dauphine had become synonymous with the idiosyncratic French movement in car design of those years. The reputation was enhanced with the launch of the Renaults 5 and 16 in later years but, by the end of the 1980s, it had faded. By the early 1990s the company was in need of a new injection of talent and imagination. It found this in the figure of Patrick Le Quément, who was responsible for a turnaround in the firm's approach to design.

LE QUÉMENT'S BACKGROUND

Le Quément was no stranger to car design when he entered Renault in 1987, having been in the business for more than two decades. He cut his teeth with Simca, and went on to form his own design studio, Style International. The industrial disruptions of 1968 caused him to seek employment once again, and his search took him to the United States, where he was to spend 17 years with Ford. It was a period that made a tremendous impact upon him. Among other benefits it allowed him to see his homeland and its car styling traditions from a distance. While at Ford Le Quément was involved with the "bio-design" movement, as

RIGHT *His interest in Renault's past led Le Quément to put forward an idea for a concept car in 1996, named the Fiftie. Its curved foms and small, sporty profile were highly reminiscent of the little Dauphine of the 1950s that had earned Renault an international reputation.*

LEFT *Patrcik Le Quément was responsible for the development of the Renault Twingo, the cheery personality of which brought it a large popular following. With its little "face" it recalled the smile on the front end of the Renault 4 of the early postwar years.*

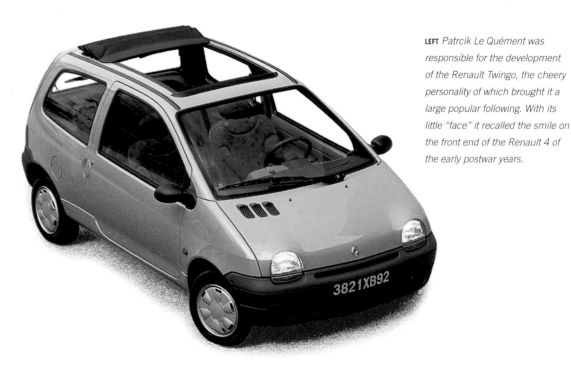

incarnated in the seminal Ford Sierra, and he learned a great deal about automobile aerodynamics. In the mid-1980s, he left the American company and, after a short time with VW, joined Renault as the head of its design team. By the late 1990s he had a team of around 260 people working for him and had transformed design at Renault beyond recognition.

Le Quément's main contribution to Renault design was to bring new car concepts to the fore, to consider design as something that operates within a broad cultural context, and to encourage original thinking. As early as 1994 the Argos concept car showed signs of a new angularity, which was to re-appear some years later. Le Quément was adamant that the look of a car, achieved through the use of angles, lines, forms, and light reflections, played a key role in the importance bestowed on certain cars: "Once they've seen them," he explained, "people should be able to remember our cars immediately, with their eyes shut." The idea of the importance of the instant impact made by a car on the viewer underpinned his approach towards the discipline of car design and helped to make many of Renault's designs so quickly identifiable and so visually memorable.

A NEW DESIGN LANGUAGE

One of the ways in which Le Quément succeeded in developing a new design language for Renault cars was through his policy of employing increasing numbers of product, rather than specialist automobile, designers who brought a different mindset to the problem of creating a car. Linking appearance very closely with overall function they tended to prioritize the total identities of the cars they were working on rather than the superficial shapes of the body-shells. In the late 1990s, for example, when the angular look had become more developed, Le Quément stated his aim to make cars borrow from the iconic power of architectural structures such as Frank Gehry's Guggenheim Museum in Bilbao, thereby providing a new metaphor for the automobile.

The project to revolutionize Renault's cars began in the early 1990s and reached its peak in the early 21st century. Le Quément oversaw the design and production of all the company's cars, both concept and production models. Three production cars characterize the success of his input in those years, namely the Twingo, the Mégane Scénic, and the remodelled Clio, while the concept cars with which his name is closely linked, the Vel Satis, the Koleos, and the

Avantime, served to take his ideas into the future. The name of Anne Asensio – the third-ranked designer at Renault in the 1990s, responsible for the design of its medium-sized cars – is also closely linked with the same three cars and she played an important role in their conception. Trained in Paris and Detroit she too had had the advantage of having looked at France from abroad and was able, as a consequence, to think radically about new directions for the company.

BELOW *Le Quément's Avantime concept developed the new look that had been launched with the Koleos concept, this time articulated in the context of a car that was a cross between an MPV and a conventional coupé.*

CREATIVE PRODUCTION CARS

The Twingo carried forward the concept of the "character car" that Renault had established in the early postwar years. Its jovial "face" gave this little car a unique identity and showed that Renault had not lost its ability to create memorable cars. The Clio also featured subtle lines and curves and, in the tradition of the Renaults 4 and 5, showed the company's lead in the area of well-conceived and attractive small urban cars. What was more, as the popular advertising campaign that accompanied the launch of the car made clear, the Clio was promoted as being, above all, the product of French creativity and style.

The Mégane Scénic, the concept for which had been created by Asensio in 1991, was one of Renault's great success stories of that decade. Building on the success of the pioneering Espace, Europe's first MPV (multi-purpose vehicle) or "people-carrier", the Scénic showed how a family car could maximize interior space without being excessively large in an urban context. Its curved forms took Renault's involvement with sculptural, aerodynamic shape to new heights.

RADICAL CONCEPTS

Le Quément's concept cars of the 1990s were more radical in appearance than the production cars. Their aim was to take Renault into the area of luxury cars, an arena France had not inhabited since the 1930s. Starting with the Vel Satis, Renault's cars for the future featured large areas of glass, sharp angles, and a highly distinctive rear end which quickly became a hallmark of Renault's late 1990s show cars. Koleos, a luxury sports utility vehicle (SUV), was launched at the Geneva show in 2000. Its radical "Mad Max" appearance attracted much attention and announced the fact that Renault was heading towards establishing a completely new car aesthetic. Moving beyond the company's reputation in the areas of small cars and people carriers it clearly had ambitions to compete with the strong German luxury automotive brands, Mercedes-Benz and BMW.

The Avantime, first shown in concept form in Geneva in 1999, also went down the luxury route, this time fusing the idea of the MPV with the more conventional coupé. In a recent interview (1999) Le Quément talked about a game he played as a child which involved putting the head of one animal with the body of another to create a new hybrid. It is a tactic that he is currently applying to the automobile and the results are extremely radical and exciting.

More than anything else Le Quément has introduced a new confidence into Renault, which enables experimentation to take place. With his international team of hand-picked experts around him he has been able to inject a level of enthusiasm and adventure into the company. He has also replaced the concept of "styling" with that of "design" and shown that there are still new directions in which to take the car of the 21st century.

PETER SCHREYER

PRINCIPAL DESIGNS

1996 *Audi A3*
1999 *Audi TT*
2000 *Audi A4 (new model)*
2000 *Audi A2*
2001 *Audi Rosemeyer*

Since the mid-1990s, the car designer Peter Schreyer has been responsible for the transformation of the design policy and achievements of the German manufacturer Audi AG. Schreyer studied industrial design in Munich before moving to London's Royal College of Art in 1979. After a period at VW with J. Mays (see pp.214–5) he took over the reins at Audi in 1994, and set about putting a new culture in place that highlighted the role of design. The policy he introduced focused on the use of a clearly identifiable design language for all the company's products and the establishment of a strong Audi brand through the creation of a family resemblance for all its vehicles.

PAST AND FUTURE

The look that Schreyer developed for Audi's products – including the A8, A6, and A4 launched in 1994, the A3 of 1996, the TT of 1999, the new A4 and the A2 of 2000 – was decidedly futuristic yet reminiscent of the aerodynamic, all-aluminium sports cars produced in the 1930s by Auto Union, a name given to a group of four manufacturers of which Audi was one. The TT had a particularly strong retro feel to it. Its evocative form was inspired by a doodle made by Freeman Thomas, who had been brought into Audi by Mays in 1991.

ABOVE *Audi's Rosemeyer sports car represents the German company's most radical design to date. This sleek, all-aluminium car with its dominant bull-nosed front is named after Bernd Rosemeyer, a renowned Auto Union racing driver of the inter-war years.*

LEFT *The Audi TT, launched in 1999, is one of Schreyer's greatest design successes. Reminiscent of the all-aluminium sports cars created by Auto Union back in the 1930s it combines a nostalgic feel with a thoroughly contemporary sense of brand identity.*

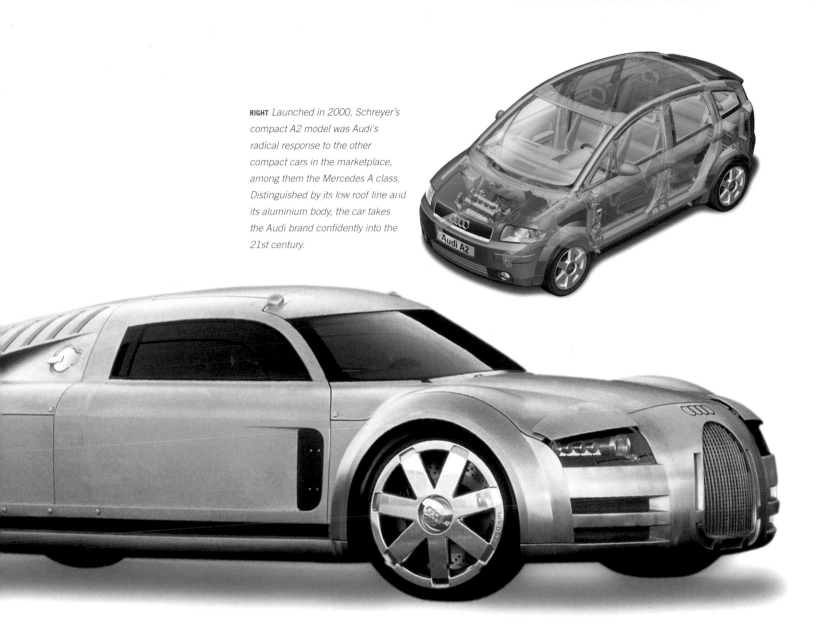

RIGHT *Launched in 2000, Schreyer's compact A2 model was Audi's radical response to the other compact cars in the marketplace, among them the Mercedes A class. Distinguished by its low roof line and its aluminium body, the car takes the Audi brand confidently into the 21st century.*

Some of Schreyer's initiatives were based on earlier developments, several of them initiated when Hartmut Warkuss (see pp.232–3) had been in charge of Audi's design policy. In 1980 the company had produced the Quattro and had begun to show a newfound confidence and a determination to compete with Mercedes-Benz and BMW in the luxury car market. In 1990 the Avus concept had gone on show, while 1991 saw the launch of the Quattro Spyder, which began to make commentators take notice. In the same year two aluminium studies were shown pointing the way forward for the Audi brand.

INTO THE FUTURE

The use of aluminium was a mark of both technological and ecological progressive thinking on the part of Audi (it also provided a means of evoking the past). Both light and recyclable, aluminium was taking on a new meaning for designers in the 1990s, and in 1993 Audi pioneered the development of what it named its ASF (Aluminium Space Frame) which made it possible to use this evocative material for car bodies. Its light silvery colour also proved to be a key branding exercise for Audi's cars of the second half of that decade and came to be a hallmark of these stylish German cars.

Schreyer's styling approach emphasized simple body-shells made of large, clear panels that looked as if they were made out of one piece of metal, a reduction of lines, the implementation of a single curved line from the front pillar right through to the tail-lights, and a continuity of line from the metal areas to the glass surfaces. Wheel arches were reduced and radiator grilles and headlights made to conform with the lines of the curved metal panels. This reductive approach resulted in a simple, sporty profile, which was more or less common to all vehicles, varying only according to the size of the model. From the large A8 sedan down to the compact A2 the Audi look is clearly recognizable, providing a coherent image for this progressive company.

"I am less interested," Schreyer has said, "in following the spirit of the age than in finding shapes that possess a timeless beauty." His commitment to such a strong aesthetic over more than half a decade confirms his belief. At the same time, each new model is a little more daring than the one before. In 2001 one of Audi's most radical designs was launched, a study for the first of its "supercars" – the Project Rosemeyer, named after Bernd Rosemeyer, one of Auto Union's best-known racing drivers. As Audi's designs become increasingly futuristic the links with the company's heritage become stronger and stronger.

ECO-CARS

As the number of cars on the streets continues to grow, one of the biggest challenges to car manufacturers in the 21st century is to respond to the moral and regulatory requirements relating to car safety, car-created pollution, and the contribution of the car to the depletion of the world's resources. More than any other single product the car is responsible for contributing to problems in these areas, primarily through exhaust emissions and the use of petrol as its main fuel. These issues have been live ones ever since the mid-1960s, when Ralph Nader published his *Unsafe at any Speed* in the United States, and the fuel crisis of the 1970s; but, with pollution becoming an everyday reality in all the world's cities and the notion of dwindling resources digging deeper into the public's consciousness, stronger demands for solutions have emerged.

THE WAY AHEAD

Inevitably the large manufacturers have taken the issues on board and are investing vast sums of money in researching the ways forward. Most energies are directed at finding an alternative fuel or fuels. A number of options are being proposed, among them the re-emergence of the electric car and the use of hydrogen, whether in liquid or fuel cell form.

The German firm BMW has made progress with liquid hydrogen and, although they are not yet available on the market, has manufactured several models in its new 7 series that can run on this new fuel. It is stored in a tank behind the rear seats. Ford has teamed up with DaimlerChrysler, and General Motors with Toyota, to explore the possibilities of powering their cars with hydrogen fuel cells, but

ABOVE *Ford's little electric THINK city car of 2000 is one solution to the problem of parking and fuel consumption. To achieve lightness a considerable amount of plastic is used in its construction. Its simple form is aerodynamic but unshowy and it exudes an air of functionality and practicality.*

LEFT *Nissan's Hypermini, launched in 1997, belongs to the family of small-scale city cars with which the problems of urban travel and the environment are being addressed. Light in weight, it is intended for short, local journeys. Once again its form is aerodynamic and its form is very function-oriented.*

RIGHT *Mazda's HR-X2, an experimental car driven by hydrogen, which was shown in 1993 along with an electric car. Mazda is one of the key Japanese companies thinking about alternative power sources for cars. They are also experimenting with new ways of making cars safer to drive.*

they are some way off from finding the solution and being able to make it available to the mass market.

Electric cars come with disadvantages attached to them which make them less than fully attractive to the mass market. The difficulty of having to plug them in to recharge them is combined with the fear of coming to a sudden halt in an inconvenient place when the batteries run out of power. While there is a place at the margins of things for electrically powered cars it is clear that they too are not going to provide the complete answer.

A HYBRID SOLUTION

The best solution to date is the hybrid car, which combines a petrol engine with an electric motor. To date the Japanese are ahead of the Americans and Europeans in this area. Honda launched its hybrid Insight model in 2000, the first eco-car to reach the market that confronted both the issues of fuel and design together. Most eco-car proposals tend to ignore the aesthetic end of things, recapturing instead the spirit of invention and experimentation that characterized developments in the "horseless carriage" in the early 20th century.

Honda rightly realized that it had to re-create the marriage of art and technology that had been achieved in the petrol-driven car as the clock could not be turned back. The result was a sleek car with a hint of retro in its 1960s-style futurism. Its highly appropriate experimental image was reinforced by the innovativeness of its technology. A petrol engine in the front was joined by an electric engine in the rear (the batteries are in the boot) and, for the purposes of weight reduction, its body was made entirely of aluminium and nylon. The Insight is the first "real" car to offer the hybrid solution to the general buying public. It offers real advantages among them 30 km/litre (83 mpg) and the generation of only half the carbon dioxide into the atmosphere of comparable small cars. Honda sees its production as an investment for the future rather than an immediate financial proposition.

Toyota has also produced a hybrid car, the Prius, and is working on a minivan and an SUV. The problem lies in developing a car with the appropriate technology that also appeals to consumers. The challenge to designers is to create an aesthetic that is "of the moment" and symbolically in keeping with the spirit of an age in which people value the planet they inhabit and the resources it has to offer.

LEFT *In 2000 Honda launched its Insight model, a hybrid car with a petrol engine in the front and an electric motor in the back. With its all-aluminium body, it is half the weight of the average family sedan. It has a retro look, reminiscent of an old Citroën.*

HARMUT WARKUSS

PRINCIPAL DESIGNS

1999 *Bugatti EB 18/3 Chiron*

1999 *Bugatti EB 16/4 Veyron*
(with Fabrizio Giugiaro)

2000 *Advanced Activity*
concept car

By the 1990s Volkswagen had become one of Europe's largest car manufacturers, responsible for four brands – VW itself, Audi, the Spanish company Seat, and the Czech company Skoda. Increasingly, for reasons of economy, the company's director, Ferdinand Piech, focused on the advantages of rationalizing production and introducing platform sharing (using the same chassis for different models). This inevitably placed greater emphasis on the skills of the designer to be able to differentiate the brands in new ways.

BRAND DEVELOPMENT

Hartmut Warkuss was head of design at Audi until Peter Schreyer (see pp.228–9) replaced him, and in 1994 he became overall design chief for the whole organization. He quickly developed a policy of putting a number of different design studios in place in order to develop the discrete brands. Peter Schreyer took on Audi at Ingolstadt, while Warkuss remained head of Volkswagen studio at Wolfsburg. Gert Hildebrand headed Seat's studio at Martorell (Walter da Silva later moved from Alfa Romeo to head the Seat studio) while Skoda had its own design section at Mlada Boleslv. In addition VW opened a small

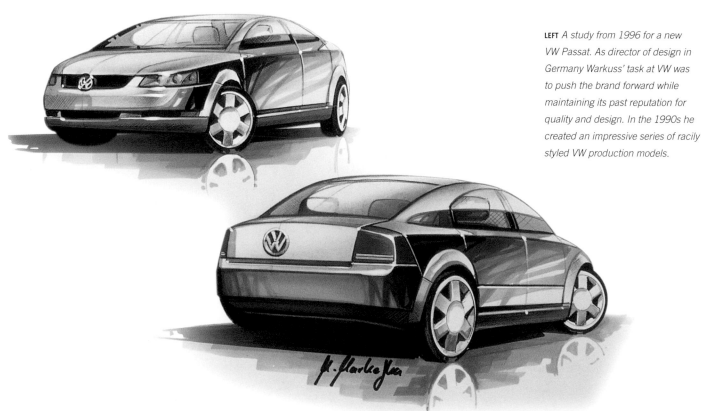

LEFT *A study from 1996 for a new VW Passat. As director of design in Germany Warkuss' task at VW was to push the brand forward while maintaining its past reputation for quality and design. In the 1990s he created an impressive series of racily styled VW production models.*

sludio in Brazil, and two research centres, one in Simi Valley in California and the other in Catalonia. Each brand took on a special identity – Audis were "sporty", Volkswagens were "functional", Seals were "young", and Skodas were "classic".

THE VW RENAISSANCE

Design at VW itself had been in decline in the years leading up to the early 1990s. The jolt needed to bring the company out of this cul-de-sac was provided by the California studio, where the designers J. Mays (see pp.214–15) and Freeman Thomas set out, in 1993, to revive the legendary VW Beetle (see pp.94–7). The project for "Concept 1" was developed behind closed doors; the idea was shown to Warkuss, then head of Audi design, and he took on the responsibility of selling the idea to VW. Two clay models were made and the words "simple, reliable, honest and original" (the last provided by Warkuss) used to sell the project. The new Beetle finally became a reality in 1998.

Mays and Thomas were soon to leave VW, the former for Ford and the latter for DaimlerChrysler. Warkuss' challenge was to continue the program that had been put in place and to ensure that VW continued to be rejuvenated. His strategy was twofold: to present a number of concept cars that would show that the company was looking to the future, and to revamp its existing production cars, namely the Jetta, the Golf, the Passat, and the Cabrio convertible. Among the concept cars to make an impact was the AAC (Advanced Activity Concept), shown in 2000, which combined the function of an off-road pickup with the comfort of a luxury sedan. The vehicle deliberately avoided the utilitarian American pickup image and instead used sophisticated styling to evoke a much more luxurious car. The recognizable signs of the VW, such as the V-shaped hood, the broad fenders, and the twin circular headlights, were included to link the product with the well-known European brand.

In keeping with the nostalgia that surrounded the success of the new Beetle, VW also looked back to another of its historical classics, the Microbus. A design study was shown in 2001 which demonstrated what the van of the future would look like.

While Warkuss' role was to mastermind the strategy underpinning VW's renaissance, he also became involved in designing, with Fabrizio Giugiaro, a new Bugatti concept. This was the W18/3 Chiron, which, along with the EB16/4 Veyron, showed the way in which Volkswagen was intending to move forward with this luxury car company that it had taken over. In the 21st century, under Warkuss' designing lead, the future for VW looks strong.

HARM LAGAAY

The reputation of Porsche (see pp.192–3) as a leader in the area of stylish, up-market sports cars was well established by the time the Dutchman Harm Lagaay took over as head of its design studio in 1988. Lagaay was not a newcomer to the company, having been a member of Anatole Lupine's design team at the Research and Development Centre in Weissach between 1970 and 1977. It was during those years that Lagaay made his contribution to the design of one of Porsche's most successful cars, the 924, but, perhaps most importantly, this period allowed Lagaay to become fully absorbed into the culture of the company such that he understood it from the inside. For Porsche, more than for many others, the concepts of consistency and continuity were key characteristics of its successful brand image and Lagaay gained a deep understanding of their crucial importance.

INTERNATIONAL BY DESIGN

Lagaay's other experiences in car styling had been acquired during a stint with Ford working on the Escort, the Sierra, and the Scorpio, and at BMW where he had worked on the Z1. A Dutchman with a German passport, he personified the accelerating internationalism of the car design profession of these years and took his talents into the global context. In 1988 he took over from Lupine, who had had a deep

BELOW Lagaay launched his 968 model in 1992. An extension of the 924/944 series, it was given a facelift to include new features, such as new wings and a new bumper.

BELOW The Porsche Panamericana was a concept car created by Lagaay in 1989. Its most striking feature was its removable glass roof. Although it pushed forward the brand its simple, aerodynamic body was consistent with the familiar Porsche look.

respect for the evolutionary nature of Porsche design, at a time when the company was experiencing fluctuations in its economic profile: the challenge was to extend that notion of evolution and, at the same time, to push it into the future.

STYLISHNESS AND INNOVATION

Porsche's image had suffered from its "yuppie" associations acquired during the buoyant 1980s and it needed to be refreshed. One of Lagaay's first strategies was to launch a concept car – a rare event for the cautious Porsche company. The Panamericana, styled by Steve Markett, a member of Lagaay's team, appeared in 1989. Its plastic and carbon-fibre body, wide wheel covers, and adaptable glass roof gave it a striking appearance, albeit with distinctive Porsche traits. Although Lagaay had hoped it would become a production car by 1992 that dream was not realized, although several of the car's novel features were to reappear in important later projects.

Nineteen ninety-three saw the launch of another Porsche prototype in Detroit, aimed to revive the interest that had surrounded the 924 and also to introduce a level of innovation into the company's production. The Boxster (the name is made out of the words "boxer", a type of engine layout, and "speedster", unique in having its engine in the middle) originated from a 1992 drawing by the American designer Grant Larsson, and was developed by Lagaay into a full-size concept car. From the outset the Boxster project set out to create an affordable Porsche that evoked such postwar classics as the 356 but combined familiar characteristics with new ideas. The interior attracted particular attention as it boasted a wide range of gadgets, including a mini television and a computer. By 1996 the Boxster had been launched as a production car and was an enormous success. It had taken three years to perfect its sleek aerodynamic form.

Lagaay's success with the translation of a concept car into a production vehicle prompted more experiments of this sort which served to take the Porsche company into the 21st century. The launch of an elegant Sports Utility Vehicle, the Cayenne, in 2000 was a dramatic departure for this tradition-conscious producer of successful two-seater sports cars, while the prototype Carrera GT, an open cockpit supercar, shown in Paris in 2000 and intended for production in 2003, served to maintain Porsche's reputation for high stylishness.

PETER STEVENS

PRINCIPAL DESIGNS

1988   *Lotus Esprit*
1989   *Lotus Elan*
1990   *Jaguar XJR-15*
1993   *McLaren F1*

From the late 1960s onward many leading car designers emerged from a postgraduate training at London's Royal College of Art. Those to achieve renown include Martin Smith and Peter Birtwhistle; Gerry McGovern, a 1977 graduate who made his mark with designs such as Land Rover's revolutionary 1998 Freelander model; Peter Horbury, who went on to head Volvo's design programme; Ian Callum, who became head of design at Jaguar; and Murat Gunak, who graduated in 1983 and who has worked on breakthrough projects at both Mercedes and Peugeot.

BRITISH CAR STYLING

Peter Stevens (b.1943) was one of the first two postgraduates to study car design at the RCA, sponsored by Ford. He left in 1969, having been taught by such figures as Tom Karen of Letchworth's Ogle Design, who was renowned for his work on the Reliant Scimitar. (Ogle was a rare instance of a freelance automotive design office along Italian lines. British car styling usually took place in-house, with figures such as David Jones of Vauxhall dominating the picture from the 1940s to the 1970s.)

Stevens began his professional career at Ford (see pp.142–5), working on, among other projects, a handle for the Granada's sliding sunroof. By the late 1980s he was employed at Lotus where he

RIGHT *A sketch from 2001 of the MG X80, a luxury, high-performance sports car that will be launched by MG Rover in 2002. Stevens developed a highly sculptural, aerodynamic body for this model.*

RIGHT *Stevens worked on the new, 1988 version of the Esprit when he worked for Lotus. This prestigious British sports car manufacturer had a high-quality design reputation to maintain and this design, with its long, low body, helped to ensure it a successful future.*

BELOW *Stevens' body for the stunning McLaren F1 of 1994 provided a sculptural form appropriate for this high-performance, road-going car which emulated racing cars destined for the track.*

worked on a number of models, among them the 1988 Esprit originally styled by Giugiaro (see pp.178–81) and the Elan of 1989. Following Chapman's death in 1982 Lotus had sought new designers to provide them with models that would keep their reputation for advanced styling alive. Stevens made a significant contribution to that project.

FREELANCE DESIGN

For much of his career, Stevens worked as a freelance designer and teacher, contributing to several international projects, including the Renault 5 Turbo Alpine and the Jaguar XJR-15 of 1990. Over the years he collaborated with numerous companies, both in the United Kingdom and elsewhere, including BMW, Subaru, Lamborghini, Aston Martin, Audi, Bentley, Chrysler, Citroën, Toyota, and MG Rover. His *pièce de résistance* was, without doubt, the supremely sensuous body that he created for the supercar of supercars, Gordon Murray's McLaren F1, launched in 1993. Murray had decided that he wanted to create a car that benefited from all the advantages of Formula 1 racing and would be the fastest car on the road. He created a concept

that depended on a combination of supreme lightness, achieved through the use of a carbon-fibre monocoque structure for the body, and advanced aerodynamics. The driver was placed in the middle although there was room for two passengers as well in the rear. Only 100 F1s were made and they sold for more than a million dollars each.

Stevens' body design for the McLaren F1 exploited all the knowledge of sculpture that he had acquired during his early student days at St Martin's School of Art, London. He believed strongly in the application of sculptural ideas and forms to car design, and the subtle curves of the front and rear wings of the F1 and the sophistication of the way in which they flowed freely into other without any visual breaks showed just how skilled he was at form creation and at understanding and articulating the symbolic potency of fast cars.

In the wake of Stevens' huge success with the McLaren F1, he was taken on by MG Rover as its design director in the late 1990s. His influence is now being felt in the radically new designs that are being launched into the marketplace by this normally most conservative of British car companies.

DESIGNER CARS

By the 1990s designer culture had invaded every aspect of the world of material goods, including cars. Since the early century modernist architects (see pp.88–91) had had a go at including cars in the sphere of their creative practice, and from the 1930s product designers such as Walter Dorwin Teague and Raymond Loewy (see pp.136–9) had included cars among the other goods – refrigerators, duplicators, railroad trains – that were touched by their skilled hands.

CAR STYLISTS VERSUS PRODUCT DESIGNERS

The world of car stylists, located for the most part within the large manufacturing companies primarily for reasons of secrecy, was generally separate from that of industrial designers, largely inhabited by freelancers. As a result, car stylists became specialists and company men. They also developed a particular philosophy of design,

exclusively car-oriented and stressing the visual component of the design process, the sculptural impact of form, and the attention to visual details, such as the fall of light on a piece of sheet metal and the shape and position of a headlight. Inevitably a level of introspection entered into this highly specialized field of activity.

Industrial or product designers retained a broader approach to their discipline, ready to work on a food-mixer, a chair, or a new brand identity as required. During the 20th century the two professions diverged increasingly. By the 1990s, it was clear that the inward-looking nature of car styling was such that in-house stylists were not always ready to instigate the radical changes that were needed to take the car into the 21st century. Patrick Le Quément (see pp.224–7) at Renault was among the first to realize this and began to employ product designers in his styling studio, with immediate results.

RIGHT *The Italian architect-designer Mario Bellini's Kar-a-Sutra minibus of 1972 was made for an exhibition at New York's Museum of Modern Art. Featuring the same lines as in Bellini's designs for Olivetti's type-writers, it was, in essence, a room on wheels intended for 12 people.*

ABOVE *The French designer Philippe Starck, famous for his interiors and furniture designs, created this plywood model for a little car that he named Toto, in 1996. The idea of the car as a pet fitted the mood of the decade, which embraced the notion of the "character car".*

Product designers approach their brief in a different way from the car stylist. They tend to think conceptually first and visually second. They are trained to think about meaning in the objects they create, and about the emotional/psychological impact of, for example, pulling a handle or turning a knob, whether on a food-mixer or a piece of hi-fi equipment. While the task of all designers is to combine the technological with the cultural, the functional with the expressive, the product designer's priorities when approaching the challenge of designing a car can be very different from those of the car stylist. The late 20th century saw several examples of product designers creating cars that made these cultural differences very clear.

PRODUCT DESIGNERS AS CAR STYLISTS

Recent forays into car design by product designers include the Frenchman Philippe Starck's Toto car, and a concept car by Australian designer Marc Newson commissioned by Ford for the 1999 Tokyo motor show. Both reflected the designers' own preoccupations, visible in their proposals for many other objects, including furniture and products for the domestic environment, from fruit-juicers to toothbrushes to watches. Starck's models for a daringly understated plywood car and the open-top Toto are basic cars somewhat reminiscent of the simple wooden shell proposed by Le Corbusier and Jeanneret in the inter-war years. Newson's 021C car was a much more developed automobile and an example of the New Authenticity style in product design. The simple exterior enclosed a spacious interior in which every detail had been thought through. The body was made of carbon-fibre mounted on a steel frame, and aluminium featured widely; the headlights consisted of LEDs and fibre-optic strips. The car was radical in various ways and showed what could happen when a product designer applied his technological, spatial, and formal knowledge to the problem of the automobile.

The examples of Starck and Newson demonstrate the important role played by product designers in pushing forward the world of car design. They will undoubtedly continue to have a role in the 21st century working alongside more conventionally trained stylists and engineers to conceive and create the cars of the future.

NEW MARKETS

As we enter the 21st century, new initiatives are visible in car design, especially in the area of concept cars, which are without doubt going to remain with us for some time to come. Various possibilities present themselves, some rooted in past developments, others exploiting new possibilities, technological, social and cultural. Many derive from new technologies, whether the use of fuels other than petrol, or computer-based navigation systems for enhanced safety.

ALTERNATIVE FUELS, INNOVATIVE TECHNOLOGIES

In the first context the Americans are hard on the heels of the Japanese. DaimlerChrysler's electric NeCar 4 has been widely promoted but cannot yet counteract the disadvantages of electric power. It is also working with the notion of the hybrid car. Opel General Motors has created a hydrogen-powered car, HydroGen 1; Ford plans

to make its SUVs lighter and more aerodynamic, and aims to launch gas and electric versions of its Escape SUV in 2003. Japan, highly conscious of environmental problems, is willing to go down the microcar route, while Americans remain enamoured of their large trucks. Europe has moved in the same direction as Japan to a certain extent. Cars such as VW's little Lupo are designed for low fuel consumption, while Pininfarina's Metrocubo of 1999 was a hybrid car.

Car safety is also high on the agenda, with technology providing many of the answers. Japan's Mazda, for example, has proposed its ASV (advanced safety vehicle), which features an internal screen to show rear and side views, has a voice-interactive navigation system, and uses a range of collision avoidance technologies.

As for the use of new computer technologies, Ford launched its 24.7 concept in 2000, a car boasting a computer that practically

LEFT *Toyota's Open Deck concept model from 1999 focused on offering its users as much space as possible, especially in the rear, open-deck area. Its innovative doors also offered the passengers plenty of space inside the car.*

covers the whole dashboard. This "cyber concept car" is based on the premise that we will spend much more time in our cars and will need a means of personalizing them as we do our computers. The 24.7 allows us to put up family photos, call our friends, listen to our favourite music, and surf the Web, all voice-activated. The car itself, unpretentiously styled, looks more like a product than an automobile.

Other technological innovations include a move to new materials, mainly to provide fuel-efficiency through lightness. Aluminium and plastics feature extensively in this context; Nissan's little Hypermini of 2000 is made almost entirely from these materials. Work is being undertaken to combine them in new ways. The Dutch company Hoogovens, for example, has worked with I.D.E.A. SpA to create a car from new materials which uses a laminated sandwich of aluminium and plastic. Increasingly the all-steel car will be a thing of the past.

CARS FOR LIFESTYLES

Perhaps even more interesting than the influence of these technological breakthroughs on cars, however, are the new socially and culturally determined directions that are emerging. One of the most noticeable, especially in Japan and the United States, is the

ABOVE AND TOP The Street Ka, a development of Ford's Ka concept, has all the sophisticated New Edge styling details of the original Ka model plus the appearance of a racy sports car. The combination results in a progressive little automobile that is very much of its era and at the same time hugely appealing. The interior of the Street Ka boasts plenty of space for its passengers together with the latest in-car technology.

ABOVE AND RIGHT *The Honda Spocket is a daring, futuristic concept car, reminiscent of "dream cars" from the 1950s. It re-uses the gull-wing door principle that featured in a number of earlier cars, among them the DeLorean. Its interior boasts several notable features, such as a double-handgrip steering wheel.*

targeting of the new baby-boomer generation ("Generation Y"). To meet the needs of this affluent generation born in the 1970s, Toyota set up a spin-off company in 1996, the Virtual Venture Company, staffed with young workers who were given the brief of coming up with new car designs. The first to emerge, designed by 33-year-old Michiro Tada, was the Will-vi concept, a retro minivan reminiscent of Citroën's 2CV (see pp.102–5). To make it a lifestyle car, several companies got together to create a Will megabrand, so that customers of the Will-vi could buy a beer or a refrigerator, or book a holiday, all under the same name and logo. In a similar youth lifestyle vein Honda launched its Fuya-jo in the same year (1999), a tall vehicle adapted from a nightclub motif, which, according to Honda's publicity, "rocks like a town that never sleeps and rides with the ease of a skateboard".

DIFFERENT SOLUTIONS, DIFFERENT STYLES

Stylistically, divergencies are occurring. In the United States cars are getting bigger and more aggressive; in Japan they are getting smaller, boxier, and taller. An interesting development is the tendency of some companies to be moving to a new simplicity of style. Labelled the "New Authenticity" it is characterized by an emphasis on interior space – more roomy, more flexible – combined with a very basic exterior which has more in common with the square housing of an electronic product than with a streamlined automobile. The hard

metal look has been replaced by the use of softer, more textured surfaces: the grille of the 24.7 resembles a woven quilt. As the car takes on more and more domestic features, borrowing the soft forms of the living room, for example, its exterior becomes more of a "container" rather than a visual symbol of power and speed.

In the search for new markets manufacturers are creating new kinds of cars by merging existing typologies. Thus the SUV is merged with the MPV, the MPV with the microcar. As society becomes ever more complex and niche markets more specialized, so manufacturers

seek new formats to meet the needs of lifestyle and aspirational shifts. There is an awareness that cars play an important role in the formation of personal or group identity, and car designers acknowledge this in their search for new visual metaphors. While Japanese companies look back to traditional aesthetics – Isuzu refers to the form of a fan in a recent concept – European designers, such as Patrick Le Quément (see pp.224–7), recognize the importance of the "brand" image of new architectural monuments, such as Gehry's new Guggenheim museum in Bilbao, and seek to align the car with this cultural arena.

The role of science fiction is as strong as ever in early 21st-century car design, as is the masculine interest in the car as a "super-gadget". Several recent concept cars are structured in new ways, their doors opening in a novel manner and their interiors showing a high level of flexibility. With manufacturing offering more possibilities than ever, the potential for change is vast. Technologically, aesthetically, socially, culturally, and environmentally, the challenges to car designers are as great as they were a hundred years ago, and the signs are that the innovations they will come forward with will be just as significant.

BIBLIOGRAPHY

General

Barker, R. and Harding, A. (eds) *Automobile Design. Twelve Great Designers and Their Work* (Pennsylvania, 1992)

Beattie, I. *Automobile Body Design* (Somerset, 1977)

Edson Armi, C. *The Art of the American Automobile* (Philadelphia, 1988)

Flink, J.J. *The Car Culture* (Cambridge, Mass. 1975)

Gartman, D. *Auto Opium: A Social History of American Automobile Design* (London and New York, 1994)

Georgano, N. *Art of the American Automobile – the greatest stylists and their work* (New York, 1995)

Lamm, M. and Holls, D. *A Century of Automotive Style* (New York, 1996)

Lewis, D.L. and Goldstein, L. (eds) *The Automobile and American Culture* (Ann Arbor, 1996)

McLellan, J. *Bodies Beautiful: A history of car styling and craftsmanship* (London/Vancouver, 1975)

Moving Objects: 30 Years of Vehicle Design at the Royal College of Art (London, 1999)

O'Connell, S. *The Car in British Society: Class, Gender and Motoring 1896–1939* (Manchester/New York, 1998)

Rae, J.B. *The American Automobile: A brief history* (Chicago, 1965)

Rees, C. *Dream Wheels: Fantasy Cars of the Twentieth Century* (London, 2000)

Tipler, J. *The World's Greatest Automobile Stylists* (London, 1990)

Wilson, P. *Chrome Dreams: Automobile Styling since 1893* (Pennsylvania, 1976)

Chapter 1

Bayley, S. *Harley Earl and the Dream Machine* (New York, 1983)

Bel Geddes, N. *Horizons* (New York, 1932)

Buehrig, G.M. *Rolling Sculpture: A designer and his work* (New Jersey, 1975)

Bush, D.J. *The Streamlined Decade* (New York, 1975)

Dominguez, H.L. *Edsel Ford and E.T. Gregorie: The Remarkable Design Team and their Classic Fords of the 1920s and 1930s* (Pennsylvania, 1999)

Ford, H. *My Life and Work* (New York, 1922)

Heinshaw, J. and Miller, A.D. *Detroit Style: Automotive Form, 1925–1950* (Detroit, 1985)

Kieselbach, R.J *Stromlinienautos in Deutschland: Aerodynamik in Pkw-Bau bis 1945* (Stuttgart, 1982)

Krausse, J. and Lichtenstein, C. (eds) *Your Private Sky, Buckminster Fuller: The Art of Design Science* (Zurich, 1999)

Meikle, J. *Twentieth Century Limited: Industrial Design in America, 1925–1939* (Philadelphia, 1979)

Sloan, A. *My Years with General Motors* (New York, 1964)

Chapter 2

Bolster, J. *The Upper Crust: The Aristocrats of Automobiles* (London, 1976)

Conway, H. *Bugatti le Pur Sang* (London, 1997)

Dalton, L. *Rolls Royce: The Classic Elegance* (London, 1990)

Georgano, N. *The Bentley* (Buckinghamshire, 1993)

Green, J. *The Legendary Hispano-Suiza* (London, 1977)

Haslam, M. (intro) *The Amazing Bugattis* (London, 1979)

Hendry, M.D. *Cadillac, Standard of the World: The Complete History* (New York, 1977)

Hunter, E.I. *Aston Martin 1913–1947* (London, 1992)

McGovern, J. *Glamorous Cars* (London, 1990)

Pfau, H. *The Custom Body Era* (New York, 1970)

"The master craftsman: the golden age of the coachbuilder in America" in *Automobile Quarterly* (ed) *The American Car since 1775* (New York, 1971)

Whyte, A. *The Jaguar* (Buckinghamshire, 1999)

Wood, J. *Aston Martin DB4, DB5, and DB6: The Complete Story* (London, 1992)

Chapter 3

Bennett, C. *Land Rover: British Four-Wheel Drive from 1948* (London, 1996)

Copping, R. *VW Beetle: The Car of the Century* (New York, 2001)

De Vreede, M. *Land Rover* (London, 2000)

Foster, P.R. *The Story of Jeep* (New York, 1998)

Golding, R. *Mini Thirty Years on* (London, 1989)

Margolius. I. *Automobiles by Architects* (London, 2000)

McLeod, K. *Beetlemania: The story of the car that captured the hearts of millions* (New York, 1999)

Marshall, T. *Microcars* (London, 1999)

Nahum, A. *Alec Issigonis* (London, 1984)

Nelson, W.M. *Small Wonder: The Amazing Story of the Volkswagen* (London, 1967)

Reynolds, J. *The Citroën 2CV* (London, 2001)

Veimeister, P. *Microcars* (London, 1999)

White, M. *Citroën 2CV: The Complete Story* (London, 1999)

Chapter 4

Egan, P.S. *Design and Destiny: The Making of the Tucker Automobile* (California, 1989)

Flint, J. *The Dream Machine: The Golden Age of American Automobiles* (New York, 1976)

Hirsch, J. *Great American Dream Machines: Classic Cars of the '50s and '60s* (New York/London, 1985)

Janicki, E. *Cars Detroit Never Built: Fifty years of American Experimental Cars* (New York, 1990)

Loewy, R. *Never Leave Well Enough Alone* (New York, 1951)

The Designs of Raymond Loewy (Washington DC, 1975)

Muller, M. *Motor City Muscle: The rise and fall of the American muscle car* (New York, 1997)

Tretiack, P. *Raymond Loewy and Streamlined Design* (New York, 1999)

Young, A. and Young, T. *Chrysler, Dodge and Plymouth Muscle* (New York, 1999)

Chapter 5

Bladen, S. *BMW* (New York, 1985)

Bluemel, K. *Ferrari: The Road Cars* (London, 1998)

Box, R. and Crump, R. *The Automotive Art of Bertone* (London, 1984)

Box, R. and Crump, R. *History of Lamborghini* (London, 1974)

Design Giugiaro: La forma dell'automobile (Milan, 1980)

Dymock, E. *Saab* (London, 1997)

Farina, B. *Nato con l'automobile* (Turin, 1968)

Forde, G. and Peto, J. *Ferdinand Porsche: Design Dynasty 1900–1998* (London, 1998)

Froissart, L. *Ferrari Pininfarina* (London, 1997)

Frostick, M. *Mighty Mercedes* (London, 1979)

Frostick, M. *Alfa Romeo-Milano* (London, 1974)

Greggio, L. *Bertone* (London, 1993)

Gregotti, V. *Carrozzeria Italiana-cultura e progetto* (Milan, 1978)

Laban, B. *Ferrari* (London/New York, 2000)

L'Idea Ferrari (exhibition catalogue) (Milan, 1990)

Lindh, B-E. *The First 40 Years of Saab Cars* (Rhode Island, 1987)

McComb, F. W. *The MG* (Buckinghamshire, 1999)

MacKenzie-Wintle, H. *Renault* (London, 1999)

Marchiano, M. *Zagato: Seventy Years in the Fast Lane* (Turin, 1998)

Olsson. C. *Volvo Cars: A Rhapsody, 1927–2000* (New York, 2000)

Pininfarina, *1930–1980: Prestige and Tradition* (Lausanne, 1980)

Prunet, A. *Pininfarina: Seventy Years* (London/New York, 2000)

Robson, G. and Langworth, R. *Triumph Cars: The Complete Story* (New York, 1996)

Rogliatti, G. and others *Ferrari: Design of a Legend* (New York, 1991)

Sparrow, D. and Ayre, I. *Maserati Heritage* (London, 1995)

Chapter 6

Bowler, M. and Wood, J. *Dream Cars: Design studies and prototypes* (London, 1999)

Delorenzo, M. *Modern Chrysler Concept Cars: The Designs that saved the Company* (New York, 2000)

Delorenzo, M. *The New Beetle* (New York, 1998)

Rae. J.B. *Nissan Datsun: A History of Nissan Motor Corporation in USA, 1960–1980* (New York, 1982)

Scharff, V. *Taking the Wheel: Women and the Coming of the Motor Age* (New York, 1991)

Sparke, P. *Japanese Design* (London, 1987)

The Car Programme: Fifty-two Months to Job One, or how they designed the Ford Sierra (London, 1982)

DIRECTORY OF MANUFACTURERS

AUDI AG
Auto-Union-Strasse 2, D-85045
Ingolstadt, Germany
Audi is a 99%-owned subsidiary of
Volkswagen AG. It has a range of
staple cars – the A3, A4, A6, A8,
and the TT sports car which has
won much acclaim for its design.

AUTOMOBILI LAMBORGHINI HOLDING SpA
Via Modena 12, 40019
Sant'Agata, Bolognese, Italy
Renowned for its exotic, highly-
styled sports car, Lamborghini is a
subsidiary of Volkswagen AG. Only
around 280 Diablos are made a
year.

BAYERISCHE MOTOREN WERKE AG
Petuelring, 130,
D-80788 Munich, Germany
Automobiles account for 75% of
BMW's sales. It also produces
motorcycles. It is known for its
classically-designed passenger
cars and sports cars.

DAEWOO MOTOR COMPANY LTD
199 Chongchon-dong, Pupyong-
ku, Inchon, South Korea
Daewoo Motors is part of the family-
run Daewoo Group,and Korea's
second automobile producer
behind Hyundai. The company
makes cars, buses, and trucks.

DAIHATSU MOTOR COMPANY LTD
1-1 Daihatsu-cho, Ikeda, Osaka
563-8651, Japan
The Daihatsu company is known
for its small, inexpensive cars.

DAIMLERCHRYSLER AG
Epplestrasse 225, 70546
Stuttgart, Germany
This car manufacturing company
is the result of the German firm,
Mercedes-Benz, and the
American company, Chrysler
Corporation, coming together in
1998. It is responsible for cars
manufactured under the names of
Dodge, Eagle, Jeep, and Plymouth.

FERRARI SpA
Via Abetone Inferiore 4, 41053
Maranello, Modena, Italy
Ferrari, with its famous rearing
horse logo, is known for stylish

sports cars, such as the Testarossa,
and become almost mythical.

FIAT SpA
Via Nizza 250, 10136 Turin, Italy
This Italian mass-production
company is known for small cars
such as the Seicento and the
Cinquecento but it also owns Alfa
Romeo, Ferrari, and Maserati.

FORD MOTOR COMPANY
One American Road, Dearborn,
Michigan 48126-2998, USA
In existence since the early
twentieth century, Ford has
produced cars for many years. It is
now America's largest manufacturer
of pickup trucks. It owns the
following brands – Aston Martin,
Ford, Jaguar, Lincoln, Mercury,
Volvo, and a portion of Mazda.

GENERAL MOTORS CORPORATION
300 Renaissance Center, Detroit,
Michigan 48265, USA
General Motors is the world's
largest producer of cars and
trucks. It owns Buick, Cadillac,
Chevrolet, GMC, Pontiac, Saab,
Saturn, and Oldsmobile.

HONDA MOTOR COMPANY LTD
1-1 2-chome Minami-Aoyama,
Minato-ku, Tokyo 107-8556, Japan
Japan's third biggest manufacturer,
making motorcycles as well as
cars. It is interested in exploring
alternative energy sources.

HYUNDAI MOTOR COMPANY
231, Yangjae-Dong, Seochu-Gu,
Seoul 137-938, South Korea
Hyundai produces cars but also
makes minivans and trucks. It is
Korea's leading producer of
vehicles and has been selling cars
to America since the mid-1980s.

ISUZU MOTORS LTD
26-1 Minami-oi 6-chome,
Shinagawa-ku, Tokyo 140-8722,
Japan
Isuzu is well known for producing
pickup trucks.

JAGUAR LTD
Browns Lane, Allesley, Coventry,
West Midlands CV5 9DR, UK
The producer of some of Britain's

most stylish cars in the 20th
century, the name of Jaguar
remains a status symbol.

MAZDA MOTOR CORPORATION
3-1, Shinchi, Fuchu-cho, Aki-gun,
Hiroshima 730-91, Japan
Mazda is the fifth largest of the
Japanese manufacturers. A maker
of cars, minivans and trucks it is
renowned for its Miata sports cars.

MG ROVER GROUP LTD
International House, Bickenhill
Lane, Birmingham B37 7HQ, UK
One of Britain's few remaining
manufacturers, this group has
deep historical roots.

MITSUBISHI MOTORS CORPORATION
5-33-8 Shiba, Minato-ku, Tokyo
108-8410, Japan
Mitsubishi is Japan's fourth largest
car manufacturer, producing a
range of passenger cars – including
the Galant, the Aspire, and the
Eclipse. It also produces trucks.

NISSAN MOTOR COMPANY LTD
17-1, Ginza 6-chome, Chuo-ku
Tokyo 104-8023, Japan
The second largest of Japan's
vehicle manufacturers, Nissan is
the country's oldest. It produces
passenger cars, pickups and
SUVs. Renault owns a 37%
share in Nissan.

PSA PEUGEOT CITROEN SA
75 Avenue de la Grande Armee,
75116 Paris, France
France's leading vehicle
manufacturer and the second
largest in the production of
passenger cars behind
Volkswagen AG. It produces cars
and light commercial vehicles.

PININFARINA SpA
Corso Stati Uniti, 61, 10129 Turin,
Italy
Pininfarina builds cars, designs
car bodies, and develops
prototypes. It also creates products
such as telephones and watches.

DR ING. HCF PORSCHE AG
Porschestrasse 42, 70432
Stuttgart, Germany

Porsche now produces two lines of
cars only – the Boxster and the
911 model. It also manufactures
watches and luggage items.

RENAULT SA
13-15 Quai Le Gallo, 92100
Boulogne-Billancourt Cedex,
France
France's second largest
manufacturer of which 44% is
owned by the French government.

SAAB AUTOMOBILE AB
Nohabs Industriomrade, S-46180
Trollhattän, Sweden
Now a subsidiary of General
Motors, Saab produces a range of
cars, among them the 9.3 Turbo
and the upmarket 9.5.

SEAT SA
Zona Franca, Calle 2, no1, 08040
Barcelona, Spain
Founded in 1950 by the Spanish
government and the Italian
company, Fiat, Seat is now a
subsidiary of Volkswagen AG.

SUZUKI MOTOR CORPORATION
300 Takatsuka-cho, Hamamatsu-
shi, Shizuoka 432-91, Japan
Japan's leading producer of
minicars

TOYOTA MOTOR CORPORATION
1 Toyota-cho, Toyota, Aichi 471-
8571 , Japan
Japan's leading vehicle
manufacturer and the fourth
largest in the world.

VAUXHALL MOTORS LTD
Griffin House, Osbourne Road,
Luton, Bedfordshire LU1 3YT, UK
One of Britain's few remaining car
manufacturers. It is owned by G.M.

VOLKSWAGEN AG
Brieffach 1848-2, D-38436
Wolfsburg, Germany
Europe's leading car
manufacturer. Volkswagen owns
Audi, Lamborghini, Rolls-Royce,
Bentley, Seat, and Skoda.

AB VOLVO
S-405 08, Gothenburg, Sweden
Having sold its car operations to
Ford, Volvo now concentrates on
the production of trucks and buses.

COLLECTIONS AND MUSEUMS

Australia
National Motor Museum, Birdwood, Adelaide, South Australia

Austria
Kröpfel Oldtimer Museum, Hartberg
Porsche Automuseum, Gmünd
Siegfried-Marcus Automobilmuseum, Stockerau
Tatra and Oldtimer Clubmuseum, Steinabruckl

Belgium
The Autoworld Museum, Brussels

Czech Republic
Narodni Technical Museum, Prague
Samohyl Motor Museum, Zlin
Skoda Auto Museum, Mlad Boleslav

Denmark
Aalholm Automobile Museum, Nysted
Jysk Automobilmuseum, Gjern

France
Collection Ferrari, Aubusson
Manoir de l'Automobile, Lohéac
Le Musée Automobile, Limoges
Le Musée de l'Automobile, Paris
Musée Cadillac, Langeais
Musée de l'Automobiliste, Mougins
Musée de la Belle Epoque de l'Automobile, Pont-l'Eveque
Musée Simca Yonnais, La Roche sur Yon
Musée Peugeot, Sochaux
Musée National de l'Automobile (Collection Schlumpf), Mulhouse

Germany
Automuseum Störy, Bockenem-Störy
Auto & Technik Museum, Sinsheim
Automuseum "Dr. Carl Benz", Ladenburg-West
Borgward Museum, Neuwied
BMW Museum Zeithorizont, Munich
EFA Museum of German Automobile History, Amerang
Mercedes-Benz Museum, Stuttgart
Motor-Technica, Bad Oeynhausen
Porsche Automobil Museum, Stuttgart-Zuffenhausen
Rosso Bianco Collection, Aschaffenburg
Stiftung Automuseum Volkswagen, Wolfsburg

Hungary
Transport Museum, Budapest

Italy
Centro Storico Fiat, Turin
Centro Polifunzionale "Ferruccio Lamborghini", Dosso
Galleria Ferrari, Maranello
Ghia Collection, Turin
Museo dell'Automobile "Carlo Biscaretti di Ruffia", Turin
Museo dell'Automobile "Luigi Bonfanti", Romano d'Ezzelino
Museo Storico Alfa Romeo, Arese
Pininfarina Collection, Turin
Museo Vincenzo Lancia, Turin

Japan
Ferrari Museum, Shizuoka-ken
Harada Collection, Yamanashi-ken
Honda Collection Hall, Mie-ken
Mazda Museum, Hiroshima
Mitsubishi Automobile Museum, Aichi-ken
Motor Museum of Japan, Ishikawa
Porsche Museum of Japan, Kanagawa-ken
Toyota Automobile Museum, Aichi-ken

Netherlands
Automuseum, Bergeijk
Daf Automobiel Museum, Eindhoven
Ford Museum, Hillegom
Nationaal Automobielmuseum, Raamsdonksveer

Russia
Moskvitch Factory Museum, Moscow

Spain
Automobile Museum, Barcelona
Collecio d'Automobils de Salvador Claret, Gerona

Sweden
Saab Museum, Trolhättan
Skokloster Motor Museum, Balsta
Volvo Museum, Arendal

Switzerland
International Car Museum, Geneva

UK
Haynes Motor Museum, Yeovil, Somerset
Heritage Motor Centre, Gaydon, Warwickshire
Lakeland Motor Museum, Cark-in-Cartmell, Cumbria
Midland Motor Museum, Bridgnorth, Shropshire
Museum of British Road Transport, Coventry
National Motor Museum, Beaulieu, Hampshire

USA
Alfred P. Sloan Museum, Flint, Michigan
Auburn-Cord-Duesenberg Museum, Auburn, Indiana
Blackhawk Automotive Museum, Danville, California
Henry Ford Museum, Dearborn, Michigan
Mark Martin's Klassix Car Museum, Daytona, Florida
Museum of Automobile History, Syracuse, New York
National Automobile Museum, Reno, Nevada
National Corvette Museum, Bowling Green, Kentucky
Petersen Automotive Museum, Los Angeles, California
Studebaker National Museum, South Bend, Indiana
Walter P. Chrysler Museum, Auburn Hills, Michigan

GLOSSARY

aerodynamics
The science of aerodynamics, which accelerated in the early 20th century, focused on the movement of solid forms through air. Wind-tunnel testing was, and still is, used to measure the effects of "drag". Engineers studying aerodynamics translated their results into new designs in car-body form. Thus emerged the curved aesthetics of "streamlining" in the 1930s, and "aero" in the 1980s.

berline
A term derived from coachbuilding that has become the European equivalent of what the British call a saloon – a closed vehicle for four or more passengers.

berlinetta
A small BERLINE.

boat-tailed
A term used to describe the rear end of a car that is curved like the prow of a boat.

bonnet (US hood)
The metal panel covering the engine, which spans the area from the main car body to the radiator at the front of the car.

boot (US trunk)
The area behind the rear seats that is used for luggage storage. The American term, trunk, refers back to the days when luggage was stored in a trunk attached to the rear of the car.

buck
The full-size wooden frame on which modelling takes place in the styling studio. It derives from the name for the body of a cart.

bumper
The parts attached to the front and rear of the car to absorb impact. They are increasingly integrated into the body of the car and are not seen as separate components as they once were.

cab forward
A descriptive term for cars in which the driver is seated towards the front of the car to give an impression of speed. The farther back the position of the driver in relation to the whole car the slower the implied pace of the vehicle.

cabriolet
A generic term originating in coachbuilding which has come to mean either a two- or a four-seater convertible.

carrossier
The French name for a coachbuilder.

carrozzeria
The Italian name for a coachbuilder.

chassis
The base-frame of the automobile. Traditionally the car manufacturer supplied the chassis, which was in effect the complete car but without the bodywork or the seats, to the coachbuilder, who then finished it off. When MONOCOQUE construction became the norm, however, the distinction between the chassis and the bodywork was eroded significantly and car design became a more holistic activity.

coachbuilder
The name given to a craftsman who utilizes traditional skills to hand-build and repair car bodies. In previous centuries it referred to the builder of horse-drawn coaches and carriages.

composite construction
This denotes a body that is made of metal but has a timber frame beneath the metalwork.

concept car
A non-production car shown at motor shows to indicate future directions and encourage the public to buy new models.

convertible
A car that can be both closed and open.

coupé (US coupe)
A car that has been "cut" at the rear to create a short back end. The term derives from coach-building, where it referred to the area between the main body and the BOOT.

crossover car
A recent term used to describe a mix of vehicle types, so that a van, for example, may be mixed with a truck to create a new typology and a new niche market.

De Ville
A term that was added to a body name to denote the fact that the model in question had a sliding roof which opened above the front two seats.

drop-head coupé
A COUPE equipped with a folding hood. The term was used most in the inter-war years and has its roots in coachbuilding.

estate car (US station wagon)
A car with a roofline that stays high to the rear and a flat back. It frequently has rear doors with windows in them, opening outward. There is no division between the back seats and the open BOOT. Estate cars provide more room for baggage than SALOON cars.

fastback
An American term to describe a car that has an unbroken line from the roof right down to the rear BUMPER.

fender
The American equivalent of WING.

GT
When added to the end of a model's name these two letters, which stand for Gran Turismo, suggest a high-performance SALOON or COUPE.

gull-wing doors
An evocative term used to describe doors that open upward, thereby resembling the wings of a gull.

hatchback
A car with a large, top-hinged rear door with access into the BOOT.

highlights
The effect of light on the metallic surface of the car's body which plays an important part in how its shape is perceived. Designers are very sensitive to this visual effect and use full-size mock-ups to be able to anticipate them on the final production car.

hood (US) see bonnet
The American equivalent of BONNET.

hybrid
A recent term for cars that are not totally dependent on petrol as a fuel but that use alternative power sources as well, among them electricity and hydrogen.

Kamm tail

A term deriving from the name of the German aerodynamicist Dr Wunibald Kamm, who worked in Stuttgart in the 1930s. One of his findings was that the presence of a short, vertical rear tail on a car assisted in reducing drag. The BMW company implemented his idea in the 1940s and it was used more widely on racing cars from the 1950s onward.

limousine

In coachbuilding the term was used to describe a large, closed car. Now it means a large SALOON car and has strong status connotations. Limousines are frequently chauffeur-driven.

microcar, minicar

The former term was used in the early postwar years to describe the small, inexpensive, and fuel-efficient cars that emerged in various countries in that era. Now the term minicar is used to describe some of Japan's recent designs.

monocoque

A metal car body that has its own supporting structure built into it and that is not dependent on an inner structural frame. The shift to monocoque bodies in car manufacturing had a transforming effect on car design as it made redundant the traditional working practices of the coachbuilder and forced the car designer to think of the body as a single unit. The term "unitary body" is also used.

mudguards (US wings)

An element of the car body positioned over the wheels to protect the car and passengers from splashes. They have gradually become integrated into the main body of the car.

multi-purpose vehicle (MPV)

The initials are widely used to describe large, single-unit cars, such as Renault's Espace, which have a considerable amount of flexible space in their interiors.

people's car

A concept from the late inter-war years and early postwar years, developed by governments and car manufacturers, to provide the mass of the population with personal automobile transportation, previously provided by the bicycle.

phaeton

One of the many terms originating in the carriage trade that moved into the world of automobiles. A phaeton was originally a well-sprung horse-drawn carriage but it came to mean an open touring car with four or more seats. See also TOURER,

pillars

The four vertical elements of the body frame that support the roof.

pontoon style

A term used in the 1940s and 1950s to describe unified, slab-sided metal car bodies that had no extraneous features attached to them and that were somewhat swollen and bulbous in look.

razor-edge

A description of a car body with sharply delineated metal panels, rectilinear forms, and sharp angles. The style was popular in the 1970s.

roadster

This term was used interchangeably with the word "speedster" to describe a two-seater, open-top car that was designed with racy lines. From the 1950s onward it was replaced by the term SPORTS CAR.

Roi des Belges

This name was used to describe a car with high-set rear seats. It derived from a particular car commissioned by King Leopold II of Belgium in 1902.

running-board

The long step that used to join the front and rear MUDGUARDS, providing entrance into the car. With the advent of pontoon-style bodywork the running-board gradually disappeared.

saloon

An enclosed car with four or more seats.

sedan

American equivalent of SALOON.

spider or spyder

A term taken from the coach-building trade which now means an open SPORTS CAR. Originally a spider was a light carriage.

sports car

An open, two-seater car for leisure use. The term was used widely in the 1950s and 1960s when the concept came into its own. It has recently experienced a revival.

sports utility vehicle (SUV)

A four-wheel-drive vehicle used for pleasure rather than for work as was the intention with original utility vehicles. It is as common a sight in cities as in the rural environment for which the four-wheel drive was originally developed.

station wagon (US) see estate car

The American equivalent of ESTATE CAR.

tape drawings

A stage in the design process when stylists use tape to create full-size profile outlines of their proposals.

torpedo

A term used to describe pre-World War I cars that had a continuous line from the BONNET to the rear panel.

tourer

This term was used generally to describe an open car that could seat at least four people. See also PHAETON. Usually a folding hood was used for weather protection.

trunk (US) see boot

Turbocharger

An exhaust-driven air pump that forces more fuel mixture into the engine, increasing power output.

utility vehicle

A term used to describe cars, such as the American Jeep or the British Land Rover, that were developed to perform specific tasks including off-road agricultural and military work.

voiturette

A diminutive of the French word *voiture* (car) meaning a small car.

waistline

This term is used to denote the horizontal line, sometimes visible and sometimes not, that is located just below the windows and extends the full length of the car. In design terms it is a crucial line as everything else on the car body relates to it visually. Some of the most elegant cars have a very straight and obvious waistline.

Weymann saloon

A SALOON car with an ash frame panelled in fabric. A Frenchman, C.T. Weymann, pioneered this kind of car body in the 1920s.

wings (US) see mudguards

INDEX

ACKNOWLEDGMENTS

The publisher would like to thank the following for their kind permission to reproduce photographs for use in this book.

Key b bottom, **c** centre, **l** left, **r** right, **t** top

1 Autocar; **2t** Giles Chapman Library, **b** Ludvigsen Library; **3** Bugatti International; **5** Renault UK Ltd; **6/7** OPG/Ian Dawson; **9** Mercedes-Benz; **10** Hulton Archive; **11** GM Media Archives; **12/13** Hulton Archive; **14/15** Ludvigsen Library; **16/17** Giles Chapman Library; **18** Corbis; **19** National Motor Museum; **20t** Giles Chapman Library, **r** Giles Chapman Library, **b** Ford Motor Company; **21** Ford Motor Company; **22t** National Motor Museum, **r** GM Media Archives, **b** Ludvigsen Library; **23** National Motor Museum; **24** Detroit Public Library, National Automotive History Collection; **25** Detroit Public Library, National Automotive History Collection; **26/27** Hulton Getty; **26b** Giles Chapman Library; **27** LAT; **28/29** Giles Chapman Library; **30t** The Norman Bel Geddes Collection, The Performing Arts Collection, Harry Ransom Humanities Research Centre, the University of Texas at Austin (by permission of Edith Lutyens Bel Geddes, executrix); **r** The Norman Bel Geddes Collection, The Performing Arts Collection, Harry Ransom Humanities Research Centre, the University of Texas at Austin (by permission of Edith Lutyens Bel Geddes, executrix); **b** The Norman Bel Geddes Collection, The Performing Arts Collection, Harry Ransom Humanities Research Centre, the University of Texas at Austin (by permission of Edith Lutyens Bel Geddes, executrix); **31t** The Norman Bel Geddes Collection, The Performing Arts Collection, Harry Ransom Humanities Research Centre, the University of Texas at Austin (by permission of Edith Lutyens Bel Geddes, executrix), **b** Ludvigsen Library; **32l** DaimlerChrysler, **r** DaimlerChrysler; **33t** DaimlerChrysler, **b** DaimlerChrysler; **34t** National Motor Museum, **b** Ludvigsen Library; **35t** LAT, **b** Giles Chapman Library; **36tl** OPG/John Lamm; **36tr** OPG/John Lamm; **36b** Detroit Public Library, National Automotive History Collection; **37** OPG; **38t** Ludvigsen Library, **l** Ludvigsen Library, **b** Giles Chapman Library; **39** Detroit Public Library, National Automotive History Collection; **40t** Ford Motor Company, **l** Ford Motor Company, **b** Ford Motor Company; **4t** Ford Motor Company, **b** LAT; **42t** Getty Images, **b** The Design Museum; **43t** LAT, **b** The Design Museum; **44/45** Giles Chapman Library; **46/47** Mercedes-Benz; **49** Giles Chapman Library; **50t** National Motor Museum, **l** LAT, **b** Giles Chapman Library; **51** LAT; **52t** LAT, **b** Ludvigsen Library; **53** l AT; **54t** National Motor Museum, **b** National Motor Museum; **55t** Giles Chapman Library, **b** Giles Chapman Library; **56b** National Motor Museum; **57t** Rolls-Royce Motors, **b** Giles Chapman Library; **58/59** National Motor Museum, **bl** Giles Chapman Library, **br** Giles Chapman Library; **59** Giles Chapman Library; **60/61** Jaguar Cars; **60t** Giles Chapman Library, **bl** Giles Chapman Library; **62tl** Aston Martin Lagonda, **tr** LAT; **63t** LAT; **63b** Neill Bruce; **64** Ludvigsen Library; **65t** LAT, **b** Ludvigsen Library; **66t** Giles Chapman Library; **67** LAT; **68/69** LAT; **68** LAT; **69** Ludvigsen Library; **70** Giles Chapman Library; **71** Pininfarina; **72** Giles Chapman Library; **73** Alfa Romeo; **74l** National Motor Museum, **r** National Motor Museum; **75l** National Motor Museum, **r** National Motor Museum; **76/77** Ludvigsen Library; **76** Detroit Public Library, National Automotive History Collection; **77** LAT; **78** Detroit Public Library, National Automotive History Collection; **79t** Ludvigsen Library, **79b** OPG; **80** Ludvigsen Library; **81t** Ludvigsen Library; **81b** OPG; **82/83** Giles Chapman Library; **84/85** Bauhaus-Archiv, Berlin; **86** VWs; **87** Bonhams; **89l** Bauhaus-Archiv, Berlin, **r** Bauhaus-Archiv, Berlin; **90t** The Frank Lloyd Wright Archives; **90b** SCE Jean Prouvé; **91** LAT; **92** Giles Chapman Library; **93t** Giles Chapman Library, **b** Ford Motor Company; **94t** Giles Chapman Library. **b** Getty Images; **95** National Motor Museum; **96l** Giles Chapman Library, **r** Giles Chapman Library; **97t** Giles Chapman Library, **b** LAT; **98t** LAT, **b** Giles Chapman Library; **99** Giles Chapman Library; **100t** Giles Chapman Library, **b** Giles Chapman Library; **101** Giles Chapman Library; **102t** LAT, **b** Giles Chapman Library; **103t** LAT, **b** Citroën; **104** Giles Chapman Library, **105l** Citroën, **c** Citroën, **r** Giles Chapman Library; **106tl** Giles Chapman Library, **tr** LAT, **b** Giles Chapman Library; **107t** Giles Chapman Library, **b** Giles Chapman Library; **108t** National Motor Museum, **b** Giles Chapman Library; **109** LAT; **110** Giles Chapman Library; **111t** Giles Chapman Library, **b** LAT; **112t** Giles Chapman Library, **b** National Motor Museum; **113** LAT; **114** National Motor Museum; **115** Giles Chapman Library; **116** Giles Chapman Library; **117t** Giles Chapman Library, **b** National Motor Museum; **118/119** LAT; **120/121** GM Media Archives; **122** Giles Chapman Library; **123** Getty Images; **124** Hulton Archive; **125t** Ludvigsen Library; **125b** Peter Roberts Collection c/o Neill Bruce; **126b** VinMag Archive Ltd; **127** OPG/John Lamm; **126/127** LAT; **128t** Ludvigsen Library, **r** Ludvigsen Library, **b** LAT; **129t** LAT, **b** Giles Chapman Library; **130t** Ford Motor Company, **b** Ford Motor Company; **131** Giles Chapman Library; **132b** Peter Roberts Collection c/o Neill Bruce; **132t** Ludvigsen Library; **133** VinMag Archive Ltd; **134** LAT; **135b** Movie Store Collection; **135tl** Ludvigsen Library, **tr** Ludvigsen Library; **136t** Loewy Group, **r** Loewy Group, **b** Ludvigsen Library; **137t** LAT, **b** Loewy Group; **138** Loewy Group; **139t** Loewy Group, **b** Giles Chapman Library; **140t** DaimlerChrysler, **b** DaimlerChrysler; **141t** Giles Chapman Library, **b** Detroit Public Library, National Automotive History Collection; **142/143** OPG/John Lamm; **142** Detroit Public Library, National Automotive History Collection; **143** OPG/John Lamm; **144t** LAT, **b** Paul Collis; **145** Ford Motor Company; **146/147** LAT; **146t** Ludvigsen Library, **b** Giles Chapman Library; **147** Ludvigsen Library; **148** Ludvigsen Library; **149t** OPG; **149b** OPG; **150** Ludvigsen Library; **151t** Giles Chapman Library; **151b** OPG; **152/153** Giles Chapman Library; **154/155** Giles Chapman Library; **156/157** Giles Chapman Library; **157** Getty Images; **158** Giles Chapman Library; **159t** LAT; **160** LAT; **161t** Giles Chapman Library, **b** Pininfarina; **162t** Giles Chapman Library, **r** Giles Chapman Library, **b** Alfa Romeo; **163t** LAT, **b** Giles Chapman Library; **164t** Giles Chapman Library, **b** Giles Chapman Library; **165** OPG/Nicky Wright; **166t** Giles Chapman Library, **b** Giles Chapman Library; **167** Bertone; **168t** LAT, **b** LAT; **169** Giles Chapman Library; **170t** Giles Chapman Library, **r** Giles Chapman Library, **b** LAT; **171t** Giles Chapman Library, **b** Ludvigsen Library; **172t** Autocar, **b** Giles Chapman Library; **173t** LAT, **b** Giles Chapman Library; **175t** OPG; **174t** Giles Chapman Library, **r** LAT, **b** Giles Chapman Library; **175b** Giles Chapman Library; **176t** Autocar, **r** Giles Chapman Library, **b** National Motor Museum; **177t** Giles Chapman Library, **b** Bertone; **178b** LAT; **178c** National Motor Museum; **179** Bertone; **180t** Italdesign, **b** Italdesign; **181** Peter Roberts Collection c/o Neill Bruce; **182/183** LAT; **182** Giles Chapman Library; **183** LAT; **184t** LAT, **b** Ludvigsen Library; **185** Giles Chapman Library; **186/187** National Motor Museum; **186** Giles Chapman Library; **187** Giles Chapman Library; **188t** Giles Chapman Library, **bl** LAT, **br** Giles Chapman Library; **189** Giles Chapman Library; **190tl** Giles Chapman Library; **191t** OPG/A Morland; **191b** OPG/Rainer Schlegelmilch; **192t** Giles Chapman Library, **c** National Motor Museum; **b** OPG/Ian Dawson; **193t** LAT; **193b** Neill Bruce; **194** Giles Chapman Library; **195t** Giles Chapman Library, **b** Giles Chapman Library; **196l** Giles Chapman Library, **r** Giles Chapman Library; **197t** Giles Chapman Library, **b** Giles Chapman Library; **198/199** Giles Chapman Library; **200/201** DaimlerChrysler; **202/203** Giles Chapman Library; **203** Giles Chapman Library; **204t** Ford Motor Company, **r** Giles Chapman Library, **b** Giles Chapman Library; **205t** Giles Chapman Library, **b** National Motor Museum; **206** Giles Chapman Library; **207t** Giles Chapman Library, **b** Giles Chapman Library; **208t** Giles Chapman Library, **b** Giles Chapman Library; **209** Giles Chapman Library; **210** Ludvigsen Library; **211t** Giles Chapman Library, **b** Giles Chapman Library; **212** Ford Motor Company; **213t** Giles Chapman Library, **b** Giles Chapman Library; **214t** Ford Motor Company, **r** Giles Chapman, **b** Ford Motor Company; **215** Giles Chapman Library; **216t** LAT, **c** GM Media Archive; **b** Ludvigsen Library; **217t** GM Media Archive; **b** Ludvigsen Library; **218t** Giles Chapman Library, **b** Giles Chapman Library; **219t** Giles Chapman Library; **b** Ford Motor Company; **220** Giles Chapman Library; **221t** Autocar; **b** Autocar; **222t** DaimlerChrysler, **b** Giles Chapman Library; **223t** Chrysler UK; **b** Giles Chapman Library; **224t** Renault, **b** Giles Chapman Library; **225** Giles Chapman Library; **226t** Giles Chapman Library, **b** Giles Chapman Library, **227** Giles Chapman Library; **228/229** Giles Chapman Library; **228t** Christine Lalla, **b** Giles Chapman Library; **229t** Audi; **230t** Giles Chapman Library, **b** Giles Chapman Library; **231t** Mazda, **b** Honda; **232t** Volkswagen, **b** Giles Chapman Library; **233t** Bugatti International, **b** Bugatti International; **234t** Autocar, **r** Giles Chapman Library, **b** Giles Chapman Library; **235t** Porsche, **b** Giles Chapman Library; **236/237** Neill Bruce; **236t** Christine Lalla, **b** Giles Chapman Library; **237** Giles Chapman Library; **238t** Philippe Starck; **238b** Mario Bellini Archivio; **239t** Marc Newson; **b** Marc Newson; **240** Toyota; **241t** Ford Motor Company; **b** Ford Motor Company; **242t** Honda; **c** Honda; **b** Citroën; **243t** Honda, **b** LAT.

Author's Acknowledgments

I would like to dedicate this book to my mother, Jacqueline Anne Sparke, who made me car-conscious in the first instance, and to the students of the Vehicle Design MA Course at the Royal College of Art who, over a period of 18 years, taught me to understand and appreciate the subtleties of car design. In preparing and writing the book I would like to thank, among many other people who have helped me and are too numerous to list here, John, Molly, Celia, and Nancy who have put up with more car discussions that they probably would have wanted to have on long car journeys; Giles Chapman, for help, advice, and inspired picture research; Emily Asquith and Kirsty Seymour-Ure for patient and rigorous editing; and Colin Goody, a car enthusiast himself, for the expert design of the book.